The Methodist Unification

RELIGION, RACE, AND ETHNICITY
General Editor: Peter J. Paris

The Methodist Unification

Christianity and the Politics
of Race in the Jim Crow Era

Morris L. Davis

NEW YORK UNIVERSITY PRESS
New York and London

NEW YORK UNIVERSITY PRESS
New York and London
www.nyupress.org

Library of Congress Cataloging-in-Publication Data
Davis, Morris L. (Morris Lee), 1969-
The Methodist unification : Christianity and the politics of race in
the Jim Crow era / Morris Davis.
p. cm. — (Religion, race, and ethnicity)
Includes bibliographical references and index.
ISBN-13: 978-0-8147-1990-9 (cloth : alk. paper)
ISBN-10: 0-8147-1990-2 (cloth : alk. paper)
1. Methodist Church (U.S.). Uniting Conference. 2. Methodist
Church (U.S.)—History. 3. Race relations—Religious aspects-
Methodist Church—History—20th century. 4. United States-Race
relations—History—20th century. I. Title.
BX8382.A15D38   2007
287'.63—dc22   2007029767

Manufactured in the United States of America
10 9 8 7 6 5 4 3 2 1

Contents

Acknowledgments

There are many people to thank for their insight, encouragement, and criticism during the shaping of this project. The staffs at the
General Commission on Archives and History and at the Methodist Library, both at Drew University, were indispensable. Dale Patterson, Mark
Shenise, and Chuck Yrigoyen at the Archives have been long-term conversation partners with me on the topic of Methodism, sharpening my
thinking, filling in many gaps in my knowledge, and correcting misper-
ceptions. Ernie Rubenstein, though he arrived at the Drew Library only
recently, has kept tabs on my work and provided timely bibliography.
Mary Kay Cavazos and Betty Adams, as they have worked in parallel on
their own research into race and American Christianity, have been invaluable conversation partners; both have also responded helpfully to
portions of this manuscript. David Evans read the entire manuscript,
providing needed polish. Chris Anderson, Kevin Newberg, and
Luther Oconer consistently kept me in mind during their own research, forwarding numerous helpful references. Colleen Shantz, Kathleen
Talvacchia, Pamela Holliman, and Lynne Westfield provided clarifying
responses to the Introduction. Chapter 3 received a good once-over by
Pamela Klassen. The scholars of the University Seminar in American
Religion at Columbia University also responded helpfully to a presentation of some of this research and have been truly beneficial to my
thinking through our regular conversations.

Ken Rowe, Terry Todd, Judith Weisenfeld, and Russell Richey participated generously, both in the project's earliest stages at Drew and as it
evolved. I now share the pleasure of teaching history at Drew with Terry
Todd and Virginia Burrus, both of whom are as wonderful, engaging, and
supportive colleagues and friends as one could ask for. Both also read
parts of the manuscript at various stages; the book is far better for all
their attention. Lillie Edwards was the first teacher to shape my thinking

about race in significant ways, and she provided guidance at the very earliest stages of this research.

Jennifer Hammer, editor at New York University Press, pressed me for clarity at crucial points in the manuscript, and was a pleasure to work with all around. Peter Paris and two anonymous readers contributed invaluable responses that assisted me in framing the project.

The Wesley Seminar at Duke University in June 2004 provided crucial research time, resources, and conversation. Richard Heitzenrater and Rex Matthews were particularly helpful, and I profited greatly from the company of the Seminar participants. Deans Maxine Beech and Anne Yardley at the Drew Theological School went far out of their way to find means to support the research for and writing of this book. It would be hard to find a better team of Deans. I am also grateful to the Leonard Hastings Schoff Publication Fund of Columbia University for a grant in support of this publication.

Finally, I am deeply appreciative of the patience and endurance of my spouse, Elizabeth Frey-Davis, and our beautiful children, Eli and Calder. It's your turn on the computer now, boys.

Introduction

In 1939 in Kansas City, Missouri, at a location intentionally selected for being only a few miles from the geographic center of the United States, nine hundred delegates representing three Methodist churches—the Methodist Episcopal Church, the Methodist Episcopal Church, South, and the Methodist Protestant Church—met at what they called "the Uniting Conference." At that conference they formed what was at the time, the largest, and arguably the most powerful, Protestant church in the United States. But the new Methodist Church—the name of the merged denomination—was racially segregated to its core. Black and white congregations had been segregated in previous church structures, but the fresh Methodist Church constitution added yet another layer of separation between racially distinct congregations. As they had been before the merger, white Methodist congregations in the new church were bound together in regional conferences. Black Methodist congregations, though, were grouped in one sprawling national conference. Black Methodists, and the minority of whites who agreed with them, saw the further institutionalization of racism as a severe setback and a lost chance for the new church to take a stand against the prevailing injustices of racist U.S. culture. As one Methodist historian put it, the creation of the segregated Methodist Church "capitulated to the countercurrents of American racist proclivities, and yielded to the prevailing morality of the society." In failing to push back against the desires for the increased power and influence that would accrue as a result of creating a larger national church, the new church surrendered its ethics to "those temporal pragmatic considerations of the world rather than the eternal claims of justice."[1] As the successful merger vote was announced at the end of the conference, and the new church officially began, the delegates rose to sing a celebratory hymn of Christian unity, "We're Marching to Zion." But in one corner of the segregated auditorium, most of the eighty-seven black delegates remained seated in protest, many weeping, even through the verse, "Let those refuse to sing, who never knew our God."

The importance of "conference" to Methodists, both as a political body and as a sacred act of gathering, would be difficult to overstate. It is the distinctive expression of "the church" for Methodists. The conference is the primary location for political power and spiritual authority, and it has two basic forms: the annual conference, consisting of local congregations and their clergy in a given area, presided over by a bishop; and the general conference, made up of delegates from the annual conferences, meeting every four years. It is in conferences that ordination is bestowed, clergy assignments are made, church property is owned, bishops are elected, doctrine is defined, and rules and policies are made and enforced. In his extended study *The Methodist Conference in America*, Russell Richey argues that conference has functioned not just as a bureaucratic body, but as a centering entity that created, defined, and maintained sacred space and time. In and through conference Methodists have understood themselves to combine the best of Protestantism in a new way for a "new continent." As a new and improved ecclesial constitution, they have "sought to imprint Methodist design on the American continent (place), reordering it according to conference rhythms (time), so as to achieve spiritual gravity."[2] It was this sense that conference held a real spiritual gravity that added to the disappointment and frustration of those Methodists who mourned the creation of a fully racialized church, because conference has meant so much more to Methodists than a form of polity. The creation of the new conference for black Methodists—called the Central Jurisdiction—meant a further instantiation of more than a century of shifts away from racial reform that flew in the face of pervasive public rhetoric about the "spiritual unity" of all Christians. Rather than moving closer to an ideal of racial harmony, the new Methodist Church appeared to be purposefully running away from it.

The trajectory forward to that moment from humble institutional beginnings in 1784—when the first Methodist church, the Methodist Episcopal Church, was formed—was a dramatic one. In the 1770s only ten white men were preachers in the Methodist movement, and there were less than 2,000 official members in what were then called "societies." One hundred years later, the Methodist movement was served by more than 53,000 preachers, had nearly three million members, and counted some two million children in Sunday schools. By that time they were not just the largest religious group in the United States, they were arguably the largest national institution in the country as well, exerting an impressive and (unlike the church leadership in the early years of the church) often very deliberate influence on the nation.[3] Ulysses S. Grant is rumored to have said that during his presidency there were three major political parties in the United States, if you counted the Methodists.[4] In that same period of stratospheric growth throughout North America, though, Methodists had also split their church into several branches. Several divisions were over issues of church polity, forming churches such as the Republican Methodist Church in 1792, and the Methodist Protestant Church in 1830. But the most significant institutional fissures emerged from disagreements over race and slavery.

Methodists in America were a multiracial and antislavery movement from their earliest days in late-eighteenth-century America, drawing white and black Americans to their revivals and societies. They produced several well-known black preachers, such as "Black" Harry Hosier and Richard Allen. Early Methodists were, as Catherine Brekus puts it, "relatively egalitarian" in terms of class, race, and gender. Many women served as spiritual leaders in the absence of regular clergy, and as exhorters alongside preachers in the public meetings.[5] But as the church gained strength in numbers and the white men in the organizational structures became more powerful, the possibility of the ordination of women became more and more remote, and the divide between black and white in the broader society became more closely mirrored among Methodists.

The most visible result of these changes was the emergence of separate black churches. The African Methodist Episcopal Church, formed in 1816 and led by Richard Allen, grew from a black Methodist congregation in Philadelphia that had walked out of a biracial church in 1787 after fellow white Methodist congregants tried to segregate it. Another group of African American Methodists formed the African Methodist Episcopal Zion Church in 1821.[6] Black and white Methodists remaining in the original church continued to debate the issues of slavery, as the denomination quickly softened its original stance on slaveholders in the church, a stance that reflected the strong opinions of Methodism's English founder, John Wesley. White Methodists in the southern United States were among the many slaveholders of that era, and the denomination succumbed to their pressure in order to remain a nationally unified church. By 1843 many in the MEC had lost patience with the denomination's continued slide toward acceptance of slavery, and a group of nearly 6,000 left the

Methodist Episcopal Church to form the abolitionist Wesleyan Methodist Connection.

Slavery continued to haunt the church, though. At its national meeting the very next year, those remaining in the church divided into two regional churches over disagreements about a slave-owning bishop in the South. These two groups became the Methodist Episcopal Church (hereafter MEC) in the northern United States, and the Methodist Episcopal Church, South (hereafter MECS) in the southern United States.[7] After the Civil War, these two churches remained separate and the process of racial segregation continued in both. In 1870, former slaves who had been a part of the southern church formed the Colored Methodist Episcopal Church. This church (hereafter CME) was heavily funded by the MECS. In 1864 the MEC began a decades-long process of segregating its own congregations, by now both in the northern states and in the southern states, by dividing conferences along racial lines.[8] While white congregations were grouped together in geographically defined conferences, black congregations were grouped together by race alone, regardless of geographical proximity to other MEC congregations. These black conferences were supervised by white bishops.

After the Civil War, the MEC continued to grow and prosper financially, benefiting from the strong northern industrial economy, and became the largest and most powerful of all the Methodist churches. The movement continued its spread around the world, as Methodists from all branches traveled the globe in the great missionary movement of the late nineteenth and early twentieth centuries. In the United States, Methodists gained national political office, acted as spiritual advisors to presidents, and were crucial to amending the U.S. constitution through women's suffrage and the prohibition of alcohol. Yet many in the two largest and white-dominated branches—the MEC and MECS—felt as if they were failing themselves and the nation through their continued regional division. 1876 marked a time of greater cooperation between the MEC and the MECS. In a meeting in Cape May, New Jersey that year, the centennial of the United States, the churches exchanged declarations of mutual recognition, respect, and affection, all couched in nationalistic language that reflected Methodists' increasing awareness and acceptance of their influence and centrality to the emerging power of the nation. The mutual good feeling continued, and the two churches worked together in several arenas, most notably in foreign missions work. By the early twentieth century, they were also cooperating on hymnbooks and other church literature. By 1910, with the Methodist Protestant Church also participating, a broad organizational outline (called the "Chattanooga Plan") emerged. This outline included an important detail: the black congregations from the MEC would remain organized together in a new form of segregated conference they would call a jurisdiction. In 1914 the MECS approved this basic proposal, but changed the plan so that the black congregations would be organized outside the new church, in a "fraternal" relationship. In 1916 the MEC approved the Chattanooga Plan in its entirety, and made no mention of the change made by the MECS two years earlier.[9]

The two churches then selected twenty-five representatives each to serve on what became known as the Joint Commission on Unification (hereafter Joint Commission). The Joint Commission was charged with the broad task of building a detailed proposal for a merger. Both commissions agreed to the basic Chattanooga Plan with the exception of their different proposals for the "status of the Negro." The MEC General Conference had approved the basic racial relationship it used, while the MECS General Conference had approved a racial relationship that looked most like its own. The Joint Commission met six times between 1916 and 1920 before finally putting forward a proposal, but they failed to agree on anything that could be approved by both churches for the next decade. That basic plan, though, was revived a little more than a decade later and approved in 1935 as the Plan of Union. The Plan called for five white jurisdictions, divided by region, consisting of all white annual conferences, and one jurisdiction made up of all black annual conferences.[10] The merger on which they voted in 1939 would culminate, so the majority of its supporters said, in the greatest and most powerful Christian church the world had ever seen, a church that would lead the greatest Christian civilization in the world.

How did these Methodists—nearly eight million strong, but certainly not the only Methodists, despite their denominational name—conceive of what they had just formed as "united" when members in the church body were racially divided? To get at this question, this book turns not to the years just prior to the merger itself, but back two decades, when the Methodist Joint Commission on Unification—made up of fifty members from the northern and southern Methodist Episcopal churches, all men, white but for two, from all regions of the United States, both lay and ordained—negotiated the basic framework that became the racially defined Methodist Church. This Commission produced an extremely detailed record of their conversations, offering historians the opportunity to observe the ways men in power talked face-to-face about race while in the midst of creating an institutionally united church. One of the central goals of this book is to move beyond standard narratives, which rightly lament the racism that made that church possible, but fail to fully explain how it was—and is—possible for Christians in the United States to hold their Christianity and their racialist thinking together. Indeed, one of the larger arguments this book supports is that it should be impossible to write about Christianity in America without assuming that it has a basic racial character. In standard treatments of the creation of this segregated church—or any segregated American church—explanations of perceived discrepancies, or discrepancies between what we might think Christians ought to have done and what they have done, yield very little in the way of explaining how such things are possible. As an alternative, we should ask not whether their thinking was Christian, but rather what kind of Christianity we are observing. Asking whether racist Christians were *really* Christians is like asking whether slaveholding Americans were *really* Americans. Neither is it constructive to ask whether the Methodists we are observing necessarily match some better, more original spirit of the movement. Again, to use the example of slaveowners: they were both quintessentially "American" and profoundly counter to many of the values that many Americans understood as central to being American.

Once we move beyond these kinds of questions, we can begin to ask better ones. The primary question posed in this book is how, precisely, did so many of these Methodists understand race and Christianity together? How did they balance the allure of cultural and political power that would come with the creation of a larger national church with their desire to adhere to Christian principles of spiritual unity? What larger desires and forces caused so many Methodists—in the middle of the twentieth century—to create a church more concretely and explicitly defined by race than ever before? How, in the spirit of unity, did they think it best to more fully divide themselves? How did they hold together the inherent tensions between what they called "Christian spiritual unity" and juridical racial segregation? To answer these questions by calling all of this "racism" is correct, but insufficient. Rather, we need to more closely examine race itself as a historical phenomenon.

Unlike their fundamentalist counterparts who were emerging as a discrete part of the Protestant front in America, Methodists in the early twentieth century were heavily engaged in fashioning a church that was integral to the idea of America and embedded in its fabric. And unlike the fundamentalists of more recent politics—the Christian Right or the Moral Majority, for example—these Methodists did not find an enemy in the government or feel that somehow they were left out or that the nation was abandoning a divinely instituted course or destiny. America and the principles they understood it to stand for were at one with the Methodist spirit. They felt as if Methodism, and especially a united church that did not waste its energies in inefficient division, offered the nation unique capabilities. Methodists had a central role to play and had been given abundant resources to carry the torch of American (Protestant) Christian civilization to the world.[11]

It is useful to focus on one denomination. Christian denominations are not just doctrinal categories with histories based on biography and theological distinctions. Denominations are also cultural categories. What is most interesting about conceptualizing denominations in this way is that, especially in the case of Methodists, members of denominations often seem most conscious, even most proud, of the cultural expressions of their denominations, and not as invested in the doctrinal and theological aspects. As the study of the history of doctrine and theology has waned, so has the study of denominations. As a result, historians have neglected the study of denominational culture, and in particular of powerfully formative cultural forces such as race that have been far more central to denominational development than has doctrine.[12]

The story I tell here is a story about powerful men and how they negotiated the creation of a large and powerful Protestant church primarily through the lens of race. Holding our focus on the Joint Commission's negotiations, keeping in mind the broader issues of southern black migration to the northern urban centers, the continued national horror of lynching, the nationalizing dynamics of the first World War, and the heightened racial unrest of the era culminating in the race riots of 1918 and 1919, this book illuminates the ways in which race undermined the otherwise well-intentioned patronage of both black and white leadership in these discussions. In attending closely to the languages the Joint Commissioners use in order to wring spiritual unity from racial division, this study builds on Russell Richey's description of early American Methodists, in which he discerns and describes four "languages" in use among them: popular or evangelical; Wesleyan; Episcopal or Anglican; and republican.[13] These four languages offered Methodists a "range of theological options, various identities, and choices as to what constituted

Methodism."[14] In particular, I attend closely—as Richey did in his volume—to languages of self-presentation among Methodists, or the vernaculars of Methodist cultures. Richey and other historians of Methodism have noted in unison that by the mid-nineteenth century, Methodists, particularly in the north in the Methodist Episcopal Church, had almost completely conflated the nation and the church. The "republican" language of Methodism, which mirrored a view of the world in which, among other things, "the fate of the republic . . . rested with the virtue or corruption of its citizens," came to be the dominant language.[15] But it is not so much the particulars of that "republican" Methodist language that concern us here as it is the basic move that this dominance entailed: that the fates of the church and the nation were one, and it was the job of the church to ensure that the American nation remained the "primary custodian," as one historian has put it, of "Christian Civilization."[16]

This book brings together two common threads of Methodist history that are normally told separately: its dramatic shift from a largely rural, working-class, countercultural spiritual movement to a mainstream, male-dominated, politically powerful, wealthy national Christian church, and a second dramatic shift from an officially antislavery church to a movement that split along racial lines, comforted slaveowners, and after Emancipation continued to draw sharper lines of racial segregation between white and black Americans. What I argue here is that American Christian nationalism and deeply embedded cultural racialism are inseparable. I do not argue here, then, that Methodists succumbed to the larger racism of the "secular" culture as they abandoned an earlier anti-establishment mode. Rather, I hope to show through this narrow slice of Methodist history the ways in which the language of race is both a sign of and an integral presence in the broader, more public, and more pervasive language of Christian nationalism. Notably, the contest for "nation" and "civilization" was pervasive among black and white Christians. In his recent book *Exodus! Religion, Race, and Nation in Early Nineteenth-Century America*, Eddie Glaude describes the process by which white and black American Christians embraced the biblical "Exodus" narrative as a way of assembling national identities.[17] Black Christians' use of the narrative to construct notions of a "black nation" "bears a family resemblance" to the ways in which the narrative was used to construct broader American nationalisms. Glaude's larger point is to "unsettle our settled accounts of nation and nationalism by showing how complicated the language of nation has been, even within the discourse of a single historical community."[18] He does this by showing how a concept of "peoplehood" or nation shaped all of black politics in the early nineteenth century. While Glaude's historical evocation of a specific period in American history is instructive—especially in its convincing description of the racial contestation over uses of the Exodus narrative—it is this larger point that is most helpful to us here. Glaude shows us that our understanding of "nation" or "nationalism" in U.S. history is often too narrowly construed as pertaining only to a group's identity as it relates to the civic nation: that body that falls legally under the constitution, including all governmental infrastructure and the attending conventional patriotic discourses that surround and uphold loyalty to it. It is at once a technical term and a term that embraces all the intangibles that decorate and enliven the structure. Rather than this conventional definition, says Glaude, we ought to more properly talk about the complex ways that "nation" has been contested and nationalism has been expressed.

Will Gravely has called for a complete retelling of Methodist history—and through it pointing more broadly to American Christian history—by attending closely to the African American presence in the historical records, even when the topic at hand is not on the surface about them. A fuller, richer, and more accurate version of Methodist history—and of American Christian history more generally—will emerge if we see that this shift in our attention and reading habits does more than fill a void in narratives dominated by white voices and figures; rather, it should transform those narratives. This book attempts just that kind of rereading.[19] What we will see in the conversations of the Joint Commission is that, in the same way that conference has been the primary building block of Methodist constitution, race had become the central thread of institutional identity, displacing other Methodist concerns and languages. The final proof of the dominance of racial identity for Methodists was a thoroughly explicit triumph of race—the complete and thorough segregation of the new Methodist Church.

The Problem of Race

It ought to go without saying, writing in the twenty-first century, that the basic assumption of this book is that race resides not in nature, but in culture. That is, racial categories are social constructions that reflect, among other things, cultural, political, and economic realities, but are not fixed, biologically determined states of nature. But much of our scholarly writing about Christianity in America still reflects habits formed when such assumptions were not as widespread. This book is not about "race relations," then, because I want to emphasize what Martha Hodes has called the "mercurial nature" of race, rather than potentially contribute to the perceptions of its biological reality.[20]

This introduction will not offer a detailed review of the scientific literature on the topic of racial taxonomy; suffice to say that nearly all the scientific explanations or theories of race fell apart shortly after their heyday in the early twentieth century.[21] Racial taxonomies then were complex and varied. Most of the racial categories of the era, in a clear illustration of their unstable mutability, reappeared after World War II as ethnicities or ethnic groups. Races such as the Celts, Slavs, and Iberians of a century ago have morphed into the celebrated ethnic groups of the cultural ethnic revival of the last several decades.[22] Contemporary racial nomenclature is divided by a dizzying mixture of skin color, geography, language, and culture, with a reigning discourse that is simplified to black and white. But while contemporary discourses on race are significantly different from the pseudo-scientific mélange of eugenics and the nascent anthropology of the early twentieth century, they contain semblances, faint linguistic and illogical inheritances, that reveal basic similarities. The most telling regards a central theme of this book—racial purity. Racialist discourse of the early twentieth century was deeply concerned with policing social and especially sexual boundaries between races. In that era widespread lynching gave witness to the violent irrational paranoia engendered by a fear of racial mixing. In the early twenty-first century a less physically violent, though perhaps no less pernicious, racialist logic opens space for the commonly accepted view that a child of a mixed-race couple may be called black but never white. In this way a core racial ideology of racial purity, exhibiting different particular manifestations in different historical contexts, holds sway over what might otherwise seem commonsensical or obviously incongruous.

It is these kinds of everyday assumptions, these hidden slips of intuitive ill-logic, that uncover the racialist ideology that is the foundation of most discussions of race and racism: race is in nature, it is nature; and, apparently, the white race is on top of the biological heap. It is no different in most academic discussions of race and racism, as disciplinary divisions give further evidence to underlying assumptions of a natural white superiority. In the study of American religion, many departments and class offerings continue to separate specialties of "American Religion" and "African American Religion." While the genesis of the separate study of African American religion was motivated by a desire to compensate for a lack of inclusion, its persistent separate life speaks volumes about how little has changed in the unspoken assumptions of what "American religion" is: *white* American religion.

But this book is not about trying to prove racial prejudice on the part of one group or another. To simply "enumerate attitudes," as Barbara J. Fields puts it, is to fall into the trap of a racialist ideology.[23] The complex and mutable social assemblages of race, its role as a primary marker of American identity in the early twentieth century, and the myriad ways in which race has been utilized as a means of negotiating social power are the primary concerns here. Finding it impossible to isolate well-defined theories of race that were held in common by the subjects of this study, I have isolated one phrase that might serve as an adequate descriptor of the general assumptions of the operating, though constantly shifting, racialized discourse among these Methodist negotiators. Representatives from all sides of the discussion called for a "respect for race-consciousness." The phrase meant something akin to self-consciousness. "Race-consciousness" was understood to be a state of mind, both for individuals within a race and for the race as a whole, in which the particular biological characteristics, strengths, flaws, and state of evolution were intimately understood. Only by this kind of racial self-awareness could any race or member of a race improve itself. "Respecting race-consciousness," as this book will show, meant that members of respective races should respect the particular manifestations and needs of other races. The complex ways in which this pseudo-psychological concept worked itself out in negotiations between blacks and whites is central to this project.

Whiteness

One of the ways in which scholars have attempted to rectify writing about race that does not attend carefully enough to the slipperiness of the topic is to talk about "whiteness." Whiteness studies refers generally to scholarly approaches used to uncover the often unacknowledged racial character of social and political privilege and power. For white scholars such as I, paying attention to whiteness means at a basic level simply acknowledging what many white scholars have not: that white people are raced too. Toni Morrison has argued that the greatest fallacy of American literary history is that it has been devoid of any black presence and thus entirely concerned with the themes of white men. To the contrary, Morrison argues, these themes are "made possible by, shaped by, activated by a complex awareness and employment of a constituted Africanism. It was this Africanism, deployed as rawness and savagery, that provided the staging ground for the elaboration of the quintessential American identity."[24] American identity, even when its racial outlines are implicit, depends on a racialized "other." Put more simply, being white is not generally regarded as racial, while being black is. To use an academic illustration again: until only recently (and this has changed nearly imperceptibly), it seemed completely natural to argue that the study of American religion needed to attend more closely to race. The primary way this problem has been resolved has been to add more studies of ignored racial minorities.[25] But what is missing in this critical paradigm is the acknowledgment that the white majority that has been referred to as "American religion" has a racial character and is primarily a racial category. The history of "American Religion" that has only accounted for white religious folk has been critiqued as unfair and incomplete. I am arguing here that it has been incomplete not only in terms of representation, but in terms of the characterization of that white majority. Not only have white religious people been in the numerical majority and maintained access to the most powerful religious institutions in America, there has also been an accompanying racial character to this position of privilege, one that has defined the notions of progress, civilization, and morality that have held sway in American religious culture. The most salient aspect of whiteness, then, is that it is unmarked, unnamed, and unacknowledged by most white people. Ruth Frankenberg has called whiteness an unremarked "location of structural privilege . . . a place from which white people look at ourselves, at others, and at society."[26] The experience of white people is often expanded to define universal human experience, which has led Kevin Gaines to describe whiteness as a "theodicy."[27] Studying whiteness, then, is discovering the implicit racial terrain for which the explicit racialization of nonwhites is necessary. Whiteness and its opposing identities have a symbiotic relationship. This is not to say, though, that white people "own" whiteness and that their racialized identity forms all others. Whiteness is a privileged standpoint that is referenced by all racial identities.

But who is white, and how is whiteness produced and disseminated? These are the central questions of whiteness studies, and there are several recent examples of how they might be addressed historically. Matthew Frye Jacobsen's *Whiteness of a Different Color: European Immigrants and the Alchemy of Race* is a comprehensive history of race and American civic amalgamation.[28] Jacobsen explains how the races, the "public fictions" of human difference common to the nineteenth-century social lexicon, have been made and remade in a long and winding process of assimilation that eventually produced the more binary racial discourse of our contemporary culture. Jacobsen describes the "vicissitudes of race" as "glacial, nonlinear cultural movements" that are nonetheless discernible in three major epochs.[29] The first period is the early republic, during which race is rather simply understood in terms of the constitutional designation "free white persons." The first massive influx of immigrants from Ireland in the 1840s, however, brought about a reconsideration of this general category. Though visually indiscernible from those whites already granted full citizenship and elite social status, the Irish were subjected to new classificatory theories of race that divided up whites into a hierarchy of races, with the Anglo-Saxons or Aryans (at times indistinguishable) generally arriving on top. Jacobsen begins the third era in the 1920s. As restrictive immigration legislation, especially the federal Oriental Exclusion Act of 1924, eased white anxieties about an overabundance of "undesirable" white races, and African American migration northward further destabilized racial boundaries, whiteness was reconstituted into Caucasian. Race scientists began describing the familiar Celts, Finns, Slavs, Jews, and the myriad other subcategories of European races as ethnicities, all falling under the racial rubric of Caucasian.[30]

The Methodist Joint Commission which takes center stage in this book met just before this shift, during the migration of the African American population, during the first major black/white race riots, and during the first world war, an event that, because it was a war between "the white races," laid bare assumptions about European racial superiority. The nearly incomprehensible array of theories on race, and especially the variety of racial nomenclature utilized by the members of the Commission, demonstrate the instability of racial discourse leading up to the 1920s.

American Civilization

Since I have characterized using whiteness as a critical approach that uncovers implicitly racialized identities from beneath a veneer of universal human characteristics, it might at first seem contradictory to analyze in this book what I have described as an explicitly racialized conversation. But this is not exactly the case. While the years of Joint Commission debate were focused on "the negro problem," there was not, in the end, an explicitly named "white solution." Rather, the delegates presented and argued solutions in the ostensibly non-racial, nationalistic language of American civilization. Grace Elizabeth Hale has described whiteness as a "broad, collective American silence" and a "denial of white racial identity." This silence acts as an "erasure that enables many to fuse their absence of racial being with the nation, making whiteness their unspoken but deepest sense of what it means to be an American."[31] This is precisely the dynamic that emerges out of the Joint Commission meetings that I want to describe in detail here.

Gary Gerstle traces these themes through the twentieth century in his *American Crucible: Race and Nation in the Twentieth Century.*[32] Gerstle argues that in the early twentieth century there were two competing and contradictory forms of nationalism: civic and racial. Civic nationalism was and is characterized by democratic rhetoric of liberty and equality for all citizens. This universalizing of basic principles of human freedom, embodied in the preamble of the U.S. Constitution, conflicted with racial nationalism, which depended on the maintenance of an Anglo-Saxon culture. This brand of nationalism posited that white Americans (defined in various ways, as we have seen) were the racial inheritors of the best of human civilization and that the American nation was the pinnacle of a long tradition of superior cultural, military, governmental, and intellectual achievement—and all the result of superior breeding through a mixture of (white) races that filtered out the weaknesses and kept the strengths of the various genetic lines colliding in American society.

But the logic of biological determinism had its limits, as Gerstle illustrates through Theodore Roosevelt and his advocacy of a racial nationalism. Especially in his recounting of his exploits at San Juan Hill, Roosevelt proudly praised the military superiority of his mongrel Rough Riders as the product of the best of each race represented. But Roosevelt was not prepared to extend the logic to the African American soldiers who were an integral part of the victory. After initially acknowledging their place in the battle, Roosevelt left out their role in his later published accounts, while continuing to emphasize the benefits of the mixed-(white) race American man. This same collision of nationalist discourses occurred in the Joint Commission proceedings, and the ensuing discussions continued to move to broader categories in an attempt to escape the contradictions.

One way to escape the contradictions was the language of "manhood," or "manliness." As Gail Bederman has shown in *Manliness and Civilization: A Cultural History of Gender and Race in the United States, 1880–1917,*[33] by the late nineteenth century the discourse of civilization—an extremely volatile and highly contested category—had been distilled to a relatively specific set of values that centered on three main factors. She identifies these as race, gender, and "millennial assumptions about human evolutionary progress." In other words, civilization was a reflection of biology, and therefore tied directly to race and gender, both in terms of human ability and in terms of the cultural signs of progress.[34] The members of the Joint Commission often enlisted the language of manhood as a central element of American Christian civilization. For the Commission members, American civilization was incomplete unless it was Christian, and Christian manhood was essential to the progress of the civilization. A man who had achieved the proper state of manhood exhibited certain characteristics. These characteristics were dependent on a high degree of differentiation from women. For example, women were fragile and "spiritual," men were strong and self-controlled; women's roles were domestic and concerned with caring for children and promoting a proper home environment, while men's roles were those of protector and caretaker of women, children, and the home.[35] In the Joint Commission's discussion of the role of African Americans in the new church, these binaries of sexual difference were conflated. This conflation debased the manhood of black men, thereby placing them farther back on the evolutionary scale of civilized progress than white men. This, in turn, meant they were less deserving of the "manhood rights" that accompanied such progress. These rights included full membership in the proposed reunited Methodist church.[36]

Put crudely, civilized American manhood was tantamount to elite white U.S. male culture. It would seem natural at this point to follow the "elite" factor in that equation and tease out the issues of class that cloud the race and gender themes I have already addressed. Issues of class are nearly indistinguishable from issues of race. In her 1982 essay "Race and Ideology in American History," Barbara J. Fields argues that the hard reality behind the ideology of race is class. Race is ideological because it has no "objective core," while class, also ideological, is wedded to "material circumstance."[37] Along with other white "bourgeois" cultural constructions, race was a tool used to shore up eroding economic and social power structures. While I do not employ Fields's Marxian language, I do assume here that matters of class fueled the origins of nineteenth-century racialist thinking as well as the continued reassembly of racial identity. What I will not do is separate race and class as separate issues in my analyses. Rather, I will highlight those places in which matters of class are clearly revealed, and at times even confessed, as driving the Commissioners' heightened fears about race.

Religion and Denominations

What rarely appears in standard treatments of race and national life in America is any substantive treatment of religion. Gary Gerstle's *American Crucible*, for instance, makes little mention of the role of religion in shaping the discourses of nationalism in the twentieth century. That religion has played a primary part in shaping discourses on nation in America, and vice versa, is not a new idea, however, and this study contributes to a growing body of literature that is attempting to eradicate the distinction between American history and American religion. Edward J. Blum's recent book is a good example of this recent work. In *Reforging the White Republic: Race, Religion, and American Nationalism*, Blum argues persuasively that it was Protestants, and northern Protestants in particular, who made a powerful and pervasive American nationalism possible after the Civil War through a rejection of civic nationalism in favor of a return to white ethnic nationalism.[38] White Christians like the Methodists in this book, then, were not following larger trends in so-called secular American culture, but were in a reciprocal relationship with that culture, a relationship in which Christianity and not-Christianity were often indistinguishable. As Blum puts it, "Protestants drove, solidified, and often sanctified changes in American society."[39]

Writing on the history of this era in Methodist history has only recently begun to build a substantial body of interpretation. One of the few books to address the MEC in the late nineteenth and early twentieth centuries is James Bennett's *Religion and the Rise of Jim Crow in New Orleans*.[40] Bennett makes several convincing arguments, but primarily shows us how religious people and institutions were complicit in the building of a solid Jim Crow culture in the United States. More importantly, Bennett and others are turning our gaze toward northern white

Christian participation in the further power and growth of Jim Crow. In their desire for a more unified America, white Christians (and Methodists in particular) encouraged the creation of a national identity deeply rooted in a fully racialized concept of citizenship. This contest between opposing views of what and whom constituted a unified Christian America was largely won not by a formal debate or a war of ideas, but by what these Methodists did, where they went, where they did not go, what they agreed to, and what they refused to do. I follow definitions of religion that de-emphasize doctrines and beliefs, and look instead to what religious people do and the ways they talk about what they do. In the particular case of the Methodist Joint Commission, we see that Methodists themselves address this difference and decide to disregard "doctrines" or "beliefs" as guides for how to constitute themselves, and instead find other ways to accommodate their desires to create a racially segregated church within an identity that was also sufficiently "Christian" and "Methodist."

So what did these religious people do, then, that should interest us so much? They reunited a very large Protestant church in America—at an institutional level—by segregating its members by race. The technical details of how that happened are well known; but how were such decisions made at a personal level—how, relationally, were Joint Commission members able to describe and argue for a Methodist unity that was only possible by separating white Methodists from black Methodists? What we learn from the sustained interrogation of the Joint Commission deliberations is how such decisions were talked about and made in public. This book does not explore the back-room negotiations, or uncover what Methodists might have said about this issue to each other in private. This study is primarily focused on the record of those conversations in which the plan for merger was developed: the three volumes of *The Proceedings of the Joint Commission on Unification of the Methodist Episcopal Church, and Methodist Episcopal Church, South* (hereafter *Proceedings*).[41] The *Proceedings* are the word-for-word transcriptions of the six meetings of the Joint Commission that took place between December 1916 and January 1920. Reading a prolonged and sustained conversation about race and Christianity among fifty individuals, two of whom were black, representing regional differences from all over the United States, offers insights different from those that emerge from simply studying the results of those conversations. In the *Proceedings* we witness personal interaction. How, for instance, did a white commissioner explain to a black commissioner that racial segregation was not racist? How would they treat each other while deciding to segregate themselves? In this way, this book is about race-talk in relationship, rather than as an institutional stance.

It is significant for our questions about the *Proceedings* that they were consciously produced as a public record. It creates an interesting tension with the face-to-face reality of the meetings. What this means is that we are not getting a glimpse into a necessarily candid conversation. Nor are we witnessing a secret process that was exposed, and thus providing us access to backstage machinations of church power brokers. These commissioners spoke, sometimes from prepared statements, sometimes *ex tempore*, with the knowledge not only that what they said had to be clear to a larger audience, but that they would also be held accountable to what they said. The participants in these meetings understood themselves to be involved in extraordinarily momentous deliberations, for both the church and the nation, and their conscious production of a public record speaks to both the heightened political stakes at that point in Methodist history and the sense of a broad national audience, both immediately and in the future, to which the participants felt accountable. Because of its close scrutiny of the transcriptions of the Joint Commission meetings, and because there is no other full-length study of the Commission itself, this book stands to illuminate a crucible moment in the history of what became one of the most powerful Protestant institutions in the United States.[42]

This book also offers a window into the history of American Christian identity in the early twentieth century. The Commission negotiations center on matters of denominational identity—that is, who were to remain members of the "true" Methodist Church. This sense of a denominational center unfolded in several ways, the primary one being along racial and national lines. Inextricably intertwined, racial and national identity functioned in the discussions as currencies of power, as ideological media through which the potential social and political influence of the new church was dispersed. Membership and its relationship to the central governing body was the key to this power and became the ground on which compromise rested. That proposed compromise was a new organizational scheme for what was referred to as the "reorganized church," in which those who were not to be treated as full members might still maintain membership in name, but without access to all privileges and powers. Race became the line drawn around full membership, and this reading of the transcriptions of the Joint Commission meetings is intended to show the contextual particularities of how race became the major currency of power. While I thus attempt to offer a sustained historical argument that race was the central impediment to the Joint Commission negotiations, the best way to categorize this historical work might be analytical/descriptive. Like a growing number of studies in the field of American religion, this project has an anthropological or ethnographic feel to it. This book has affinity with Susan Friend Harding's *The Book of Jerry Falwell: Fundamentalist Language and Politics*,[43] a work that is decidedly anthropological, but in which Harding's practice of descriptive close reading leads to analysis of a cultural logic very similar to my analysis here. Harding describes the "languages of faith" she studied in Falwell's world as her "field site." She uses the words of fundamentalists not as "evidence for something else," but to show how their faith language "persuades and produces effects." While I am using the transcriptions as evidence for larger arguments about American Christianity and its cultural character, I also use them to examine the language of race. This book explicates the ways the language of race persuaded these Methodists, and how it and the language of Methodism inhabited the same space.

The material for this book is closely circumscribed, but read in wider contexts. To locate the Joint Commission negotiations in broader national conversations about race, I have read the primary newspapers from both churches (in particular the *Christian Advocates* published in New York by the MEC and Nashville by the MECS, and the primary newspaper for black members of the MEC, *The Southwestern Christian Advocate*); books and pamphlets written by the primary actors on the Joint Commission; the church newspapers of the AME, AMEZ, and CME; regular publications of the missionary societies of the MEC and MECS; and a long span from *Crisis*, the publication of the NAACP, and *Opportunity*, the journal of the National Urban League. The transcriptions themselves, though, form the basis of the analysis. Like an anthropologist, I have isolated the Joint Commission as a discrete discursive community. As such, I have tried to describe not so much the differences among the commissioners as the ways they construct their differences. With only a few personnel changes over the four years of its existence, the Joint Commission was a unique group of interlocutors focused on a single problem. The scope of my analysis does not include to any great degree the sources of their ideas, nor the political motives behind what they said and did. I do not, for instance, divide the Joint Commission into different alliances or racial groups or even regional groups and then trace their differing political moves over time. Rather, I spend time following the language of difference that Joint Commission commissioners used about themselves and others. Readers will encounter here the process of constructions of difference that unfolded over the course of the negotiations.

The chapters in this book are centered topically, but their order follows the basic chronology of the Joint Commission meetings. Chapter 1, "Birth of a Nation, Birth of a Church," serves both to describe the institutional history of the Joint Commission and to set up the issues that were addressed in the Joint Commission negotiations. By looking at a few examples from publications, we will also begin an immersion into the complex language of race, region, and American civilization.

Chapter 2, "The Baltimore Meeting: Saints, Cemeteries, and Savages," addresses how the Joint Commission established the terms of the debates. It begins in Baltimore at the Joint Commission's opening ceremonies, and presents an analysis of the use of history, story, place, and sacred objects in the ceremonies as a means of performing Methodist identity. This performance, staged in a sacred Methodist place and at a sacred Methodist time, presented a Methodist identity that was focused on the particularities of American Methodist-ness through descriptions of and stories about past heroes. We will explore the ways in which sacred objects, sacred spaces, sacred stories, and sacred time were assembled into an identity that was distinctly Methodist and distinctly indigenous to American soil. The next section of the chapter begins in Baltimore but ranges through the discussions in all the meetings. We see how the Joint Commission leadership purposefully steered the negotiations away from arguments that used theology, doctrine, or "Christian ethics"—in other words, away from the explicitly religious world they had just performed. While not arguing that the ensuing negotiations were necessarily "profane," the chapter shows how many in the Joint Commission constructed a hierarchy of spirituality that placed large-scale institutional unity as a more worthy spiritual ideal than racial equality in the ecclesial sphere.

Chapter 3, "Race Consciousness," explores the development, primarily in the Baltimore meeting, of the language of "race consciousness." I distill the wide-ranging discussion into two competing versions of this concept: northern race consciousness and southern race consciousness. These labels reflect not regional differences, but rather regional interests. In other words, the two strategic variants were not employed or presented solely by one church or the other, but were used interchangeably by commissioners from both churches.

Chapter 4, "The Savannah Meeting: The Bogey of Social Equality," is focused on the Savannah meeting and the shift away from race consciousness to a discussion of "social equality." It is through this discussion that we discover what fears undergirded resistance on all sides of the debate to a fully integrated church. No member of the Joint Commission ever spoke out in favor of social equality among the races. MEC members—the two black members and the acknowledged "radical" white bishop especially—expended great energy distancing themselves from any hint of advocacy of such a principle. To illustrate the centrality of a "conservative" position on the social equality of the races to the success of any position taken in the negotiations, the chapter lays out detailed examples of the wide array of theoretical approaches to race that were argued at Savannah, and shows how they all agreed that "social equality of the races" was a serious and grave danger not only to the new church but also to the American nation itself.

Chapter 5, "The Final Three Meetings: The Problem of Missions and the Urgency of Patriots," details the final three meetings and the shift to language of nationalism, patriotism, and debates over who in the new church would be considered the objects of mission activities and who would be considered missionaries. Here discourses of racial and civic nationalism collided as black Methodists, hopeful in the wake of their participation in the war effort, pushed for recognition of their voluntary patriotic sacrifices. In response, many of their white counterparts in the Joint Commission—some from within their own church—called on them to do their patriotic duty by compromising even further for the sake of unity and at the expense of "mere rights."

1

Birth of a Nation, Birth of a Church

In 1915, D. W. Griffith's monumental film *Birth of a Nation* "wrote history with lightning," as President Woodrow Wilson supposedly said. The film cast the civil war in the United States as a horrible but eventually purifying event in the life of the nation. The America that was born of the conflict was stronger and wiser. It was a natural reunion. It repaired an unnatural cleavage in the family of the white race in America, a mongrel race melded from the best genetic stock of Europe—though primarily by the greatest strain, the Anglo-Saxon.

The film begins with a few scenes that establish the blame for all of America's troubles: the arrival of African slaves. First it shows the arrival of the slaves, the central problem in American life, and then those good-hearted but sadly misguided figures in the narrative, the northern liberals. They are shown in the early scenes of the film in their abolitionist phase, not helping the black man at all, we find out, but instead altering natural relationships in ways that nearly destroy the entire nation.

The central racial theme of the film is the evil of miscegenation. Of all the characters in the film, the mulatto seductress and the puppet mulatto governor are the most evil and misguided. In fact, they are the only characters with misguided intentions. Neither the Union nor the Confederacy is portrayed as the malevolent aggressor. The Union, and northerners in general, to be sure, are not gallant heroes in the same way the Confederates are. They are rather, like the Confederates, tragic figures, caught in an inevitable confluence of opposing political needs bred by unnatural alliances with blacks and greed. They are a part of a community torn apart by past sins. Lincoln, especially, is portrayed as a heroic leader, trapped between equally abhorrent choices. What takes the northern leadership astray is the self-interested meddling of mixed-blood troublemakers. Well-intentioned northern liberals are duped into thinking they are helping blacks and making up for the wrong of slavery by integrating them fully into white American society on a socially equal basis. But the film firmly contends that race mixing only leads to disaster, no matter what the intentions of the participants.

The South, before the war, is portrayed as an idyllic land of right relationships. Everyone is in his or her place: masters are kind but firm, slaves are obedient but happy. Trouble arises from the improper relationship between the white northern abolitionist senator and his mulatto mistress; he also keeps many blacks in his company. This senator and others like him move the North to war. After the war, it is the mulatto leadership, which is clever but finally unable properly to handle the mantle of authority, that nearly destroys the South entirely by encouraging ignorant blacks in the Union Army to seek revenge on southerners. The turning points for this world turned upside down are two sexual encounters: one in which the mulatto governor makes sexual advances on a white woman, and another in which a confused black Union soldier lusts for a white girl and chases her until she jumps to her death. These incidents rouse the southern men to don the white uniforms of the Klan and ride to the rescue. They defeat the mulatto-led reconstruction government and return southern society to its proper order. Blacks and whites, both South and North (though not mulattos), are all happy in the end as the natural racial order is preserved, and the nation is reborn from the cleansing fire of war.

These scenes do not suggest that blacks are inherently evil or sexually uncontrollable. They do imply that improper racial ordering will lead blacks out of their place and cause them to do evil. Mulattoes in particular are singled out as the evil spawn of race mixing. And the black Union soldiers are only rapists when in a soldier's uniform and given authority they are unable to handle. There are many blacks in the film who do no evil. Several even participate in the fight against black Union soldiers. These blacks never step out of their "natural" roles into improper intimacy or illegitimate authority. They know their place, and they are perfectly capable of a good and happy life in their place. They are loved by their white owners/bosses, and they love them back.

The themes and concerns of this film closely mirror those that drove the discussion of unification among Methodists: race and social order, regional identity and national unity, and a racialized program of national progress toward civilization. Perhaps most importantly, it is the fears of whites that become so horribly realized in the film's scenes of sexual predation and its Frankensteinian mulatto characters twisted by experimentation with unnatural social intimacy. Initially glossed over or only vaguely referred to, the question of "social relations" between whites and blacks was a primary concern of white Methodists. What became known as the "bogey of social equality" among the Methodist conversants was also one of the few things they all agreed on: that black and white Methodists should never be "socially" equal, and that to eliminate segregation even in a church would be to suggest that they were. Both black and white Methodists went to great lengths to say that they had absolutely no interest in even discussing the prospect of "social equality." The most self-consciously "progressive" white Methodists expended their strongest rhetorical dismissiveness on this matter. Advocating "social equality" was considered an extremely radical position of "agitation." In the same way, black Methodists made abundant gestures of disgust in answering the accusation that they were interested in "social equality."

Like the makers of *Birth of a Nation*, who were looking for a more perfect reunion of North and South, Methodists were looking for a reunion of the regionally defined branches that would not only return them to their original structure but also move them beyond, to something new and better. Like the unified American nation, Methodists needed to leave behind old divisions and return to proper relationships with each other. Unification was necessary if they were to hold their place as the carriers of American Christian civilization. That unified church had to conform to the standards of American civilization, and had to reflect the social relationships there as well. What precisely "American Christian civilization" meant for the church, or what proper social relationships looked like, were of course disputed.

"The Long Road"

Methodist Episcopals of all persuasions had been pondering a reunion of the northern and southern churches from the moment they split. The General Conference of the Methodist Episcopal Church of 1844 brought about a formal division that reflected sectional differences within the Methodist Episcopal Church that had been brewing for several decades, and provided enough fuel to stoke vociferous and consistent debates over property, blame for the split, and the rights to the claim of "true" Methodist Episcopal heritage. Methodists in the MEC generally contended that the split was the result of differences over the slavery question, while many in the MECS argued that the slavery question merely revealed deeper ecclesiastical issues. In his book about the unification of the MEC and MECS, Bishop John Moore, an MECS bishop who was a member of the Joint Commission, wrote that an earlier division in the MEC, one that produced the Methodist Protestant Church, reflected the very same issues that caused the split of 1844. The creation of the Methodist Protestant Church has been generally accepted as a matter of divergences concerning ecclesiastical power.[1]

The phrase that came to represent this MECS position was that "slavery was not the cause, but the occasion" of separation. It took twenty-five years and the end of the Civil War before the two churches engaged in formal discussions. One of the first things to be discussed was reunification, as many MEC members and leaders assumed that the end of slavery meant the end of division. In 1869 the MEC sent a delegation of two bishops to the MECS General Conference in St. Louis. They presented a formal plea for unification. In response, the MECS sent a letter to the MEC College of Bishops putting forth the case that reunification was not a simple matter, and that the occasion, not the cause, of the separation had disappeared with the emancipation of the slaves. More important, perhaps, was the lack of agreement about the status of the action of the 1844 General Conference. At its 1848 General Conference, the MEC declared that the Plan of Separation of the 1844 General Conference was null and void. This meant that the MEC did not formally recognize the MECS as a legal church, and thus that (in the view of the MEC) the MECS was illegally holding property and carrying on work under the name Methodist Episcopal Church.[2]

No formal meetings on the question occurred until the American centennial, 1876, when two commissions, each appointed by their respective General Conferences, met in Cape May, New Jersey. The meetings were friendly and conciliatory, and included a crucial exchange of official mutual recognition. The dispute over the Plan of Separation was resolved when the parties accepted a statement that both churches represented legitimate branches of the original Methodist Episcopal Church of 1784. This was the beginning of real attempts at union.[3]

Other important changes occurred after the Cape May meeting. The MEC dropped objections to MECS expansion into "northern" territory, as MECS congregations appeared in the Pacific Northwest and Illinois. The MEC was already sending missionaries to the South, especially among ex-slaves. This extensive missionary enterprise, which often resulted in separate MEC and MECS congregations serving the same communities, led to one of the main rallying cries in support of unification, as the state of "altar against altar" embarrassed some Methodists, infuriated others, and reeked of inefficiency to the younger church leaders who had been following the early-twentieth-century trends in "scientific" church management.[4] This condition also offended the patriotic sensibilities of many Methodists in both churches, something we will revisit later in this chapter.

By the late nineteenth century, the MEC leadership was moving quickly in the direction of ecumenical cooperation. This movement culminated in the first Ecumenical Methodist Conference in London, England, in 1881. In 1888 the General Conference appointed a commission on Interecclesiastical Relations, with the purpose of promoting general Christian (read Protestant) unity. At the MECS General Conference of 1894 a Committee of Federation of Methodism was formed, and a request was sent to the MEC General Conference asking that they do likewise. The MEC General Conference approved, and the two committees met in January 1898.[5] From this meeting several broad recommendations for cooperation emerged, especially in regard to liturgical and congregational level issues. A common catechism, hymnbook, and order of worship were called for, as well as cooperation in foreign mission work. The Commission also recommended, without many specifics, that domestic cooperation increase in order to allay overlap and redundancy at the local level. These recommendations were approved by the MECS General Conference that same year, but were not recommended by the MEC until 1904.

In the realm of foreign missions, the two churches divided up work by geographic regions, with the MEC responsible for Puerto Rico and the Philippines, the MECS for Brazil and Cuba. A common publishing house was established in China, and they combined their separate Japanese mission churches into the independent Methodist Church of Japan in 1907. The establishment of an autonomous church in Japan was to be a significant event for the black congregations in the United States, as those who wanted the black congregations to set up their own independent church used the Japanese church as a successful precedent.

One move made by the MEC General Conference gives some indication as to how far apart, despite the cooperation that had been achieved, the MEC and the MECS were, and also how much the problem of race factored into that distance. The 1908 MEC General Conference passed a proposal to the Methodist Protestant Church for unification. The Methodist Protestant leadership accepted the proposal with enthusiasm and in response proposed that along with the MECS, the three churches organize another committee to study the possibility of a union among the three Methodist bodies. As a result, the Joint Commission on Federation was formed, and held its first meeting in Cincinnati in January 1910.[6] From this meeting emerged a subcommittee, composed of three members from each church, to work out the details of possible union.

This Committee of Nine produced a proposal that would set the stage for the creation of the Joint Commission on Unification, which would not include the Methodist Protestants and which began meeting in late 1916. The committee of nine met in Chattanooga in May 1910. The report from this meeting proposed a merger without many specific guidelines, but also included an addendum that suggested the black membership be separated into its own jurisdiction. The only other major topic of discussion was the nature of the General Conference, which was largely a problem between the MEC and MECS and did not affect the Methodist Protestant Church. Recognizing that the major obstacles to a viable plan of union lay between the other two denominations, the MP delegation recommended to their General Conference of 1912 that they continue the appointment of delegates to the Commission, but that they not participate until the MEC and MECS settled their differences.[7] This proposal was accepted and the MEC and MECS continued meeting alone.

The recommendation that was eventually passed on to their respective General Conferences was essentially the same proposal from the 1911 meeting in Chattanooga, Tennessee.[8] Official approval by the 1916 MEC General Conference in Saratoga Springs, New York, finalized MEC support for the Chattanooga proposal, but made no mention of the change made by the MECS General Conference of 1914.[9] The resulting reaction in the MECS was mixed. Some took the silence as a sign that the MEC was willing to negotiate and might compromise on the issue of black membership. Others understood it to be a firm stance, and used it to express the worry shared by many MECS members, that any unification would only result in the "absorption" of the MECS by the MEC. Black MEC members and whites who supported their presence in the new church, for their part, worried that over-eager leadership from their church would compromise too far in their desire for a larger, more powerful reunited church and accept a racially segregated compromise. Despite these fears and heated exchanges between the various church serials, the movement toward unification continued. The Joint Commission on Unification scheduled its first meeting for late December 1916.[10]

The Working Conference on the Union of American Methodism

An event outside of denominational planning gave one more push toward the meetings of the Joint Commission, and is indicative of both the level of national attention to this issue between the two churches and the concern from outside the MEC and MECS that Methodism's regional division reflected badly on the state of national unity. In February 1916, delegates from seven Methodist denominations—the MEC, MECS, AME, AMEZ, MP, CME, and Methodist Church of Canada—gathered at Northwestern University at the behest and expense of the John Richard Lindgren Foundation for the Promotion of Peace and International Unity for a conference titled "A Working Conference on the Union of American Methodism." For the most part the Foundation awarded prize money to papers prepared by students on the topic of ecumenism, but the board of the fund felt that the Methodist cause was important enough to assist directly. Representatives were bishops, editors of denominational publications, seminary professors, and prominent laymen. Invited presenters were asked to address specific issues, which included sectional problems, polity, doctrine and ritual, church discipline, "the Negro," foreign missions, domestic missions, property, "connectional enterprises," and "federation vs. organic union." Perhaps in recognition that it was the most contentious issue, the session on "the Negro" was scheduled for more speakers than any other. The topic also took up much of the time in the roundtable discussions afterward.

It was the first gathering of Methodist representatives at which there was reasonable hope whatsoever that any of the Methodist denominations would soon be uniting. Indeed, the Foundation had high hopes. They were spurred forward on the one hand by the fear and apprehension that broad war in Europe could threaten "Christian civilization," and on the other by the optimism of modern progress and all that it held out for the spread of "Christian civilization" from America.

In that spirit, the meeting opened with the adoption of a "Call to Prayer for Methodist Unity." This opening statement was animated by a sense of urgency because of what those gathered perceived as the potential for global disaster if Methodists remained divided. No one had dreamed, it said, that

the twentieth century would witness almost world-wide war, involving nearly all the great Christian nations, and that in hatred and savage

cruelty, enormous loss of life and immense loss of property, it should
stand without a parallel in all the centuries of man's existence on this
planet. Men's hearts have begun to fail them because of fear. . . . The
hopes of international peace seem bankrupt . . . men's hopes of international peace are blasted. The world is in despair. Civilization is halted
and Christianity dishonored and disparaged. Men ask, is god no longer
a god of peace? Is the god of war to overthrow the kingdom of the
Prince of Peace? If the Church of Christ fails to restore the spirit of
brotherhood in the world, then may we despair of the race. . . .

The world they saw before them could not appear more bleak. Under this
sense of impending worldwide doom, these Methodists from all over
North America saw themselves and their proposed task as a crucial piece
of saving the world from self-destruction:

We are called to consider the question of Christian Unity in the interest
of international peace itself. The brotherhood of man is at stake as well
as the belief in the fatherhood of god. . . . Able and candid discussions
have shown that there are no insuperable barriers to Christian Union,
provided the spirit of Christian Unity becomes a passion among us.
Only the elemental fires can give final shape to the continents and fuse
the metals in the rocks. Only divine fires can make the true superman superior to hate and bloody strife. . . . Methodists of the continent, pray,
pray everywhere, pray without ceasing, for Christian Unity among the
sons of Wesley, for, as a great Congregationalist leader has well warned
us, "As goes Methodism, so goes America."[11]

Responses to the Conference were mixed among MEC and MECS members. Among MECS members of the eventual Joint Commission, at least,
the presence of the black denominations instilled a fear that those denominations would want to participate in the formation of a new all-in-
clusive North American Methodist church. This fear was baseless, as the
AME, AMEZ, and CME church leadership had little interest in joining
their white counterparts.[12] There had been some animosity already between the CME and the African Methodist Episcopal churches over the
CME's dependence on MECS philanthropy. There had been erratic conversation among those churches about a national union, but the most viable plan fell apart in 1918 after bishops in the CME withdrew their support for it. These churches valued their independent status and were at

times a bit amused at the MECS presumption that they would want to join the white denominational ranks. The trustees and planners at the John R. Lindgren Foundation were also perhaps a little too optimistic in their broad and enthusiastic vision for cooperation and eventual union, and their well-intended inclusion of the various denominations only served to heighten the suspicion among MECS opponents of union that their smaller church and its distinctive identity would be lost in a crowd of white northern aristocrats and black Methodists seeking revenge on their former slave-holding brethren.

Among black MEC leaders who did have a tremendous amount at stake in the conversation, the meeting at Northwestern served to inspire their hope that a new racially inclusive church was within reach. In the lead editorial of the *Southwestern Christian Advocate* following the Working Conference, Robert Elijah Jones, the paper's editor and eventual ministerial delegate to the Joint Commission, reported positively on the conference, encouraging his readers that "it was clear that union was desirable and that there were no insuperable difficulties."[13] Jones (1872–1960) lived and worked in New Orleans, Louisiana. He was born in North Carolina, and served his first pastorates there until he was made assistant editor of the *Southwestern Christian Advocate* in New Orleans in 1897. He was editor from 1904 to 1920, when he was elected bishop. He and Matthew W. Clair were the first African American bishops in the MEC. Under Jones's leadership, the Gulfside Assembly in Waveland, Mississippi, was purchased and established as the first major MEC retreat center for black members. It would be difficult to understate Jones's influence on the Joint Commission. His presence was formative and his carefully chosen interventions were influential.

Jones's presentation at the conference was prescient in two ways: he addressed from the outset the issues that lay at the heart of white opposition to an integrated church, and he proposed the organizational scheme that would form the basis of the eventual Plan of Union, a position he maintained for the duration of the Joint Commission meetings. Showing that he understood what whites feared most, he began his speech not by outlining the organizational details of his proposals, but by addressing the "social" fears of whites.

Jones drew a careful distinction between two kinds of social interaction, what he called "sociable" and "social." "Sociable" interracial interaction was kind, polite, and perfunctory, and it facilitated necessary cooperation for church work. Interracial interaction that was more than this, that engendered meaningful relationships—both platonic friend-ships and romantic encounters—was "social." Sociable interaction be-tween blacks and whites was acceptable. Social interaction was anathema to both races, argued Jones, especially when it led to interracial marriage. Jones considered sociable interaction possible, and testified that he had witnessed interracial cooperation that never moved to the level of the "so-cial." The experience Jones relied on was the MEC work in the southern states among blacks. For years, he said, white MEC representatives had worked in the southern states on sociable terms with blacks. Whites had "eaten and slept in their [blacks'] cabins. We do not know of a single mar-riage that has grown out of this relation."[14] Jones referred to a paper given by (white) fellow Methodist John R. Mott, the internationally known YMCA leader and future Nobel Peace Prize winner, in which Mott outlined the dangers inherent in interracial contact. Mott warned of a marked decline in morals when different races are brought into more in-timate relations due to "the shrinkage of the world." The loss of guiding traditions and social customs, the clash of different ethical systems, and a general relaxation of moral restraints in the face of differing value sys-tems all lead to general decline in a society's moral life. All of this is only possible, Jones argued through Mott, if there is the "restraining and transforming influence of a greater human power."[15] In other words, in-terracial contact moderated and regulated by the proposed Methodist church would present no danger to the social balance that was of primary importance to whites. There would be no need for mixed-race congrega-tions, he said, and besides, "mixed societies are not desired even by the colored people." Jones's attempt to pacify white fears of racial intermin-gling was echoed by Bishop George W. Clinton of the AMEZ. The "plane of Christianity" is the only plane upon which real brotherhood is possi-ble, Clinton said, but he quickly circumscribed his use of "brotherhood" and "brothers": "and when I say brothers, I mean brothers in Christ, and no [sic] brothers-in-law, because I am glad that this bogy of social equal-ity and all that kind of stuff has no more weight with the intelligent Negro than it has with a black-snake." Matters of social equality were not mat-ters of law, said Clinton, but matters of individual taste. Both of these black leaders used strong language and dismissive rhetoric to prove to whites that they did not care at all for the agitating arguments for social equality. They seemed determined not to let the issue even linger long enough for discussion.[16]

Jones offered several other arguments in favor of a merger plan in which black and white Methodists were members of the same church but segregated by conference—essentially laying out the basic plan that would be implemented more than twenty years later. Like many black and white Americans of his day, Jones argued that "the Negro" had an essential nature with "his" own particular religiosity. Blacks are loyal, have a strong faith, and possess an "almost universal belief in the personal and immanent presence of God." They exhibit a "forgiving spirit" and a strong humility. They have a powerful talent for music, and "his emotion add[s] greatly to present Christianity." Jones developed the notion that blacks are humble and forgiving. It was of utmost concern to whites, both northern and southern, that black Americans would be likely to harbor bitterness and animosity toward whites in the South. But when blacks were not as angry or resentful for the wrongs of slavery as whites expected them to be, this was also held against them as proof that blacks lacked dignity and personal strength. Jones attempted to find a way around this double bind by arguing that blacks who found a "forgiving spirit" toward whites were not revealing a flaw of "racial subserviency [*sic*] but a real strength of character." Alluding to growing hostilities in Europe, Jones suggested that this strength, if it existed among whites, might have paved the way for "an entirely different world situation."[17]

Jones was also concerned about the appearance of inconsistency in black arguments for a place in the new Methodist church. White Methodist leadership grumbled that MEC black membership wanted the best of both worlds—autonomy and access to leadership—while remaining within the larger Methodist church. Jones and others advocated Methodist union that included blacks, but blacks were to be organized within their own jurisdiction in order to retain their own sphere of influence. To make this argument many pointed to the success of the African American Methodist denominations—the AME, AMEZ, and CME churches. Separation from whites had many advantages, said Jones, and the "distinctive colored" churches were strong and had grown tremendously on their own. But it would be "paying the Negro too great a compliment" to say that they could continue their success as far as white churches had gone. "Negroes" lacked complete development, and so while they needed autonomy in order to find their own way, they would never realize their full potential without contact with whites, "this world's best civilization."[18] The arguments for autonomy within the institutional fold of the new church, then, were not inconsistent, but pragmatic. Christian civilization could not be achieved without regulated contact and mentoring from whites, who were the progenitors and keepers of the world's highest civilization.

Jones was not always so deferential. While he made a point of regularly complimenting whites on their achievements and reminding all that there would be no black progress without white influence, Jones also found room to criticize white Methodist leadership. He occasionally, as in this speech, hid his chiding in the guise of a compliment, or at least a nod to white minority domination in a decidedly nonwhite world. One of his arguments in the Evanston speech was that Methodist unification would be beneficial for the Anglo-Saxon.[19] While whites were the "world's masters," and may have possessed in "large measure" apostolic leadership, they were not the largest group in the world, and may have been one of the smallest. Jones suggested that whites needed to consolidate their resources and leadership, lest overwhelming numbers who have not yet achieved their fully civilized potential swallow them up. As the world's colored races develop and achieve "race consciousness," they will begin to "resent discriminations." To avoid this, whites must not only consolidate and streamline their programs, but also begin early to show those races not as fully developed as whites that brotherhood in Christ really means something. A "world-wide program," warned Jones, would be impossible without reassurances from whites that they care about the less developed races. The Anglo-Saxons of the Methodist churches must be careful that they do not abuse the advantages and strengths they have in the world and tread on "helpless Negroes." The famous Anglo-Saxon sense of justice and fair play must show itself promptly, warned Jones, or history will judge them harshly as those who were given much, were expected to give much in return, and instead gave very little indeed.[20]

The conference gave some speakers the opportunity to air various theories on race and race history. In particular, several speakers dealt with the problem of God's role in the institution of slavery in America. The presence of ex-slaves in Christian churches that also housed former slaveowners, in a nation the church claimed was ordained by God as the chosen vessel to spread Christian civilization, presented a sticky theological problem. How were American Christians to reconcile their view that the existence of the United States was ordained by God, that it was built on Christian principles and was destined to spread its superior Christian civilization to the world, with the fact that that same nation participated in the promotion of human slavery? This problem haunted Methodists, especially those in the MECS—not in terms of culpability, but because the resolution of the problem affected the bargaining power of blacks in contemporary disputes. If enslaved Africans were simply another society of human beings like the Americans who enslaved them, then slavery was an ignominious act of immoral aggression. Slavery became in this case barbarism. But if enslaved Africans were in fact better off in some way because of their transfer to America and their contact with American Christian civilization, then there was an undeniable benefit to both slaves and their descendants.[21]

The theory that slavery was, in the long term, beneficial for black Americans was espoused by both northern and southern white Methodists, and it was not unheard of among black Methodists either. During the Working Conference, several speakers who represented different sides of the union debate advocated some version of the theory. White MEC Bishop Wilbur P. Thirkield, who advocated a racially inclusive new church, argued that slavery had been part of a divine providential plan that would culminate in the full integration into one Methodist church of all the descendants of slaves who were now on their way to becoming completely civilized.[22] Slavery, argued Thirkield, was "a tutelage," giving Africans lessons in "ideas of law and order, in the civilizing power of sustained work, in the English language, in the knowledge of God's Word, in the rudiments of Christian religion."[23] On a different side of the union debate, Henry N. Snyder, an MECS Joint Commission member and president of Wofford College in South Carolina, used a similar logic of divine planning for the fate of the Negro race.[24] Yet Snyder did not seem as awestruck with the way God had chosen to find salvation for the Africans. His more circumspect version of the history of the Negro race ran more like a tragedy than a melodrama. For Snyder, the tragedy was not concluded. The ending might only be happy in that the Negro race would be better off because of its contact with (white) American Christian civilization. It would remain tragic, though, because separation, no matter how much the "idealists" might scorn it, would remain the reality for the races. America was not and never would be home for former Africans. Snyder praised former slaves' ability to adapt to the new American environment, but nonetheless they were not "at home in his new world . . . [not] a welcome citizen in the household of the American political family, [but rather] an intruder, and that even in the church of Christ he is still, as one sitting by the Beautiful Gate of the Temple, stretching forth begging hands."[25] While Thirkield and others envisioned all non-Anglo-Saxon races eventually achieving a high state of Christian civilization and living more intimately, Snyder sustained a similar race history but articulated a different future in which the races, while perhaps all progressing toward greater civilization, would nonetheless remain separate.

Perhaps the one major development of the conference was the discovery by white Methodists that the leadership among black Methodists held widely differing views of a proposed reunited church. Many whites, especially in the MECS, assumed that the strictly black Methodist denominations would be clamoring at the door of the new church in order to take advantage of its immense resources. Several leaders of these churches scoffed at the idea, not only during the conference but also in their church newspapers and in correspondence with MEC leadership. Leadership of the black denominations was especially divided, not only in opinions on union but on how to approach the problem in the first place. Bishop Charles H. Phillips (CME), for instance, thought that the black congregations of the MEC and the CME should merge, the white congregations of the MEC and the MECS should merge, and then at some later date the two resulting churches might attempt a merger. This would be a more efficient way to go about it, said Phillips jokingly, because these two groups of black congregations were "white folks' negroes," unlike the strictly black AME and AMEZ.

The only participant at the conference to approach the question of race and union from a biblical standpoint was Bishop Levi J. Coppin (AME). His presentation was brief, without deference to racial superiority, and clear. With a short exegetical sketch, Coppin argued that racial segregation in Christian churches was unscriptural. Not only was he alone in his approach; his subject matter did not receive much response either. Many who disagreed with him saw Coppin's focused biblical approach as judgmental and offensive. This same negative view of the role of scripture, doctrine, and theology in the debate on race and union would profoundly shape the direction of the Joint Commission debate.

The Final Push in Print

As the reality of a face-to-face meeting between the MEC and MECS on the topic of unification began to sink in, strong proponents and detractors of unification began finding ways to make their message heard.

Those with the influence or the means published books or pamphlets arguing their position. Others battled it out via letters to the editors of denominational papers. The more prominent members of the Joint Commission published books on the prospect of union before the meetings began. Some publications did not explicitly address the union debate, instead making broader cultural arguments meant to influence the negotiations. Several general trends and themes emerged that would shape the Joint Commission discussions: definitions and descriptions of race, the role of region in shaping the new church structure, and a deep concern with the role of Methodism in the maintenance and spread of American Christian civilization.

All three main groups in the discussion—whites in the MEC, blacks in the MEC, and the all-white MECS—were preoccupied with the place of the church in the American national consciousness, but all to different degrees. The national scene and the Methodist place of prominence there concerned especially the MEC leadership, and they went to great lengths to show that Methodists were not falling behind the current progress of the nation at large. White Methodist leadership, especially in the MEC, conceived of themselves as the guardians and carriers of American civilization. Jay Douglas Green has explored how MEC missionary campaigns both in Africa and among blacks in the United States, particularly in the South, were part of a wider program to bolster the church's self-perception as the carrier of American civilization. Green argues that foreign and domestic missionary efforts took part in an "Africanist" discourse that upheld broad cultural notions of white Protestant superintendence and paternalism.[26]

Green's thesis that Africa was at the center of much of Methodist work to establish the denomination as the leader of American Christian civilization is accurate, but perhaps not broad enough. This is because Methodists, like most other Americans, conceived of race more broadly than white and black, or Anglo-Saxon and African. Methodist notions of American Christian civilization were rooted in the conviction among whites that American-ness had a racial component. The American nation was a race nation, and its white race was superior to those from which it sprang. For example, the growing war in Europe was drawing the attention, and the criticism, of many in the United States. The Methodist periodicals of the MEC and MECS devoted a tremendous amount of print space to the war prior to the U.S. entry into it, and even more after. The war was both explained and described in terms of race. Some writers described the war as a race conflict, and understood the lack of American presence in the war as a matter of racial superiority. (White) Americans were above such self-defeating interracial bloodshed between sub-groups of the same white race family.[27] The need for a "Christian America" to keep the nation pure and out of the "fratricidal conflict" in Europe became a rallying cry for church leaders. Northern Methodists especially, more so than southern, considered American Methodism to be the epitome of "Christian America" and imagined that Methodism upheld the ideals and values of the nation. Often the rhetoric of the United States as a "chosen nation," and even a chosen (white) race, energized the discussion of church planning. An article in the New York *Christian Advocate*, "A Foreign Missionary's Plea for a Christian America," by Bishop William F. Oldham, bemoaned the loss to interracial war of the "great white races" of continental Europe. It is worth quoting this article at length to get a sense of the drama that fueled enthusiasm for white America as God's chosen race-nation:

> In that great unevangelized heathen world lying beyond the borders of Christendom there have hitherto been three great gospel burden-bearers—the German, the Briton and the American. Of these three, alas, two are locked in fratricidal strife. God forgive them both! They are destroying and crippling each other's energies. One great gospel burden-bearer remains untouched. Tell me, why, do you think, this America of ours is untouched? It is the restraining purpose of the living God. God has kept one great reservoir for the refreshment of humanity, for the re-inspiring of hope, for the re-enforcement of courage, and for the possibilities of still carrying on a great world-program for Christ.
>
> In this strained hour God calls to this, the youngest born people of His family, saying, "Children of God in America, to you I commit the high and holy task, the unspeakable privilege, of being the pathfinders for humanity, of leading a perplexed and troubled world to find the answer to all its perplexities and the enlightening of all its darkness at the foot of the cross."[28]

In the midst of this enthusiasm for the emergence of the United States as a great Christianizing power with Methodism at its center, the problem of regional differences remained central. Leaders in both denominations were publishing their opinions and arguments in a long-distance dialogue as they indirectly addressed and responded to each other. Two good examples of books published on the eve of the Joint Commission meetings are MEC Bishop Earl Cranston's *Breaking Down the Walls*[29] and MECS ministerial delegate John M. Moore's *The South Today*.[30] Both of these books attempt to downplay the regional differences, or at least to show how the differences that existed either did not matter or were necessary to a union. Cranston, for instance, argued that white southerners were, because of experience, best acquainted with the "problem of the Negro." They were thus indispensable to discussion of the problem and integral, he hoped, to a union that included black Methodists in some "fraternal" relationship.[31] Moore, on the other hand, tried to reassure his counterparts in the MEC that the MECS did not represent a backward and self-referential society and that they were, as a new generation of white southerners, more attuned to their place in the national scene than to the preservation of regional tradition and identity.

Moore's optimism notwithstanding, regional identity among whites in the MECS stood center stage for much of the unification debates. Perhaps for lack of any kind of corresponding cultural articulation of a northern regional identity, or perhaps because of the imaginative and romantic seduction of the idea of "the South" for northerners, commissioners on both sides engaged the imagery and language of southern-ness throughout the Joint Commission negotiations. While "southern-ness" was a crucial part of the MECS identity and the standard lexicon of their institutional identity, "northern-ness" functioned as a foil to the grand civilized culture imagined as "the South."[32] MEC periodicals and publications were filled with references to American Christian civilization, but there were no references to "the North." Political and regional identities among white MEC members were subsumed by national identity, but they were nearly always willing to play the part of the spoiler in the southern drama. White MEC members, in deference to their peers in the MECS, assented to the accusations of northern aggression and shared in southern hand-wringing over the tragedy of the loss of "the old plantation." In this way, southern identity was not the sole possession of MECS members. Rather, the "idea of the South" was a discursive tool wielded for different purposes by both black and white members of the Joint Commission from both denominations.[33]

Besides the perceptions of deep regional divisions, Cranston and Moore wrote to introduce language that might be used to negotiate racial membership. They offer distinctly different languages, but they don't necessarily reflect clearly regional positions. Their differences do reflect the

tension at the time between discussing race in the more complex nomenclature of Anglo-Saxons, Celts, Negroes, and so on, and a simplified binary of white/Anglo-Saxon and black/Negro.

Cranston's was the binary language of race. The differences between
races were identified by their progression toward manhood and civilization. His basic argument in *Breaking Down the Walls* is that both denominations agreed that black Methodists were "men." As such they
were "eligible to full citizenship in the kingdom of Christ" and they had
proven themselves worthy to be accorded "manhood, fidelity, and
courage." White Methodists had invested them with "manhood-con-
sciousness" and "freedom of choice in matters affecting [their] own destiny." But while black Methodists were men in the eyes of God, they were
not fully men in the church. Their progress toward "manhood's full estate" was not complete, and therefore they were not yet capable of handling the responsibilities of ecclesial administration on a large scale. It
was up to black Methodists themselves to make this progress. Cranston
takes the familiar "uplift" position espoused by some whites and blacks
in the MEC in regard to its racial segregation. Segregation provided the
proper arena in which black Methodists could help themselves grow and
prosper. Integrated congregations would not only limit the necessary opportunities for black leadership to grow, but would also thwart black
Methodists' "preference for pastors of their own race."[34]

Besides making clear that segregation remained the policy of the MEC,
Cranston had another message to members in the MECS who resisted
union: the black membership of the MEC might not even want to join a
unified church. He asks the central question: "Will the Church South
agree to any plan that includes Negro membership and Negro representation in the General Conference?" But rather than address this problem
directly, he suggests that they would only have to address it provided "the
Negro desires such a relation to the proposed reorganization." Cranston
was offering the possibility, though without any indication of such from
the black MEC membership itself, that their increasing "manhood consciousness" would give them the desire to join one of the established
black Methodist churches or create their own separate church in which
to enjoy their newfound freedom.

Moore's book addressed race and region from a more variegated theoretical ideology. Though published by the Missionary Education Movement of the United States and Canada, *The South Today* served more as an
apology for his home region than as a textbook for future missionaries.

Moderate in tone, and de-emphasizing the separateness of the region, Moore labored through many pages of economic data and cultural observations, all the while hoping that the study would "serve to awaken a new regard for the resources and potentialities of the Southern States, a new appreciation of the efforts and achievements of the Southern people, and a new estimate of the part which the South in the future is to have in the affairs of the nation."[35] Directly aimed at readers from the northern United States, and at the MEC in particular, the book strikes a balance between regional isolationism and a distinctive yet "progressive" regional identity. The book also outlines a specific taxonomy of the racial makeup of the South.

In the opening pages, in his general description of the South, Moore gives a portrait of the races represented there. Moore begins at what he considers the bottom of the racial hierarchy, with the Mexican population. After the Mexicans come the Germans, then the French-Huguenots, and finally the closest relatives of the Anglo-Saxons, the Scotch-Irish. Moore likes the Scotch-Irish, and sees in them the greatest promise for becoming civilized by the influence of Anglo-Saxons. The Scotch-Irish, he claims, are more victims of environmental and political circumstance than of "bad breeding." The final category is Anglo-Saxon, in which he places himself; it gets but a brief description that is almost reverent and seems to assume that any reader would be familiar with the virtues and strengths of that race.[36]

It is worth noticing that Moore did not include "Negroes" or "Indians" in his description of the population. Chapter 5 of the book is devoted to an exploration of "Human Problems" in the South. These problems are three groups of people left out of the original list—black Americans, Native Americans, and those he calls the "belated people of the hill country."[37] As part of the "Scotch-Irish race," Moore excuses the "belatedness" of this last group on the basis of factors of environment, especially the difficult life in the mountains (by hill-country he means the Appalachians) and their lack of access and exposure to "civilization." He dismisses Indians as a backward people by way of their inferior breeding, but admits they have not been treated too well either. Blood and breeding are at the core of the problem, though: "Some Indians are frugal, industrious, and are desirous of building up some wealth," Moore admits, "but the vast majority, and especially the full bloods, look to the government award for support."[38] Notice the implicit assumption that a little interbreeding has helped in some cases. For all these groups he laments that the mission organizations have not done enough.

For black Americans Moore reserves the most space, as he sees them as the source of most of the difficulties in the South: "The Negro has been the occasion of what too many have been free to call the race problem. . . . The problems of racial relations will diminish and slowly disappear as the intellectual, moral, and religious problems peculiar to each race shall be worked out."[39] In the midst of his discussion of the Negro, though, Moore slips out of his multiracial language into a binary scheme of black and white, or Negro and white. In a discussion of professions and growth of trades and the professional classes, for instance, he writes, "In many instances the white professional men in law and medicine are turning much of the Negro patronage to the professional men of the Negro race. In the case of the ministry there is no competition, as each race requires its own."[40]

This slippage from a complex multiracial taxonomy to one that reduces the racial picture to blacks and whites was not uncommon in the Joint Commission discourse on race. In relation to the broader national discourse on race, this move matches a shift to a more concretized "whiteness." In his 1967 study of nativism, *Strangers in the Land*, John Higham traces the convergence of what he calls a hyper-Anglo-Saxonism and nationalism. Nineteenth-century nationalism, says Higham, was not generally fused with racialist thought. But by the turn into the twentieth century, Anglo-Saxon identity had been so popularized and successfully fused with nationalist feeling by northern intellectuals that it was able to morph, at the grassroots level in the U.S. South and West especially, into a white supremacist nationalism.

But economic improvement is not the most important path for uplifting the race, says Moore. He argues that there is a "finer emphasis," an emphasis on less tangible needs such as moral improvement, cultural and social refinement, and spiritual maturity. This kind of improvement is possible, as there are already examples of its success: "There is a steadily increasing group of educated, cultured, and refined Negroes, many of whom are of mixed blood."[41] Contrary to the widely expressed fears about race-mixing, Moore seems to imply that these "ennobled" members of the Negro race might owe their success to that portion of their lineage that is white. Later in the chapter he writes, "Many individuals among them have risen to commendable strength, intellectual and moral. Many of these are mulattoes and chafe under the restraints incident to the race."[42] Like many aspects of racial theorizing, the existence of "mulattoes" was often played more than one way. Mulattoes who were seen as successful and developed were proof that a little white blood could improve the bad breeding of a "pure" Negro. But at the same time whites argued that miscegenation was an evil to be avoided at all costs, since, though those mixed-race individuals might be a little more evolved than their full-blood black relatives, they were not as evolved as their full-blood white relatives. The mulatto was not a race, just a hybrid fluke.

Moore concludes his assessment of the "human problem" by reminding his readers that "[Negroes] are still a child race," and that all planning done for them must take that into account. The race can be only lifted and enlightened "by forces beyond his power."[43] The Negro race was capable, like a child, of maturing and joining adults in the normal progression of American civilization. But like children, they were incapable of reaching adulthood without help and guidance. Fully matured human potential was impossible, because of natural causes, for the Negro race without the uplifting assistance of the members of the Anglo-Saxon race. In a later section in which Moore is discussing Protestant organizing in the South, he asserts the inability of the Negro population to contribute to the progress of Protestantism. Because of their "economic, intellectual and social development they are not in a position to contribute very largely to the religious influence and force of Protestantism except in their own race." The Negro leadership needs assistance, and while Negroes are "demonstrably religious," they insufficiently grasp the teachings of Christianity. He goes so far as to say they are not always "intelligently and practically Christian." The masses of the Negro population have mixed superstition with emotionalism to produce a religious practice that is "far removed from that of developed humanity."[44]

The section of the chapter on "human problems" that seems to illustrate most starkly that Moore was addressing the book to an MEC audience is the section titled "Appreciation." For several paragraphs Moore expresses praise for MEC workers who had started and funded education programs among southern blacks since the days just after the Civil War.

But even the present state of progress would not have been possible without that magnanimous assistance that has come from the North, and the people of the South are profoundly grateful to the men and women of other sections who by their gifts of money and personal self-sacrifice have helped the South to educate this backward and dependent people. The late munificence of the great foundations can never be lightly regarded but the constant, unfailing, and sacrificial gifts from

Northern Church bodies for the last fifty years stand out to-day as love's and religion's regard for a cast-off and neglected people.[45]

But in his moderating and mediating way, as if he could hear the grumbles of protest from some of his white MECS readers, Moore assures them that the indignities and affronts suffered by white MECS members at the hands of MEC missionaries would not be forgotten: "This is not to say that all their acts were and are approved. Many of these zealous souls were not discreet in the condition in which they labored, but their integrity and high purposes no one questions. To-day the unpleasantness is in the past and the South rejoices in the labors of those who gave themselves so that those in darkness might have the light."[46]

2

The Baltimore Meeting
Saints, Cemeteries, and Savages

At the official archives of the United Methodist Church, a visitor can find far more than dusty books, crumbling diaries, and stacks of bureaucratic records. There is a substantial array of other kinds of Methodist records on display and in the vaults. In particular, the collections contain many personal items that were used, owned, touched, in the close vicinity of, or even sat upon by important Methodist figures. In these collections, items connected to John Wesley figure most prominently: his eyeglasses, one of his clerical cuffs, his cashbox, his grandfather's Bible, the key to his prayer room, a piece of plush velvet upholstery from one of his chairs. There are even several pieces of wood that were taken from trees under which he either stood or preached. One piece of wood came from a pear tree in England from which Wesley supposedly enjoyed picking fruit. The most unique of the pieces is one that connects the power of the founder with the final moments of his life: kept in a glass case with many other pieces is a reproduction of the "death mask" that was made of Wesley's face after he died. The original remains in the vault.[1]

But Wesley is not the only Methodist figure represented in the collections. Many of the items are connected not with the founder of the Methodist movement, but with the leaders of the movement in North America. There are several saddlebags that were used by the early circuit riders; there are communion chalices used by William Otterbein and Jacob Boehm, leaders of early German revivalist groups who eventually joined with Methodists; Bibles, clothing, diaries, powder horns, preaching stands, benches used in revivals, more pieces of wood from famous trees where revivals were staged and converts won. Even a piece of bone, carefully displayed in its own case, that may be part of the thumb of George Whitefield, perhaps one of the most influential preachers in the eighteenth century, and one of the early Methodist leaders in both England and America, whose body, kept in a crypt beneath a church in North Hampton, Massachusetts, was slowly taken apart by curiosity seekers and the faithful, over a period of many years.

These collections of objects were not (necessarily) assembled for the purpose of creating a museum that would educate visitors about aspects of Methodist life. Very little, in fact, is known about their provenance. But what we do know is that the objects were collected from, or donated by, a broad spectrum of individual collectors, most of whom were Methodists of one stripe or another. Some were kept by the families of those early Methodists who first received or kept the objects. Some, like John Wesley's cashbox, were found in attics of deceased Methodists. About some objects we know nothing. In other words, the trickling down of these disparate physical traces of Methodist history had no single or central guiding force, but can best be explained by an apparently general sense among many Methodists that there was some value, indeed some *sacred* value, in these objects that were, in one way or another, touched by Methodist divines. As Thomas Tweed has shown us, United Methodists have also been eager to assign sacred designations to physical spaces and places.[2] Methodists, it would seem, have not always been afraid to associate the divine with the material world. They even seem to have found great power and meaning in those associations.

Among the Joint Commissioners, an easy use of sacred objects, places, and times became a part of their negotiations. Juxtaposing the ways American Methodists have used commemorative objects, stories, places, and times with explicit descriptions of their sources of Christian authority tell us a great deal about them. We learn, first, that Methodists, as Thomas Tweed argues, have not been as conventionally Protestant in their approach to the sacredness of the material world as many scholars have assumed, and thus are not that anomalous in the history of religions. Second, as Russell Richey argues, history and memory are central to Methodist identity.[3] Third, we find specific clues to this Methodist identity through a close observation of their choices, descriptions, and use of the material and temporal realms of ritual. Finally, through a comparison of Methodist rituals with what Methodists actually said in the process of institutional self-constitution, we learn about the role of these rituals and spaces in the way Methodists constituted themselves. What relationship is there between the power performed and enacted in their commemorative rituals and the values that emerge in the formal negotiation of institutional power?[4]

Juxtaposing the initial ritual performance of Methodist identity at the first Joint Commission meeting in Baltimore with the immediate abandonment, or at least apparent derailment, of the explicitly religious language used in those memory-making rituals exposes an apparent contradiction in Methodist self-presentations. The performance of Methodist identity—which involved stories about "heroes of the faith," sacred objects, attention to sacred space and time—does not seem at first glance to address the central problem: race. But after the ceremonies and their presentation of an explicitly religious identity, the Joint Commission moved into another discourse that was consciously not theological, doctrinal, biblical, or even particularly Methodist. While they defined themselves as the representatives of the best in all these categories, it was not to these categories that they turned to frame the discussion of how to (re)unite their churches. Instead the leaders of both commissions, and the majority of the commissioners, laid out other values, not explicitly Methodist, that they hoped would suffice. They acknowledged that they would not be able to agree on a view or theory of race relations expressed in the language of Christianity. They admitted this openly. So instead they proposed alternate values that were not explicitly Christian. Primarily they spoke in a language of values generated by a broader national reliance on models of big-business empires: expediency, efficiency, order. Bishop Earl Cranston, in particular, attempted to argue that the question of "God's will" was settled: God wanted their Methodist institutions to unite, and so it had been left to the Joint Commission to find the path to union, not to discern God's will about the nature of that path.

Exploring the material and spatial choices the Joint Commission made, and the ways they incorporated the sensual and material world in expressions of their religious identity, offers clues to the denominational identity about which they began to negotiate. This identity was ruled by concerns about authenticity, indigeneity, cultural influence, national identity, and the future of "American Christian civilization." While more traditional Christian sources for authority—scripture, theology, and doctrine—were present in the negotiations, a majority of the Joint Commission, spurred by outspoken leaders from both churches, made a conscious attempt to avoid or suppress use of those sources in the negotiations.

The Opening Ceremonies

Baltimore was a deliberate and careful choice for the first meeting of the Joint Commission, not only as a geographically central location between the northern and southern states, but also as a historically significant location that lent a sense of authenticity and originality to the task. It was also indicative of the expectation that this would be the Commission's only meeting. The meeting was held in First Methodist Episcopal Church, the successor church to Baltimore's Lovely Lane Chapel where the Christmas Conference of 1784 organized the Methodist Episcopal Church. It was hoped that the Commission could iron out their differences all at once and reunite the church where it began.

The Methodist leaders who assembled in Baltimore in December 1916 understood themselves to be gathering in the shattered pieces of the sacred Methodist conference that was begun there. The sense that they were negotiating a return to the proper, whole, and original form of their movement pervaded the opening sessions. The commissioners exhibited this sense of gravity not only in their literal words, but also in their repeated homage to Methodist leaders of the past and in their use of sacred space, objects, and time.

There were other spaces in Baltimore that were sacred to Methodists, and the year in which they were meeting added to the significance of their gathering there. 1916 was the national sesquicentennial, as well as the centenary of the death of Francis Asbury, Methodism's first bishop. Asbury was buried there, as were more than two hundred other Methodist preachers. The commissioners were invited to a prayer service at Mount Olivet cemetery, where they would give "proper honor during this centennial . . . and show [their] respect, recognize [their] obligation, and interpret [their] affection" for their (white) founding father.[5] In the presence of the (white) Methodist dead, the commissioners gathered together and prayed and sang hymns and bound themselves tighter to a shared sense of history that figured powerfully in the dialogue and rhetoric of their negotiations.

John Franklin Goucher (1845–1922) was the host of sorts for the Baltimore meetings. Goucher was one of the most influential ministers in the MEC at the time. An ordained minister, president of Goucher College, author, and active proponent of foreign missions, Goucher was one of the strongest voices throughout the five-year life of the Commission. His was the voice of modern American civilized progress, dramatically advocating the potential of modern Protestantism to reform the world. He viewed white Methodists as the epitome of modern Christianity and the only hope for worldwide progress. His language and arguments helped shape the discourse of the negotiations. And on the first day of the meetings, Goucher set the grave tone, establishing the sense that what they would accomplish carried great historical weight. Introducing the speaker for the opening worship service, Goucher held a copy of Bishop Coke's Christmas Conference sermon at which Francis Asbury received episcopal ordination. Goucher paralleled Coke's sermon and audience with the sermon and audience of that day, emphasizing the great increase in numbers from a band of eighty-one young and untrained ministers and less than 15,000 communicants in 1784 to 28,000 ministers and nearly 6.5 million communicants in 1916. But the audience also included, said Goucher, "American Methodism," meaning all the variegated denominations that traced their lineage to 1784, as well as "all evangelical Christianity." These Methodists considered themselves not only the central and authentic strain of Methodism, but also the central powerful voice of worldwide Protestantism. It was as if the "epochal" address Goucher held in his hand, and the physical space of that occasion in which he stood, more powerfully authenticated the sacred mission the group had gathered to discharge.[6]

There was more. At the beginning of nearly every session in Baltimore, Goucher used a historical object with an accompanying story to remind them of the occasion. He called attention to the furnishings of their meeting room. The table where speakers stood came from the Alexander Warfield house, where it furnished the "prophet's chamber," a small room where Francis Asbury was thought to have spent much time in prayer while visiting the home of one of the first Methodist converts and society members. The table provided for the Commission chairman was where Asbury supposedly wrote much of his journal. Bishops McKendree and Richard Whatcoat, two of the most famous and influential of the early Methodist Episcopal bishops, also used the table. Another chair in the room was made from the tree under which Robert Strawbridge, the first Methodist in Maryland, had been buried. One of the gavels used by the Commission chairmen was made from the oak tree under which John Wesley is said to have prayed when he first arrived in Savannah in 1736. John Evans, the first convert to Methodism in America, used the pulpit during the forty-three years he was a class leader, and Robert Strawbridge, Asbury, McKendree, and Whatcoat all preached from it. Draped on the arm of the pulpit were the saddlebags of one Henry Smith, who was "closely related to Bishop Soule." Soule became the senior bishop of the MECS after the split of 1844. Goucher read scripture several times from the pocket Bible found beside the dead body of Bishop Thomas Coke, who was sent by John Wesley from England to America. The Bible was "doubtless the last material thing he had grasped while on earth," added Goucher.[7] Reading from that Bible at the first business session in Baltimore, Goucher read the same scripture John Wesley had read at his first sermon in America.

What significance did they find in the fact that the Bible they used was "the last material thing" touched by a Methodist divine? What was the point in repeating the grasp of a dead man, an otherwise morbid act? Or re-performing a first sermon or scripture lesson? Or meeting in the presence of the saddlebags of a Methodist hero? In this particular context, in the meetings that were about re-forming the original Methodist Episcopal Church, these gestures and objects were a claim to the spiritual power that was lost in the split of 1844. This was the split that tore the fabric of what they considered original Methodism—the authentic "ecclesial existence," as Richey puts it, of an indigenous American religion. And it is this sense of indigeneity, this striving for a proven authenticity and original physical connection with the beginnings of the American nation, that imbues the objects and stories these Methodists tell with power and meaning. In repeating the first scripture lesson Wesley read on American soil, the Commission not only reminded themselves of their history and connection with the colonization and evangelization of the North American continent, but they found purchase on the shores of a new America. The new America they were hoping to build would be healed of the old wounds and divisions that had split the nation and the Methodist Episcopal Church.

But we must also see the obvious gaps in that original ecclesial existence: The sacred memory narrated in their rituals made no connections to Methodists who were not white men. The imagined indigeneity of the white men in charge of these meetings was diverse only in its regional representation of white men. Nor did these memories include the divisions of African American congregations into the AME and AMEZ, or the radical abolitionist Wesleyan Methodist Connection. One wouldn't know from these commemorations that the early Methodist world was a radically egalitarian one. Congregations and revival meetings and society meetings alike were spaces where women and slaves and freed blacks, all from a wide spectrum of economic and social strata, were active participants and often leaders. It was only at the place of institutional conference that the pool of leadership was made shallow for literate white men.

A final example of a sacred object is perhaps most illustrative of the way these Methodists understood their place in a sacred history. Goucher introduced a second gavel that was used in Baltimore. This gavel was made of two different woods from two significant sources: the handle was made of olive wood from the Mount of Olives in Jerusalem, and the head was made from a tree called by Methodists "the Strawbridge Oak." Strawbridge was one of the first important lay preachers in American Methodism, and the ground under the oak tree from which the head of the gavel was made marked a place where he is said to have preached when his chapel wouldn't hold the crowds who came to hear him. That the head of a gavel was made from the wood of this oak tree represents the way Methodists understood their authority and power in America. The symbol of order and authority in their deliberations, the hammer of rule, possessed authority by the merit of success and by the measure of overflow. Methodist Episcopals in the early twentieth century considered themselves the inheritors of evangelical success.

What was significant about the crude image of the successful frontier preacher holding forth in the woods was not that the new Methodist church wanted a return to that scene of origin, but that this scene represented a kind of innocence. In 1916, Methodists were numerous, powerful, and wealthy. If churches overflowed, they built bigger ones. But this material success and the cultural power of its leaders were at times difficult to reconcile with the identity and ethos of early Methodism. The history to which they paid homage in Lovely Lane and Mount Olivet cemetery was the history of circuit riders who spent long years on horseback, for whom personal sacrifice, poverty, and loneliness were normal. As Donald B. Marti has shown, the shift to a wealthy Methodist Episcopalism was a shift to a whole new identity, both within and without, and it was explained in broader terms of American cultural narratives of "rags to riches."[8] In other words, the historical narrative they celebrated and reinforced focused on "progress" in terms of church growth, wealth, and influence on the American continent—their hammer of authority, the proof of the rightness of their religious inheritance. Blazing frontier trails, early Methodists staked a claim on a "new" world, began a new sacred history, and like many American Christian groups, the history they told of themselves looked no further for spiritual inheritance than their own church. Authenticity was the lesson of the gavel: American Methodism inheriting the power of Christianity from Jerusalem to a new world, free from the fetters of European Christendom.

The Indian Oak

The Strawbridge Oak from which the gavel used at Baltimore was made had another history with no specific Methodist connection. John Goucher told this story at the opening meeting as well. The Strawbridge Oak was first known as "The Indian Oak." During the French and Indian War, a small group of Indians attacked settlements in European Atlantic colonies. At one homestead in Maryland, they killed the father of the family living there, and took the wife and three children prisoner. When the captives and their captors stopped to camp for the night, the mother instructed her two older children to remain awake and wait for their captors to fall asleep. When she gave a signal, each was to take the axe of the nearest Indian and kill him. Each child was to kill one, and the mother was to kill the remaining two. The family carried out their plan, and ran into the woods. One of the Indians, apparently only dazed by the blow from one of the children, managed to fire his rifle into the woods in the direction of the escaping family. The bullet lodged in an oak tree, which was later named "The Indian Oak." When the tree was cut down, after it had been known as the Strawbridge Oak, a bullet was found, and the evidence of the rings and the French origin of the bullet confirmed, said Goucher, the truth of the story.

That Goucher took time in the meetings to tell this story is in itself instructive of the importance of story, history, and place. But what about the story itself? The details reveal subterranean themes that are central to the very structure of the racialized discourse of these meetings.

This "captivity narrative" has a long history in American culture, and the basic structure and characters of the genre appear in this version.[9] The savage, uncivilized Indian, who, in this case, is also a "foreign" Indian from French-dominated Canada, is a familiar villain and central foil to the protagonist, the virtuous white woman. The Indians, while fierce fighters who gained the early victory in their surprise attack on the family, are finally unveiled as somnolent weaklings, unable to remain vigilant or to foresee the braver plan of a mere housewife. The white woman in this story is cunning, fearless, patient, and loyal to her family. Thus tensions of savagery/civility, chaos/order, dark/light, state of sin/state of innocence are at play, as the barbaric, un-Christian Indians' lack of planning and self-discipline are overwhelmed by the civilized Christian woman's shrewd planning and patient action. Like the film *Birth of a Nation* for white Americans in general, this story serves to heighten the awareness of the white Commissioners' own sense of being part of a civilization in a precarious position. That position was threatened by the presence of a dark, dangerous, uncivilized, un-Christian, and unmanly subspecies.[10]

But the point of the story, of course, is that civilization always wins—even when a woman represents civilization. In this way the story also serves to further separate the barbarians from civilization by feminizing their male warriors, which reveals their lack of one of the primary characteristics of civilization, "manliness." In the Indian Oak story, a white civilized woman takes on the mantle of "manliness" in the absence of her husband and defeats the men of the uncivilized Indians.

What is perhaps most telling about the Indian Oak story is that the denouement involves a threat of sexual violence to white women. The sexual tension implicit in this story revealed itself within the Joint Commission's racial discourse as the fear of "social equality" and miscegenation. A fear of even the perception that they were creating a church that promoted "social equality" or encouraged miscegenation was at the root of the Commissioners' (both white and black) negotiation of the place of the black membership in the new church.

The gavel represented a physical connection to a complex assortment of themes. The marriage of Methodist evangelical success on a new continent with the wood from "the Holy Land" evoked dreams of America as a "new Israel." Methodists were reminded of their simpler roots and the progress they had made. They had, by the measure of that success, the authority to influence the nation in the name of God. America was also a land threatened by savagery, but the power of civilization would always win out. As he dropped the gavel on the table to begin their deliberations, Bishop Earl Cranston (MEC) pronounced the assembled commissioners prepared to tackle the problem that confronted them: "We are ready to consider what the essence of Methodism is."[11]

"The Ground of Expediency"

What the essence of Methodism was, as it turned out, was an extremely slippery problem. It would probably be fair to say as well that, in the end, this Commission certainly did not think it had solved that problem. One of the difficulties was, of course, that *who* was to be included in this particular branch of Methodism was the primary point of disagreement. The opening ceremonies also included, as would be expected, a sermon, in this case delivered by Bishop Warren Candler (MECS).[12] Titled "The Church: The Fullness of Christ and the Hope of the Universe," it reached great rhetorical heights. Candler explored the development of the concept of "the Church," and spun ornate theological meditations on the relationship between it and Christ. But he did not make connections to the problems they all knew they had to address. He did not reference the problem of reconciling the spiritual ideal of a unified church with the ecclesiastical problem of a membership that was decidedly dis-unified.[13] This serious disconnect between a theological ideal and a political reality pushed the Joint Commission to employ identity as the primary mode of negotiation.

While there were sermonic speeches and the occasional interpretations of "New Testament ethics" or "the ethics of Jesus," the Commission—and the leadership in particular—steered itself far away from the kinds of discussions that would force the commissioners to decide whether one church or one position on unification was "more Christian" or "more spiritual" than another. The ensuing debate over the next four years was pitched at a high spiritual register, but in the decidedly non-spiritual language of race. This is not to say that the discussion was not religious—indeed my point is that all that the Joint Commission produced was religious—but that the more conventional and traditional religious language was relegated either to the discussion of the unification ideal or was an unwelcome interjection. There were also several instances in which a Joint Commission delegate presented theological or scriptural reasons why theological or scriptural reasoning did not apply to the problem at hand.

As we saw in chapter 1, the only presentation at the Working Conference to offer a scriptural approach to the problem of race in the church received little to no attention. This, and the fact that only one speaker addressed the problem in this way, was a clear indication that the leadership of the MEC and MECS were not disposed toward fighting a theological battle. Whether or not the leadership of the two churches planned together to squelch this kind of discussion I have not been able to discover. But it is obvious from the *Proceedings* that they did not want to tackle the problem in that way.

The guidance from the Joint Commission's leadership was at times subtle, and at times blatant. MEC bishop William F. McDowell, who chaired the MEC delegation, for instance, made it clear that there was only one goal before the Joint Commission, and that was unification.[14] McDowell often took on the task of trying to center the discussion. Several times during meetings he stood and attempted to focus the discussion or trim away some of the extraneous issues. He openly worried about the delegates' inability to discern their immediate task. The goal of unification, said McDowell, was to be achieved without attempting to discern "God's will" or to find a "biblical solution" or to search for a theological imperative. The best thing for the church was what was in God's will, and so it would do them no good to try to work out amongst themselves a clear statement of "God's will."[15] McDowell also worried about the divisive effect such a discussion would have among the members, and he often interrupted a discussion to try to reassure one side or the other that there was no question as to the spiritual intent of all the members present. At one particularly tense moment during the Savannah meeting, he asked that they all assume "that everyone [sic] of us is equally moved by the spiritual motives of this great thing."[16]

MECS Bishop Collins Denny, like McDowell, refused to sit still for appeals based on claims to a higher Christian ideal.[17] During his first speech at the Baltimore meeting Denny said he would be willing to hear any proposal from anyone, but "he was not yet willing to sit and accept somebody's interpretation of the mind of God as the divine solution of this question."[18] Feeling as if they were being put on the defensive, Denny and other MECS leaders repeated this sentiment whenever a delegate attempted to argue from scriptural or theological grounds. Not only did they find it insulting to be told that they were not as righteous as the speaker, they would say, but interpreting the will of God was a foregone conclusion in that environment: they would not be able to come to an agreement on God's will, and unification would fail. After MEC lay commissioner Alexander Simpson accused the MECS delegation of ignoring the Gospel and turning a blind eye to their own "common humanity," MECS Bishop Edwin Mouzon defended himself and his fellow commissioners, saying that they "enjoy being preached to. But we do not appreciate being reminded continually that in the opinion of some we do not manifest Christian principle."[19]

But it was MEC Bishop Earl Cranston who made the strongest and most sustained arguments against theological and scriptural discussion. For Cranston the central goal was unification, and he was firmly convinced—and he was almost certainly correct—that the quest for unification would fail if they attempted to address the racial issue theologically. Cranston's substitute value was "expediency," and he preached expediency throughout the negotiations. The very existence of the Joint Commission, and the proposals they put forth from the respective General Conferences, relegated the "negro question" to "the ground of expediency." Individual or institutional views on the "ethical teachings of the New Testament" were so radically different that there was no chance of finding agreement or achieving unification. The Joint Commission was a "treaty," and an official acknowledgment that whatever expedited unification was acceptable in the discussion.[20] In terms of his personal view of the relationship of the black MEC membership, Cranston was willing to compromise with the MECS and to consider making the new church an all-white church.

To further buttress this argument, Cranston and others attempted to construct the notion of "equality" as a shifting phenomenon dependent upon the situation being addressed. Cranston distinguished between "spiritual equality" and "ecclesial equality." "Christian fellowship is spiritual," he argued, and it "does not inhere in any ecclesiastical scheme, nor can it be given or taken away by any human authority." All races are "one in Christ," in other words, but this spiritual unity does not transfer to human society in general, to social interaction among races, or even to ecclesiastical structure. This distinction between the "spiritual" realm and the "merely ecclesial" became the escape hatch for white Methodists when answering critics who attempted to argue that there were Gospel principles that weighed in the race issue. So to what were they to turn, then, to find a racial model for church structure? What was expedient where the Gospel, doctrine, theological debate, and Methodist tradition were not? Cranston addressed this directly, supporting the general trend of the negotiations: they had to look to the communities in which the church found itself and model themselves after those. They had to concede, said Cranston, that "involuntary community existence"—by which he meant the race one was born into—"and community life in community organizations such as our Churches must be governed by the same rules and principles that necessarily obtain in such community organizations and cooperative movements in general."[21]

This approach reflects what one finds throughout the *Proceedings*. American civilization, American government, the U.S. Constitution, the U.S. legal structure, and the idea of the American nation all get vastly more attention as models for church governance, structure, and "manhood rights" among the membership than do any models culled from church history or biblical principal.

At times, though, Cranston eased into making theological arguments himself, even during the St. Louis Meeting claiming that "expediency" was itself a New Testament ethic.[22] During the long Savannah debates he pled desperately for the discussion to be turned away from the right or wrong of integrating the new church. The "status of the Negro," he argued, was not "fundamental in any doctrine of salvation through Jesus Christ." Thus the matter was taking them away from the "fundamental conception of the Church of Jesus Christ," by which he meant the unification of its strongest elements. By continuing to debate a "New Testament" approach to the question of the black membership the Joint Commission was subordinating "the spiritual ideal to the conventional." Rights, status, historical consistency, ethics—all of these things were conventional and not spiritual, because all of them were incidental to the most crucial aspects of the negotiations: (white) unification and "our common obligation for his ['the Negro's'] moral and religious uplift."[23]

Cranston also employed a tactic that was intended to re-spiritualize what he had vociferously tried to de-spiritualize. He went on in this particular speech to add that blacks in the MEC were improperly preoccupied with the trappings of political power.[24] Characterizing the positions and rights that the black membership was fighting for as "superficial distinctions and barren recognitions," Cranston belittled the quest for equality in the new church while he elevated the alternative to a spiritual ideal. "Self-direction" and a racial sphere of influence were more spiritually viable options than the fleeting illusion of political power. The longer and less immediately gratifying road of racial segregation and self-motivated growth would best serve the greater spiritual good of "the race."[25]

Some delegates went to greater lengths to prove that "heredity [and] race prejudice" could "scarcely yield even to the gospel."[26] Frank M. Thomas, a ministerial delegate and one of the eldest delegates from the MECS, frustrated at what he considered the inappropriate moralizing of the MEC commissioners and the MEC press, presented a prepared speech at the Cleveland meeting in which he tried to reason out more carefully why the "status of the Negro" was a problem that could not be solved by recourse to the New Testament.[27] That the New Testament had any bearing on the problem was a fallacy, he said, and would not stand "searching inquiry." Thomas argued that the New Testament is not a guidebook for the "details of human life." Rather, it sets out certain broad principles: the "Fatherhood of God," the "Sonship of Jesus Christ," "His Universal Atonement," the "Gift of the Holy Spirit," the "Brotherhood of Believers." None of these principles, though, qualify the "Negroid" for equal standing with whites in a church. Any true Christian would rejoice that all humans are equal on the plane of salvation and their relationship to the spiritual "kingdom." But this is an entirely different plane of existence from the ecclesial and "fraternal" plane. Christians can be equal "brothers" in the matter of salvation and in relation to God, but that equality does not translate to the non-spiritual realm of church structure. To claim that the phrase "all are one in Christ" translates to "all are one in Christ's church" would not hold up "at least in Methodism, the acid test of the facts. A man's spiritual relations do not determine his ecclesiastical relations." As an example of how this played out in the church in other areas, Thomas pointed to the itinerant system of Methodist ministerial assignments. He asserted that Methodist preachers, "free-born, with the blood of patriots in their veins," do not retain their level of spiritual equality because they are moved around year to year from charge to charge. If it were not for the "high spiritual values involved" they would simply be at the whim of the "appointive power." Without any sense of irony, Thomas claimed that it would be "difficult to find a more pronounced form of human slavery."[28]

Similarly, MEC Bishop Richard Cooke tried to find a way to explain the vast differences between the two churches by outlining the compartmentalized version of social ethics that were espoused by many, he said, in the American South, as well as in certain European intellectual movements.[29] Cooke used the language of "spheres" to describe the way those opposed to racial integration understood the "ethics of Jesus Christ." There are limits, he argued, to those ethics, because they pertain only to certain areas of life. The MEC could not adopt such a system of ethics, but he hoped he could assure some MEC commissioners that those not willing to hear a "Gospel" argument were not disagreeing about the interpretation of Jesus' words, but rather understood the nature of "Gospel ethics" in a different way. He tried to convince his colleagues that their differences were not irreconcilable. Rather, he argued, the commissioners needed to find another way of approaching the problem.[30]

MEC Bishop Frederick Leete outlined this notion of spheres even more sharply. Rousseau, not Christ, advocated social equality, he argued.[31] Jesus was not a "leader of society" and did not "mingle much with society." Jesus did teach principles that had some bearing on society, but not any principles that would indicate that all members of society should have equal social footing. Rousseau taught much worth considering about the "rights of man, but very little or almost nothing about the higher duties and privileges of man." Talk of "social equality," argued Leete, had its source in French (not Anglo-Saxon!) philosophy and not in the Gospel. Christians, as this line of thinking went, could think and apply Christ-taught principles in three distinct spheres: politics, society, and the life of the Church. In this way the Commission could advocate equality among church members without advocating the social equality of those same members. With this reasoning Leete attempted to extricate the Commission from the "social equality" dilemma by diverting it into another "sphere" of Christian thought.

"God Brought Us the Negro"

But it was inevitable that theological thinking would make its way into such negotiations. As we have seen, even those arguments against using scripture and theology were by their very nature theological and scriptural arguments. So while for the most part the stronger players in the negotiations were able to guide the discussion in different directions, there were still several strong speeches that made arguments based on scripture and/or scriptural theology. There were several isolated interventions by delegates who attempted to persuade their opponents that the position they advocated in regard to the "status of the Negro" was not a position that could be defended in terms of Christian thinking. I say they were isolated because the few incidents were immediately shut down by one of the leaders or else simply ignored. These speeches were delivered by white MEC members and were aimed at their MECS counterparts. In this way, it was the MECS that was put on the defensive most of the time, though MEC leaders such as McDowell often came to their rescue.

One of the most outspoken MEC delegates was Alexander Simpson, a lay delegate from Philadelphia.[32] He was one of only two commissioners, along with MEC Bishop John Hamilton, who openly advocated a full racial integration in the new church. On several occasions Simpson attempted to pull the Commission into a discussion of a solution informed by New Testament thinking. Unlike most of the delegates, Simpson was rarely deferential, and he held little of his opinion back when accusing others of hypocrisy and ignoring their own Christian values of love and unity in Christ. Simpson argued outright that it was inexcusable for any Christian to argue that, in the face of Gospel teaching, a Christian church could exclude from its midst any group on the grounds of race. His arguments were met with either a watered-down restatement from members of his own delegation, or indignant refusal from MECS members to acknowledge that the teachings of Jesus had anything to do with the subject at hand.[33]

Others did not attack as openly as Simpson, but they tried to talk about Gospel notions of love, humility, unity, and brotherhood. The telling reaction to these speeches was the silence that followed, or the lack of engagement from the next speaker. A good example of this occurred during the Cleveland meeting in 1919. Ira E. Robinson,[34] an MEC layperson, entered the discussion in an attempt to stop a shift in momentum toward legal solutions that were being discussed.[35] Like many lay delegates, Robinson rarely spoke to the entire Commission. But obviously disturbed by the discussion taking place, he made an emotional plea for them to abandon questions of legal solutions and return to the "simplicity of faith and love." Robinson's speech reads like a short sermon, gently chastising his fellow Christians for abandoning the basic principles of their faith and looking instead to the convoluted and corrupt world outside the Church for guidance. What is most instructive about this moment is not the speech itself, which was directed at the entire Commission rather than at one party within it, but the fact that no one engaged its substance. The appeal met with silence.[36]

Several speeches played off older theological musing about the presence of slavery in a "free" Christian nation. The old slaver's argument that slavery was God's will, or was at least used by God to introduce Africans to Christianity and to remove them from the evil influences of idolatry and sin, was used by members who were arguing for competing sides.[37] For those who advocated racial integration, the argument that God intended the Africans to be sent to America as slaves boosted their contention that God did not intend for whites and blacks to remain separate. Their version of the history of the slaves revealed a natural progression from a destitute and godless existence in Africa to the civilizing and Christianizing influences of slavery to a fully integrated Christian society in America. Those who advocated a racially segregated church argued that of course God intended Africans to be enslaved into good Christian influence, but that slavery was a purposefully separate and unequal relationship between unequal races.

Some repeated this theological argument explicitly. MECS Bishop Collins Denny argued boldly that slavery was "God's plan." He answered the criticism that God would not have willed such a horrible fate on anyone by comparing the slavery of Africans in America to the journey of the ancient Israelites. Exile and slavery in Egypt and Babylon were sore trials during which God wiped, ground, and stamped out the "tendency to idolatry" in the Israelites and purified God's chosen people to bring them back to righteousness.[38] So too did slavery remove the innate tendencies of Africans to look to pagan ways for religion. In a more implicit use of this kind of divine history, Denny and others often expressed great joy and pride that, by their accounting, the blacks in America were in a "higher" position, with better opportunities, better social standing, and better civilization, than any other black people in history anywhere in the world. This would not have been possible without the African diaspora of slavery, for it was only by direct contact with and long observation of white Christian civilization that the black races could reach the great point of progress at which they found themselves in America in the early twentieth century.

In the minds of the Joint Commissioners, America was a special place and they were in a special time, ordained by God to make way for a fully restored American Methodism. The opening ceremonies and the sacralizing of the Joint Commission's mission reveal an identity-centered concern for claims to cultural authority in America. The Commissioners' emphasis on objects and people associated with America reveals a desire to establish their Methodist identity as the authentic American Christianity. They hoped to secure their role as the bearers of an indigenous religion.

The struggle over the "essence of Methodism" was fought from conflicting versions of Methodism's representation of America and the continuance of its cultural authority. One version of this authenticity was concerned that authority was lost if two separate churches remained, and that institutional merger was worth remaining a racially segregated church. The other side worried that authenticity would be lost if racial unity were discarded. Those who knew that theological, doctrinal, or biblical debates would never lead to a merger won this struggle, as those categories were successfully suppressed in favor of "expediency."

3

Race Consciousness

With the release and widespread viewing of the racially charged and virulent *Birth of a Nation* in 1916, the ensuing revival of the KKK to which it gave energy, and the publication of Madison Grant's *The Passing of the Great Race*, public and scholarly debates over theories of race were gaining momentum. Madison's book, in particular, captured much of the American public's attention and imagination, as he mapped out an accessible description of the races of the world and argued that the "Great White Race" was in danger of disappearing due to increased global migrations and new levels of racial intermixture. Much of the debate was spurred on by the thinking of Franz Boas, who, in *The Mind of Primitive Man* (1911), turned the prevailing thinking about race as a fixed, biologically determined state on its head. Grant's work countered this position decisively, noted Henry Fairfield Osborn. In the preface to Grant's book, Osborn claimed that the "great biological movement" of which Grant's book was a part proved "environment and . . . education have an immediate, apparent and temporary influence, while heredity has a deep, subtle and permanent influence on the actions of men."[1] Grant intended his scholarly work to be influential far beyond the confines of academia; *The Passing of the Great Race* was a jeremiad for the American republic, and he hoped that it would awaken the children of the Anglo-Saxon founders to guard against the race-mixing that threatened the very foundations of the nation. He warned that those who did not possess the attributes of the "higher types" were, out of resentment, trying to turn the conversations about race in their favor by claiming the primacy of environment. Not only were "those individuals who have neither country, nor flag, nor language, nor class, nor even surnames of their own and who can only acquire them by gift or assumption" attempting to spread questionable science, they were also attempting to re-narrate the history of the United States. Contrary to what children were being taught in schools at the time, wrote Grant, the writers of the Declaration of Independence were not motivated by "philanthropy and noble purpose." Rather, "equality," in their minds, "meant merely that they were just as good Englishmen as their brothers across the sea. The words 'that all men are created equal' have since been subtly falsified by adding the word 'free.'"[2] Grant was right, of course, since most of the founders, he eagerly pointed out, were slaveowners who despised Indians. But his larger point was that the steady march of civilization, led by American offspring of the Anglo-Saxons, was primarily the march of heredity, and that civilization was endangered by the false theory that environment was more powerful in the development of humanity than was biology. Race consciousness, he lamented, had been greatly impaired by the pervasive belief that education and environment can erase any human differences. "True" race consciousness, according to Grant, had to be revived among the Anglo-Saxons of America if civilization was to survive.[3]

In the spring of that same year, 1916, at Howard University, a young scholar and future leader of the Harlem Renaissance named Alain Leroy Locke gave a series of groundbreaking lectures. In a set of arguments that surveyed the most current thinking on race theories, Locke turned away from the prevailing fad for biological determinism in dramatic fashion and set the platform upon which other writers could begin to accumulate ammunition for an assault on the prevailing racial ideologies. He began his arguments from the anthropological theories of Franz Boas and tuned them to the particular details of the African American experience.[4] Paying particular attention to Boas's contention that physical, mental, and cultural characteristics of each race were mutable in response to environment, Locke argued in his first lecture that race is not, as so many believed at the time, a fixed, biological phenomenon. Locke turned the prevailing ideologies of race on their heads, arguing that culture, not biology, produces race.[5] But his lectures did more than develop Boas's anthropological theories in the context of African American life; he also diverged from Boas's work in significant ways. In particular, unlike Boas, Locke advocated an embrace of "race consciousness" by African Americans.[6] In his view, race consciousness was necessary for African Americans to assist in a "rather more rapid assimilation of the . . . general social culture, than would otherwise be possible." By "assimilation" Locke did not mean a simple conformity to the social practices and culture of dominant white America. Rather, in his view assimilation was more akin to the way in which an individual person is unable to function as a self-sustaining adult until he or she gains a certain level of self-awareness and self-respect. Race consciousness appeared to Locke as "the social equivalent to self-respect in the individual moral life."[7] To use more contemporary language, Locke understood that race was constructed in a mix of environment and culture. For Locke, this meant that race consciousness was more than merely determinative for "the race," and thus there was a kind of liberative quality to his position. It also meant that race was plastic enough to be formed and shaped in ways that would benefit African Americans. Locke understood that while race was not biologically determined, it functioned that way in American society, and therefore that African Americans needed to foster a consciousness of the beautiful and unique aspects of their race. Doing so would allow them to "mature" and develop into a strong and vibrant people, a people who could then engage the dominant white world on its own terms, rather than having to make the choice between confrontation and acquiescence. In this way, Locke was striking a balance between the most commonly engaged strategies, patterns associated with either W.E.B. Du Bois or Booker T. Washington.

The set of speeches Locke delivered had little immediate impact, according to Jeffrey Stewart, despite their distribution in printed form.[8] But they are reflective of the ways in which "the negro question" was being discussed in American society. The phrase itself—race consciousness—was making its way into the national conversations about race, and thus also taking on new shades of meaning as different sides in the debate vied for control of its use. There was considerable tension even in the juxtaposition of the two words—"race" referring to a group, and "consciousness" invoking the mind of an individual. Locke's use of the phrase provided a richly layered image of what this kind of consciousness might look like.

As the Joint Commission searched for a discourse on race that avoided theology, doctrine, and scripture, they settled initially on the phrase "race consciousness," and their uses of it reflected the larger national contests, such as the differing positions of scholars like Grant and Locke. The language of "consciousness" tapped into the discourse of civilization, especially in ways reflected in the story of the "Indian Oak": civilized peoples were not restrained by the base and animal-like power of the unconscious. To be civilized one had to be conscious of one's race. A lack of race consciousness belied a lack of self-knowledge and general knowledge, and the yet-untamed savagery of instinctual behavior.

Race, Consciousness, and Morality

If, as Toni Morrison has suggested, it is against "rawness and savagery" that American identity has been defined, it is civilization that provides the terms of that identity. At the Baltimore meeting the terms of racial difference were circumscribed by competing discourses of "consciousness." At the Savannah meeting the state of that racial consciousness emerged in terms of the discourse of civilization. Civilization is the wakeful captive—virtuous, strong, selfless, and white—who must endure the presence of the savage hordes "who throng our streets and are in all our homes."[9] The victory of civilization is a moral imperative beyond questions of bias or prejudice or racial superiority. Such questions were incidental to the question of the civilized progression of American Christianity. If the savages remained unconscious, then they would suffer their own fate.

In chapter 2 we analyzed the ways in which the Commission performed and displayed its Methodist identity. Sacred history, place, time, and objects were used to establish and reaffirm a common denominational identity among the assembled disputants. The rubrics of identity at the opening ceremonies and the ensuing early discussions were decidedly "religious" and dependent upon explicitly Methodist denominational language and discourse. Yet after they laid the groundwork and underlying assumptions about "who they were" and "what the essence of Methodism was," the commissioners left this explicitly religious field to establish membership parameters in terms of race and modernist values of expediency. All the commissioners agreed that the religious aspects of Methodism were acceptable.

But very few white commissioners were willing to say, or even willing to accept themselves, that "race" on its own was a legitimate means of defining membership. They needed to be convinced—or to convince themselves—that race was useful as a concept. Race needed to inhabit a moral space. All the commissioners knew that the only reason they were unable to arrive immediately at a compromise was that they disagreed about what relationship black MEC members would have to the new church. This was unavoidable. The MEC commissioners knew that black membership was the central issue, and they also knew that even to consider or discuss the possibility of a separate denomination on racial grounds was anathema for the majority of MEC membership. They also knew that such a proposition would be considered outrageous to those outside of Methodism—non-church interests as well as Church interests—especially in the North.

But the pressure for union was as strong or stronger than the fear of a reaction to a new church with a racially segregated membership. Many outside of Methodism were watching the Joint Commission meetings closely, and this pressure, especially after the United States entered the War in Europe, was immense. Before the United States became involved, Americans considered themselves above the fray. The war was widely interpreted as the result of a lack of modernization and a lack of racial progression. Methodists criticized the churches of Europe in this regard as well. The European churches lacked the broad vision and modern polity of American Protestants that allowed the Americans to missionize the world and enjoy great success at home among the immigrants. Modern methods of efficient and civilized church management led to institutional growth, an explosion of programs of all kinds, and the gathering of vast resources. All this success paved the way for American Protestants to exert great national cultural influence while maintaining a strict legal separation between church and state. European Christians, on the other hand, were clinging to outdated polity and were rife with corrupt administrations that were tied to state governments. The influence of the Roman Catholic Church, of course, contributed greatly to the state of cultural stagnation and the lack of civilized progress that dragged Europe into what was basically a civil war. Once the United States was drawn into the war, of course, this view changed somewhat, and Americans had to view themselves more in the role of savior. To properly play this role, though, Americans had to look like the superior culture and civilization they claimed to be. For Methodists, this meant that their regional division had to be resolved if their claim to be the primary bearers of American Christian civilization was to be accepted.

So, with the pressure of national influence on their minds, the commissioners were confronted with this basic problem as they attempted to resolve their lack of unity: racial inclusivity was the issue upon which they disagreed. The MEC status quo was unacceptable for the MECS; the MECS demands were impossible for the MEC. Each Church, of course, had to solve the problem by answering to different interests. A compromise between the two positions allowed the MECS to look "progressive" to most anyone. A compromise meant the southern Church would move closer to the juridical equality of the rest of the nation. But there were elements in the MECS—some strongly represented in the Joint Commission—

who wanted no compromise at all. For the MEC commissioners, their task was perhaps more difficult. To the far larger national audience—MEC and otherwise—who considered the Jim Crow South a backward and debilitating drag on the nation's march toward the penultimate civilization, any participation in a juridical "color line" was a serious blow to that progress.

The range of opinions within the MEC itself ranged from this "no compromise" position to a modified and segregated racial inclusion, to outright calls for the black MEC membership to "do the right thing" and withdraw for the cause of union. The MECS had to negotiate its way through an older and fading Civil War–shaped generation while keeping itself in tune with many younger leaders who were attempting to find a way out of a more constricting regionalism to a larger nationalist consciousness. The MEC, on the other hand, while it did not have to contend with an explicitly competing regionalism, did have to find ways to draw southern regionalist sentiment toward the discussion of nationalism.[10] This could only be accomplished by praising the value of local interests and communities within larger community rubrics. It was within this tension between community identities that "race consciousness" found purchase and grew in the Joint Commission negotiations.

This meant two things, then: first, that union—or re-union, depending on one's view of the nature of the original split—had to be presented as a sacred duty and principle, both in the Church and in a national patriotic discourse; and second, that race had to be defined and understood in ways that shaped the terms of "race relations"—discrimination, segregation, prejudice, etcetera—into terms of morality. In the end, the Joint Commission had to construct a solution that spun a racially divided union as a sacred and civilized relationship, one that, while built on the principle that unity was a sacred and spiritual national cause, divided some of its members for the sake of that cause. Unity was impossible without division. Division in the new church had to exist also as a sacred and civilized relationship. The way to begin that argument was to build a discourse that flowed naturally out of moral discourses—both explicitly Christian and otherwise—common to both MEC and MECS interests.

It was the nature of "race consciousness" that served as the first major platform of the debate on race at the Baltimore meeting. Two versions of what this phrase meant emerged. At the risk of using glib nomenclature, but to help alleviate confusion, we will generalize the use of race consciousness among the Joint Commission members by means of a regional shorthand: northern race consciousness and southern race consciousness.

These regional distinctions often obscure or confuse other issues, but in this case, the two competing notions of race consciousness do reflect positions that each church commission took. Both versions, however, slip in and out of clear and distinctive usage. Often the difference between the two is a simple matter of emphasis.

Southern Race Consciousness

In southern race consciousness, generally ascribed to MECS members, race was closely akin to national, regional, or cultural identity. Thus race consciousness resembled nationalism, patriotism, or civic pride. Race was one's primary community identity. One's race was the central marker of one's progress toward civilization, and it determined many of one's primary strengths and weaknesses as an individual. Improvement or progress was measured at the macro community level, not at the micro individual level. While individuals certainly could progress beyond or lag behind their race, it was the aggregate or median level of civilized progression that held sway over the individual.

Those Joint Commission members who emphasized racial community over an individual's racial-ness used southern race consciousness as a way to describe an individual's awareness of the traits of one's race. This awareness entailed a confident knowledge of one's race—its strengths, weaknesses, idiosyncrasies, exoticisms, and history.[11] Race consciousness in the southern sense also meant pride and a desire for racial distinctiveness. This is similar to what is described later in the twentieth century as ethnic or cultural pride. Southern race consciousness differs greatly from this later variant in that it envisioned race consciousness leading to racial segregation, not a celebration of multicultural or multiracial diversity. Southern race consciousness was a position from which members advocated racial segregation as a means of providing a safe haven where a race could grow. In this view, purity was a primary value. The strengths of a race could only be fostered properly in a context in which a racially aware community could properly and knowledgeably propagate itself. Like staking a tomato or over-watering a garden, too much assistance from outside the race would only serve to create pathological dependence. To continue the garden simile more directly, mixing races would also dilute the genetic strengths of each race, just as mixing plants produces hybrids that may blunt the beneficial characteristics of the original.

These garden comparisons are intended to sound vaguely Mendelian. Southern race consciousness—like most racial discourses of the time— borrowed from the sort of conventional, clean, arithmetic logic of Gregor Mendel's agricultural theories on selective breeding. In the hybrid race theories behind southern race consciousness, some cultures cross-pollinated to produce a culture superior to either of the originals. Others produced weak, mongrel offspring that only exhibited the enhanced weaknesses and muted strengths of the originals. While no clear consensus emerged among race theorists—and certainly not among the members of the Joint Commission—as to precisely which races mixed well, or even who belonged to which race, it was clear that white Americans did not mix well with black Americans.

It is in this way that southern race consciousness fit nicely with the general view of the MECS Commission. The MECS members repeatedly voiced their concern that the MECS not be overwhelmed and lost in a merger with the larger MEC. This concern was not simply a matter of protecting political interests in the future united church. It was also a matter of protecting "the South" as a discrete cultural entity. Thus, by arguing for a "respect for race consciousness," MECS members were arguing for a separate sphere of distinction not only for black Methodists, but also for white southern Methodists.

The commissioner who first developed the phrase in the Commission meetings was MECS Bishop Elijah Embree Hoss.[12] He delivered the first major speech on race, and his introduction of race consciousness as a desired state for the church was formative. His speech was a response to the unification proposal Goucher had put before the Commission. In his address supporting the proposal, Goucher introduced language and ideas about the "world-wide work of the Church" and "world-wide Methodism."[13]

Hoss's speech is notable first for what he did not say. Hoss was responding to the first formal proposal presented by an MEC member. Goucher had just offered an articulation of the MEC proposal different from the language of the MEC General Conference. Goucher's proposal did not offer a racial differentiation among conferences, but rather regional conferences of different "classes." These "classes" would be determined by qualitative criteria. The implication was that the black congregations would not meet the criteria for full conference status. This proposal was offered by Goucher as an opportunity for the MECS membership to negotiate racial segregation in terms other than race.[14] But

Hoss ignored this in his response, as he was apparently more irritated by some of Goucher's incidental language.

Rather than hear what Goucher offered as a way to avoid charges of racism, Hoss heard language of a "world church." This vision for a united Methodism, said Hoss, "consorts well with the genius of Romanism" and is "distinctly hostile to the genius of Protestantism."[15] The genius of Protestantism was that it provided for race consciousness. Hoss had spent four years in Brazil with the MECS mission work, and he used his experience there as an example of how a "world church" would not work. Despite his best efforts in Brazil, said Hoss, he had to contend constantly with "the national feeling" and the "race feeling" that caused the Brazilians to desire to "regulate their own affairs." "The only thing that enables us to perpetuate our grasp upon them," he lamented, "is that we furnish the funds. Otherwise, they would go out overnight."[16]

The problem Hoss had with the situation there was not the possibility that the Brazilians would "go out"—after all, he was advocating just that for black MEC congregations—but that they were not prepared to manage their own church without the help of MECS missionaries. They were not "fully developed," said Hoss, except "in connection with liberty." Here Hoss formed a central element of his race consciousness position. As races develop and become more conscious, one of their first and natural inclinations is to be free from any control from outside the race. "National" churches are inevitable, argued Hoss: "You might as well try to stop the operation of the law of gravitation as of [sic] this feeling inherent in the human heart."[17] This desire for liberty, a natural developmental stage in the progression of a race, was the brightest development in Methodist mission work around the world.

Hoss not only reinforces the race theory behind southern race consciousness, but also inaugurates a sustained attempt by proponents of an all-white Methodist Church to harness the ideals of American national identity. The picture of a future Methodism Hoss paints is a racially segregated one, but that segregation is not the result of racism. Rather, that segregation is the result of a natural human inclination toward liberty and independence. The delimitation of racial segregation as a matter of liberty, justice, and independence reveals the centrality of American national identity to American Methodist identity. In this large committee divided by a bitter history of regional disputes over doctrine, social policy, and power, it was the cultural ideals of America to which they turned for common ground. In the same way that the ideal of unity had to be restructured to include room for racial segregation, so too did liberty have to be re-imagined to include a forced racial independence. As MECS ministerial delegate Edwin Barfield Chappell put it, black Methodists should be "free to work out their own racial destiny in their own way."[18]

"The Large Demands of Race Consciousness"

For delegates advocating it, race consciousness was a state of nature—not a chosen path, but one that demanded to be followed. All races had a consciousness. It was not something they chose. All races had to come to terms with themselves as they became more conscious. So if each race was properly to relate to other races, race consciousness had to be "respected." This call for respect allowed those who called for racial segregation to distance themselves from the segregation aspect of their plan.

Horace M. Du Bose, MECS ministerial commissioner, went on to present the first MECS proposal.[19] Du Bose was probably chosen for his enthusiasm for union, as he was one of the strongest proponents of union from his church. He was also probably one of the most willing, eventually, to consider a compromise on the issue of the "status of the negro." His initial proposal, in line with the instructions from the MECS General Conference, called for the black membership of the MEC to form a separate denomination outside the denomination formed by the white membership from the MEC and MECS. Du Bose's tone was friendly and fatherly. Mostly he sounded generous:

> Let that colored connection be in every sense a part of the reorganized Church, only having its own General conference, starting out with the same constitution that we have used, modified to meet their needs, but of course to be modified by them as they may find it necessary in the course of the years. . . . In this wise maintain a most perfectly fraternal intimacy, one that will grow and will secure confidence, and by that means give to our colored brethren an arena of activity, a theater of operations, that will fit them for complete independency, so far as that is needed, and strengthen their self-reliance and in every way meet the large demands of race consciousness.[20]

It is the language of rights and "proper relationships" that comes through strongly from most MECS members. Du Bose argued for an "arena of activity" for the black congregations that would preserve the "natural" relationships between the races while providing the independence (properly supervised and patronized by the white denomination) the black congregants needed and to which they had a right.

MECS Bishop Edwin Mouzon chimed in to support Du Bose and his version of race consciousness by responding to critics of this language.[21] Several delegates, especially MEC Bishops McDowell and Hamilton, had warned that there was a serious danger in advocating race consciousness. Bishop McDowell worried that exaggerated regionalism would contribute to the spread of the worldwide conflict. He hoped that the Joint Commission would not achieve unification "in such fashion as to lend our Church's support and countenance to that very thing that is breaking the heart of the world to-day—race assertion, race prejudice, exaggerated national emphasis that does not look toward humanity, but looks toward the other thing [race and national division]."[22] No matter how it was defined, thought those who opposed it, race consciousness could lead to racial strife. More than one delegate suggested that the war in Europe was the result of too much race consciousness. Mouzon took issue with this position, discriminating between true race consciousness and "race conceit." The war in Europe was the result of racial conceit, he said. He then equated race consciousness with national consciousness: "Race consciousness respects race consciousness. The race consciousness of America respects the race consciousness of Great Britain, and the race consciousness of Great Britain respects that of every other nation."[23]

In this short space Mouzon suddenly shifted the discursive platform, and accomplished several rhetorical moves at once. First, he equated racial difference with national difference. This primarily lent some dignity to his opponents, the blacks in the conversation, by offering them a comparison with the international power Great Britain. Second, and most importantly, he argued that there is a difference between race consciousness and racial conceit. This again moved the moral discussion away from any contest as to whether there should be an established difference or segregation at all between blacks and whites. Separation here is further naturalized and upheld by its equation with nations. By doing this, Mouzon moved the moral argument to what should be done between groups that are naturally separate, rather than addressing whether there is any difference at all. The other subtle shift Mouzon only hinted at was that the white Methodists were one nation—that is, they were true Americans— and the blacks were not quite fully Americans. They were their own race nation, and thus did not truly belong in the American national community. They would be forever just outside it because they were their own race nation living within the national boundaries of the true (white) American nation.

Northern Race Consciousness

While the emphasis in southern race consciousness was on race as a community, those who advocated and/or used northern race consciousness described the behavior and characteristics of a race in terms of an individual. While southern race consciousness depended on agricultural logic for its metaphors, northern race consciousness looked to Darwinian models of biological evolution for the basic framework of its social evolutionary logic. In northern race consciousness, races followed a developmental path like a human individual. A race began like a child, and could, depending on and responding to its environment, evolve toward "maturity." Thus in this scheme, some races were "child" or "immature" races while others were "mature." What distinguished northern race consciousness was that, as with an individual, environment made all the difference.[24] In the southern race consciousness model, races maintained fixed characteristics that evolved only as the group progressed on its own intimate agenda. Those fixed characteristics could be improved upon or remedied, but not changed. In northern race consciousness, while individuals in a race did have certain common characteristics, those characteristics were not as fixed. Like an immature child, an entire race could be guided and shaped. If placed in a proper environment and given access and room to learn from a mature race, a child race could progress and change.[25]

This social progressive paradigm for understanding race—the family model of races and civilizations—produced a meaning for race consciousness completely different from, and in competition with, the southern model. While in the southern version race consciousness meant awareness of one's racial community and thus knowledge of one's core racial self, northern race consciousness meant that an entire race could awaken—or be awakened—to awareness of itself and who it was. The race could then move on from that point, changing, adjusting, learning, and (given the correct environment) progressing. Achieving race consciousness was like a child becoming conscious of itself as a child. An immature race had in it all the potential and ability of a mature race. Like a child, an immature race would continue to respond and react automatically from simple biological impulses. These impulses were racially determined, and so it was not until a race, as a group, became conscious of itself and its unconscious racial impulses that it could begin to improve itself. In northern race consciousness this awareness was accelerated with assistance from model races. In southern race consciousness, this accelerating patronage only taught the wrong lessons.

So in the negotiations and plans for compromise, this was the key difference. Northern race consciousness fit the MEC plan for compromise because a race could be made conscious of itself and mentored like a young human. As a commission—meaning not all members agreed with this—the MEC hoped to find a compromise that did not retreat too far from its current racial arrangement. At the time, the MEC organized black congregations into black Annual Conferences. These Annual Conferences had equal and proportionate representation in the General Conference. This did not mean, however, that blacks in the church had proportionate representation at the national level. There was not a black bishop until 1920. In fact, there was a strong movement that led to a motion before the MEC General Conference that called for a special election of a bishop for "colored conferences." This was defeated at the 1916 General Conference, but it illustrates the level of frustration among black MEC members. It also shows that white MEC members acknowledged that juridical equality did not necessarily mean equal opportunity or access. It was widely acknowledged in this debate that a great divide existed between the black and white MEC communities. The MEC commissioners acknowledged among themselves that this status could not be maintained if they hoped to achieve unification. But in their use of northern race consciousness they hoped to support their expected basic compromise position: that black MEC members would remain members but be organized as a separate body within the new Church. Northern race consciousness provided a theoretical position from which to argue that the black membership would be best served if it were organized separately but close to the influence of white Methodists.[26]

John Goucher was the first MEC commissioner to respond to Hoss's use of race consciousness. Goucher moved quickly to restate race consciousness in a way that fit MEC needs and de-emphasized the "community interests" aspect of the MECS arguments.[27] He argued that race consciousness was more like self-consciousness, a consciousness that would be a first and necessary step toward the "self-development" of a race. Racial self-consciousness was discussed in light of missions and "missionized races" as mission efforts remained a primary point of comparison for the "home" problems with "the American negro." Racial self-consciousness sounded like individual "self-awareness."

Goucher also argued that blacks needed a certain amount of self-consciousness and "self-interpretation." He put together the most explicit version of a "racial uplift" ideology, arguing that blacks must only be given the freedom to discover who they really are, and that they would then learn by doing. This Goucher referred to as "self-interpretation," an absence of which leads to "no possibility of development":

> When the privilege of making one's own mistakes is accompanied by the necessity of correcting one's own mistakes, you are going far toward the development of self-consciousness and self-interpretation, which are the fundamental elements in personality. . . . Speaking for them, they need an autonomous existence, not outside Methodism but so related to Methodism that they may find self-interpretation at the same time they are developing self-consciousness. Otherwise, our nation is in danger, and the Church is in danger, and the colored people are absolutely in danger in all their relationships.[28]

The danger to which Goucher refers is entangled with the notion that individuals who do not know themselves completely, who are not fully aware of the dynamics of their race, do not possess "race-consciousness," are "undeveloped" and thus a threat to the social order of the American nation. This lack of conformity with the social order of the dominant group, called "racial immaturity" by Goucher and others, was the major concern and the major source of fear for white Methodists who wanted racial segregation in the unified church.

MECS delegate William N. Ainsworth also contributed to the discussion of "race consciousness."[29] Ainsworth had not yet spoken in the meetings because the discussion of the "negro problem" was the "crux in these negotiations." He publicly acknowledged that he felt it was useless to discuss anything else until the "status of the negro" was worked out. "Race consciousness" was of the utmost importance, said Ainsworth: "[R]ace consciousness on the side of the negro race and race consciousness on the side of the whites. It seems to me that this is fundamental, that it is absolutely essential to the largest development of the Church among [*sic*] both races that there shall be a full recognition of this consciousness."[30] Races are like families, argued Ainsworth, and like families, "proper development" is hindered when races are not properly separated. Ainsworth proposed—and he was the first MECS member to do so openly—that the black MEC membership continue into the new unified church but be placed in a missionary jurisdiction under the control of a Home Mission board. The intention of his proposition, he said, was to "recognize the race consciousness that is involved, but . . . at the same time furnish to our colored brethren the largest counsel and the widest brotherly assistance in working out their highest Christian destiny and also secure to them the largest liberty in the management of their own ecclesiastical affairs."[31]

The northern version of race consciousness worked well for MECS interests too. MECS delegate William J. Young asserted that a "large growth of self-consciousness among the negroes . . . has led them to feel that they must assert their own independence and work out their own salvation."[32] He chided black delegates I. Garland Penn and Jones for their naiveté concerning the blacks of the South, arguing that "negroes of their [Penn's and Jones's] type do not understand the negro of the South as thoroughly as do the white people of the South." By "type" Young did not mean northern, as both Penn and Jones were from southern states; he meant educated, middle-class black Americans who had frequent contact with and exposure to white Americans and their world. Their "condition" set them apart from the majority of black America, but they were not advanced enough in their cultural progress to allow them the advantage of white objectivity. Thus, they did not understand the real condition of most black Americans as whites did. Young counseled Penn and Jones:

I believe that men like these colored men who sit beside me, if they had the courage or heroism to do it, could solve the problem for themselves and for the colored race by going out and being brave enough to face their brethren and to speak the truth to them as the Southern white people who love the negro understand it, thus solving the great problem that has been agitating the Churches ever since the war by bringing about the formation of the negro Methodists into an entirely separate ecclesiastical organization in sympathetic touch with their white brethren.[33]

The Failures of Baltimore and Traverse City

The Baltimore meeting ended with "the question of the Negro" much less resolved than many had hoped. The discussion of race consciousness had proven divisive. For many it had only served to illuminate fundamental differences among the delegates. After days of increased tension and a growing awareness of their differences, McDowell suggested that the Joint Commission create a small committee to approach the problem of black membership. MECS commissioner P. D. Maddin protested vehemently, arguing that each commission had been given specific instructions from their respective General Conferences. He pleaded that "individual opinions" had no bearing whatsoever on the discussion.[34] Despite such protests, the "Committee on the Status of the Negro" was formed and instructed to meet separately. The Committee was to present a proposal at the next meeting.

The Joint Commission met at Traverse City, Michigan, in June 1917.[35] All the committees that had met in the intervening months submitted reports at the beginning of the meeting, including the committee studying the question of regionally organized conferences and the "Status of the Negro" committee. The regional jurisdictional conference report was addressed first. This question also divided the Commission, and they spent a day wrangling over the details of powers and composition of regional conferences. The central issue was whether regional conferences would have administrative powers or legislative powers—in other words, whether regional conferences would be able to write their own laws. Many commissioners—a few MECS delegates included—feared that regional legislative bodies would prove unnecessarily divisive in the unified church. A core of MECS delegates favored regional legislative powers in order to protect southern interests from being overrun by majority votes from the former MEC regional conferences in the General Conference. But the primary fear behind the discussion on both sides was, again, the "Negro question." Many in the MECS adamantly refused to accept regional conferences without legislative powers because they worried that whatever compromise the Joint Commission worked out on the black membership would be undone in an all-powerful General Conference. Likewise, MEC members worried that the attempt to create powerful regional conferences with the power to make their own rules would allow the compromises they had worked for to be overturned.

At the end of the discussion on regional conferences, before any discussion had taken place on the organization of the black membership, Penn spoke up in protest. The Commission was prepared to vote and fix the number of white regional conferences. Penn questioned what was behind the rushed vote, since the implication of such a vote was that there would be no such corresponding regional conference for black members, which would essentially amount to a tacit acceptance of the Associate General Conference scheme. Penn demanded that the question and vote be delayed until the race question had been settled. Jones rose too, nearly in panic, and claimed that their "enemies" in the South would use such a vote as a wedge to argue that the regional conferences were fixed.[36] The Joint Commission finally agreed that any settlement on the white regional conferences would not preclude the possibility of a black regional conference.

Only a slim majority within the Committee approved the report from the fourteen-member Status of the Negro committee: seven to five. The dissenting votes made for strange bedfellows. Black MEC delegates Irvine G. Penn and Robert E. Jones, and white MECS delegates H. H. White, Bishop Collins Denny, and future Bishop John M. Moore all opposed the report for different reasons. The report proposed that a new structure called an Associate General Conference be created for each mission, foreign, ethnic, or racial group. The General Conference, the final lawmaking body of the Church, was to be composed of all white regional conferences in the United States.[37] Black conferences in the United States and African mission conferences were to be organized together. A minority report was submitted by Denny and H. H. White in which they reiterated the MECS proposal for a separate body of black Methodists outside the new Church.[38]

By the end of the Traverse City meeting the Joint Commission could offer the public nothing but a statement of their tentative agreements on a few issues. They also had to admit that they had not even discussed the committee report on the question of black conferences and membership.[39] This did not go over well with the churches at large, in both the MEC and the MECS, and it increased the pressure on the delegates at the next meeting in Savannah to try to find a way to tackle their differences more directly.

4

The Savannah Meeting
"The Bogey of Social Equality"

Lynching—the word used to describe the public murder of black men and women by civilian white mobs in the late nineteenth and early twentieth centuries—and the large-scale violence of race riots hovered like a ghost over the Joint Commission deliberations, infused their discussions, and occasionally even broke through the surface of their conversations, especially after a particularly horrific episode had made its way into the news. Despite years of activism and struggle against it by people like Ida B. Wells-Barnett, there seemed no end to the scourge of lynching in American life. While many elite whites often condemned the practice, the federal government never managed to pass a law specifically addressing lynching until after World War II.[1] Disbelief and disillusionment among black Americans about lynching and a generalized sense of the pervasive threat of violence against African Americans became more pronounced as the United States entered World War I in 1917. Many black Americans—including Methodists like Robert E. Jones—hoped publicly that the thousands of young black men who eagerly volunteered to fight for the United States despite Jim Crow at home would provide proof to white Americans that black resentment was not to be feared and that black Americans were willing to make the ultimate sacrifice for the country they considered their own. But this hope was not to be realized, as white commanders segregated black soldiers into their black regiments. Moreover, while General Pershing refused to allow white Army regiments to be commanded by foreign officers, he sent black regiments to fight under the command of the French army.[2] In effect, the white-controlled U.S. military transferred Jim Crow laws and practices to Europe, segregating eating and sleeping quarters on bases, but also entering towns and cities in Europe where they were fighting and closing off access to certain sections of those towns to the African American troops. The message was that while white and black soldiers had an equal right to fight and die for their country, those rights were not to confuse the issue of racial hierarchy. It was in the social spaces, what would normally be shared living and socializing spaces, spaces where white and black bodies would be in close proximity, that the clearest messages were to be read: races were not meant to be mixed, and equality of national citizenship did not imply equality of race. Putting black and white soldiers together was wrong. Mixing races was wrong. Even allowing soldiers of different races to share common living space was to imply that "social equality" might be acceptable whereas clearly it was not. Clearly, there was something more to the appearance of "social equality" than racial bias or prejudice. The fear of "social equality" and the horrific violence of lynching were tied to the same obsession with racial purity that so many white Americans, South and North, considered a linchpin of American Christian civilization.[3] Beneath the frantic protection of social hierarchies, then, loomed a very real threat of brutal violence.

The plague of lynching went on so strongly, so relentlessly, and the race riots across the United States after the return of black soldiers were so dispiriting, that many African American leaders called for stronger action. The NAACP, among other organizations, began systematically to survey the problem. One fearless researcher was Walter White, who, taking advantage of his light skin, traveled in the southern United States passing as a white man to investigate specific cases of lynching. He interviewed white participants, politicians, and witnesses, and he returned to the North just in time to escape certain death himself after his identity was discovered. But he survived to write about what he had found in *Rope and Faggot: A Biography of Judge Lynch*.[4] In that book, White analyzed the roots of the problem, including the roles Christians and their churches played in allowing for and taking an active part in the maintenance of the pervasive culture of racial violence in the South. White's work even pointed directly at specific Christian churches as being particularly culpable: Baptists and Methodists. While he allowed that not all white Baptists and Methodists participated directly in incidents of racial violence, White contended that they did actively promote a climate of racial hatred and fear. In his chapter "Religion and Judge Lynch," White surveyed the state of seminary education and the racial ethos generated by southern white churches. White made the connection between the fear of "social equality" and the threat of lynching, characterizing reactions to the phrase as irrational or worse. He quoted a "prominent Southerner" who knew much about various denominations: "Whenever I speak to Methodists or

Baptists I almost always preface my remarks with some sort of careful statement regarding 'social equality.' If I do not—it matters not what I say about Negroes or lynching, 'social equality' is about the first thing they think of and it makes them go into a sort of insane rage. The Methodists are now worse than the Baptists."[5]

The Methodists in the Joint Commission, from both churches, while not appearing to go into an "insane rage," did respond disproportionately and in rare unison to the idea of "social equality." The scenes of exchange over the issue of race illustrate a larger point about its "mercurial nature": it also depends on a certain amount of stability in the public sphere, or, to use James C. Scott's cogent image, it depends on a "public transcript" of race.[6] It is useful to think about the Joint Commission's negotiations over racial power in this way because both those with most of the power—the white Methodists—and those with less—the black Methodists—were constrained by broad tacit agreement in American culture about the basic terms of race. That "public transcript" provides a stable reference point for negotiation by all in a society, whether they are dominant or not. And while we might expect that those victims of domination would be bound to a discourse of power that oppresses them— such as race—the "public transcript" also places limits on those in the dominant group. For the Methodists in the Joint Commission, their public transcript, that place where they all felt comfortable and in agreement and where they established that each of them could prove that they were not a threat, was an endorsement of the total unacceptability of the "social equality of the races."

It was at the Joint Commission meeting in Savannah in January and February 1918 that, after the two notable failures in Baltimore and Traverse City, the delegates began to speak more candidly about their individual views of race. What ensued was a parade of speeches on "the negro problem" by nearly all the delegates. For the first time, many of them felt unconstrained by any particular church position, and many disagreed openly with colleagues in their own commission about how to proceed. Despite the wide range of positions taken at Savannah, there emerged consensus on one concept: that the "social equality of the races" was completely unacceptable, and that anything they agreed upon would clearly avoid any structure that would appear to promote it in the future. This position was always portrayed, in a strategic way, as a "conservative," "civilized" position, and as the only moral position to take. Racial equality in the social sphere was not negotiable. It took many days of

debates and speeches in Savannah for the delegates—black and white—
to reassure each other of that bottom line. Having reached this much consensus—and that was the only consensus on race they had reached—they
nearly reached agreement on a plan before they left Savannah.

In particular, the two black delegates, Irvine Garland Penn[7] and
Robert Elijah Jones, expended a lot of floor time at the meetings reassuring their white counterparts, both northern and southern, that they were
in no way campaigning for anything resembling "social equality." In a
phrase from his first speech at Baltimore, repeated often both in print and
on the floor of the Joint Commission, Jones said that he believed in a
color line, and had no fears about it. Penn added that he himself had written the color line into the MEC book of discipline.[8] This was why social
equality was called a "bogey"; like the bogeyman in the woods, there was
never any evidence that social equality was in their presence. But for the
nervous delegates of the Joint Commission, any unidentified noise about
equality was reason to run for the cover of the color line.

The language of "the color line" was the same as the language of "social equality." Social equality was the kind of equality that would lead to
black and white Americans eating together, chatting together, walking
down the sidewalk together, and, if taken to its extreme, marrying and
having children together. At its heart, it would seem, were issues of class.
White delegates admitted outright that they were concerned that equal
representation among the races in the new church would lead to social interaction that would compromise the whites' "social standing" or "social
position." But while such seemingly shallow concerns did have some
bearing, the implicit concern in these strident repudiations of social
equality was the preservation of clear racial categories. The color line
protected white privilege and power. Social equality threatened the very
place where race could be undone: sex and reproduction. Law and cus-
tom in white America had struggled to keep up with forces that threatened to blur the color line. Interracial sex was the act that muddled the
fragile clarity of objective racial distinction—that is, skin color—upon
which so much of American culture was built. Social equality was anathema to these white Methodists because they considered it the beginning
of a slippery slope to interracial sex. It was anathema to black
Methodists—whether they really detested it or not—because to advocate
social equality would signal the end of any political power they held. Social "conservatism" was the only acceptable platform from which they
could negotiate in the Joint Commission.

Donald Mathews has described this obsession with racial distinction among white southerners as a search for authenticity and purity. The search, he argues, was exacerbated by the social and psychological devastation of the South's defeat in the Civil War. The search manifested itself in religious and social reforms, such as, among Methodists, a return to sanctification as a more authentic Methodism, and, more generally, the sabbatarian and temperance campaigns. But it was most vividly in racial segregation that the widespread white desire for clarity and purity revealed itself. Racial segregation was at first widespread but informally enforced. But as social taboo became gradually more institutionalized, whites in the South perceived themselves as safer and purer.[9] Lynching was the dramatic product of a desire for purity sexualized by fantasies of rape. In this way, racial segregation made "collective punishment of African Americans a sacrificial rite that purified the community."[10]

Mathews's analysis accurately describes the fear of social equality in the Joint Commission, except that it functioned as a given for all sides of the debate. The only difference, among white delegates, was perhaps the degree of passion with which social equality was attacked. The regional differences in the Joint Commission were rarely clear or consistent. And while the powerful desires for purity and authenticity among white southerners that Mathews describes might be exactly right, it is less clear how uniquely southern those dynamics are. The negotiations of the Joint Commission at least suggest that region may not be the primary factor in explaining white American fears of racial mixing.

Those in the Joint Commission suspicious that there was a plot to attach social equality along with full black church membership were of course concerned about the natural extension of the very discourses of freedom and equality that were integral to discourses on American cultural ideals. How were the white delegates, who praised and made allegiance to the cultural and spiritual ideals of freedom, democracy, equality, and liberty, to reconcile these ideals with racial segregation or reduced representation in church governance? And how were the black delegates to explain their own agreement to inequitable treatment in light of these very ideals, but with the added pressure of black activists such as W.E.B. Du Bois who used these same discourses along with revolutionary and abolitionist rhetoric to argue that no true American would ever be complicit in his or her own oppression?[11]

No matter how they made use of various racial ideologies, all of the delegates attempted to situate themselves in terms of a conservative racial discourse over and against a radical or "agitating" discourse on race and race relations. This conservatism was expressed not only explicitly ("I am a conservative, no matter what you think"), but also implicitly in a Commission-wide dismissal of the "bogey of social equality."

Race and Caste, Mass and the Individual

Along with only a few other MECS delegates on the Joint Commission—most notably Bishop Collins Denny, E. C. Reeves, A. J. Lamar, and later, Bishop James Cannon—H. H. White, a lawyer and judge from Louisiana, represented the extreme end of racialist thinking in his church.[12] The section of the MECS they represented, though, was large and powerful. Its power came primarily from the age and influence of many of the leaders in the MECS. The older generation remembered the Civil War and the Reconstruction era and the personal pain and social chaos that they entailed. Delegates often referred to this powerful faction in the MECS and how one might explain certain decisions to them, or package a compromise to please them.[13] In the final days of the Joint Commission, Bishop Cannon had to admit to an incensed Robert E. Jones that his insistence on a seemingly meaningless point in the compromise proposal was only to pacify this major faction.[14]

Not far into the debate at Savannah, White presented a prepared speech. In it he said what no other delegate had yet said: that there were many in the South—including, he argued, a majority of MECS members—who believe in the supremacy of the "Caucasian" race. Race, he argued, was the central issue around which the new church should to be organized. "Caste," he said, was the artificial distinction that would provide the structure for any plan that attempted to place the races together in the new church. When caste replaces race, he said, individual blacks are given false power that they neither deserve nor can handle. An arrangement based on artificial caste would only "fool the brother in black" and "amuse him with the shadow of equality while the substance is denied him."[15] Any such relations in church governance based on what White called the "equal status theory" would only lead to a breakdown in social relations outside of equal representation in the church. Race relations built around the reality of race, on the other hand, are built on solid differences. Race differences are real, he argued, and cannot be erased by toying with race relations.

White quoted an unnamed southern writer who used language that is worth repeating here:

> he who supposes that the South will ever waver a hair's breadth from her position of uncompromising hostility to any and every form of social equality between the races, deceives himself only less than that other who mistakes her race instinct, the palladium of her future, for an ignorant prejudice and who fails to perceive that resolution to maintain white racial supremacy within her borders is deepest rooted and most immutable precisely where her civic virtue, her intelligence, and her refinement are at their highest and best.[16]

The "highest and best" of southern refinement was found in the churches, argued White. Because of this, it was imperative that of all institutions in the South, the churches should be the first to maintain that racial separation that protected "her virtue." Here the image of civilization as the woman under attack by the black race returns to the conversation. Civilization is strong and willful, but at the same time delicate and weak, like a woman, because of its sophistication and refinement. It suffers harm only because it operates on a higher and more refined plane of existence, one that needs the manly "ride to the rescue" by the Anglo-Saxon men who lead it. It was this role that White and others were playing. White's speech had the quality of Martin Luther's famous "here I stand" pronouncement, and indeed one of White's MECS counterparts, Bishop Mouzon, invoked that very image of Luther as the lone vanguard against truth.[17] White took his stand and offered what he considered to be the only options available to the Joint Commission in light of how he understood the MECS position.

First, he claimed that the MECS would not be willing to enter an arrangement for the new church in which black members had any representation whatsoever in the General Conference or any general judicial body. Second, the black membership of the MEC would settle for nothing less than full representation in the new church. Third, the MECS would not enter into any agreement that did not also "take care of" the membership in the historic black Methodist denominations. In light of these claims, White said the only option outside of quitting the negotiations was the formation of a separate church outside the white church in which all black Methodists would be together, but under the "tutorship" of the white Methodist church. Recognizing that the black MEC membership would not agree to their ejection by the whites that out-numbered them, and also recognizing that they had the legal ground to appeal such action, White suggested some tactics to the white MEC del-egates. Basically, White proposed that the white Methodists threaten their black counterparts with decreased monetary assistance if they did not voluntarily leave the church. The black membership would then be "as-sured" that monetary assistance would be resumed and increased as soon as they "adopted the white view."[18]

White's confidence that his view was a fair representation of the MECS majority is puzzling. Most of his colleagues in the Joint Commission did not subscribe to anything close to it. But this view, and his steady advo-cacy of it and its consequences, weighed heavily on the negotiations. Not only did his colleagues on the MECS side feel as if they had to clarify their own positions in light of this, but White's unapologetic language of Cau-casian racial superiority coupled with almost deferential politeness to Penn and Jones added yet another difficult angle to the negotiations. White's view was difficult to deal with because his racial discourse dif-fered so greatly from the main thread of the conversation. While he said in substance nearly the same thing as many of his more politic counter-parts on the Joint Commission, his explicit use of the language of white supremacy set him apart and complicated the negotiations for everyone.

Bishop Hamilton: Equality but not the "Horror" of Miscegenation

Bishop Hamilton was probably one of the loneliest men on the Joint Commission.[19] Except for Alexander Simpson, no one else on the Joint Commission came even close to embracing the ideal of equal and full rep-resentation for all Methodists that he advocated. Hamilton's radical stance served the MEC commission well, though, since he offered an ex-ample of the radical position that frightened the MECS. His isolation in the Joint Commission proved that his position was not the norm. Penn and Jones, especially, did not want to be associated with Hamilton's views; he was considered a radical, but a black Methodist with the same views would have been considered a social "agitator."[20] Hamilton had been known for decades for his opposition to class and race discrimina-tion in the MEC. In his first major appointment in Boston he had fought the institution of pew rents, and had organized well-funded programs to assist the large immigrant populations of the Boston area. Later in his career he worked with the Freedmen's Aid Society, and he was considered by many the strongest voice in the MEC for the rights and privileges of the black membership. He was also known as an independent thinker. When most thought he would automatically support the creation of a bishopric that would provide an episcopal position for blacks, Hamilton ignored these expectations, and the expectations of many black Methodists, and opposed it on the grounds that it was not enough.

For these and many other reasons, Hamilton is a good example of the ways in which "progressive" racial thinking was deceptive. In his first major speech at Savannah, Hamilton combatively argued against all forms of segregation in American churches. He spoke angrily against white government-backed discrimination in the American West against Asians; he fumed about rich Methodists who left his churches when he welcomed "servant girls"—meaning recent immigrant women—into MEC congregations; and he boasted that he had never by "any 'consciousness' lifted myself above any other human kind."[21] But while he did not make the explicit argument that whites were better than others, his language often revealed an acute consciousness about class distinctions and the need to draw a line at some point between racial and ethnic groups. This attention to matters of social class tied his thinking to the basic prevailing racial ideology. The most dramatic example of this occurred in an exchange between Hamilton and MECS delegate A. J. Lamar.[22]

Hamilton's speech at Savannah was attacked or mentioned deprecatingly by nearly every MECS delegate that spoke. Lamar admitted more clearly than the others what bothered them about Hamilton's speech. Lamar's interpretation of MECS reactions to Hamilton's use of equality is instructive. Hamilton's discussion of equality is the "awful specter" that haunts the people of the South: "[It] is the fear that at some time in the future, through the lower strata of the white race, there shall be the amalgamation that will give us a composite citizenship in these Southern States instead of the purest block of Anglo Saxon American citizenship that exists in this nation." Proof, said Lamar, could be found by simply comparing Mexico, Cuba, or other Central American nations with the United States and asking "which is the strongest and which the best civilization?"[23] Lamar revealed the strange and elliptical nature of the racial ideologies that these Methodists made use of. He admits here that races are not pure. One's race does not guarantee one's level of civilization, but it does guarantee that one will be treated like the "mass." There was a "lower strata" in the white race, Lamar admitted, that threatened the very foundations of "Anglo Saxon American" civilization. But he would not be willing to force them out of the church because of their blood right to the privileges attained by the aggregate level of civilization of their race. Penn and Jones were, as individuals, civilized men of intelligence, grace, and talent. But they were not entitled to any privileges by their own accomplishments, even though they would never, by their own public admission, even consider racial "amalgamation" like the "lower strata" of the white race.

On hearing Lamar's response to his speech, Hamilton rose immediately in protest. Hamilton claimed here and at other times that he was either completely misunderstood or that there was a concerted effort to misrepresent his views in order to give the MECS a bargaining foothold.[24] By arguing for "mingling" or "equality," said Hamilton, he only meant equality at an institutional level, and "the very thought of miscegenation was not in my mind. I was as far from it as the Kaiser from the desires of the American people."[25] But despite his protests, Hamilton had to rise several more times to clarify this point, each time more vociferously than the last. MECS delegate W. N. Ainsworth basically repeated Lamar's accusation. He said that Hamilton's remarks—though "extreme"—"give our people pause in their desire for unification."[26] This time, MECS delegate E. C. Reeves took up his defense before Hamilton could stand. Reeves interrupted his southern colleague and said that Ainsworth had misquoted Hamilton. Hamilton stood after Ainsworth had finished and said that people simply expected him to favor "social equality or that horror of miscegenation, and everything I say seems to be interpreted through those glasses."[27]

What we learn from Hamilton's angry defensiveness is that even those whites who supported full and equal representation in the church made a clear distinction between equality in church governance and equality in social situations. And Hamilton, a living hero to many blacks in the MEC because of his advocacy for their causes, did not think "social equality" and the apparently inevitable miscegenation that followed it was merely a bad idea or awkward or something to be avoided. It was a *horror*.

Jesus Was "the Greatest Social Democrat"

Hamilton was not completely alone in his position. One other MEC member, Alexander Simpson Jr., argued for full representation for all

Methodists. Simpson, a lay delegate and famous Justice for the Supreme Court of Pennsylvania, was also one of the few who felt free to say that his position was the more biblically sound. Simpson's major speech at Savannah was distinctive not only for its open condemnation of the MECS position in New Testament terms, but also for its sweeping characterization of the South as a backward region.

Simpson made broad statements about the state of the world and its progress toward economic equality. He praised the rise and reforms of the labor movement, and cheered the fall of the robber barons and their monopolies. He hoped that soon "the high salaries of the supposedly great men of this country, the great fees of the lawyers, the great profits of the merchants, are all going to be more or less submerged in the rising wages of the laboring man." But his support of worldwide leveling was circumscribed. All the recent reforms, he hoped, would one day put all people on a more "common level." But this common level, he was careful to say, was only on the planes of politics and economics. Jesus might have been "the greatest Social Democrat the world has ever known," but he was also "of an inferior race . . . and despised even by a conquered people." And since Jesus did not teach or struggle for his own social equality, this was not a principle that was a product of his teaching. Jesus did not teach "social equality, but, please God, He taught us religious equality, and not one word or act of His, so far as the Bible shows, taught anything else."[28] These general distinctions in the application of the notion of equality—economic, political, and social—that Simpson made were accepted in some form by most of the delegates. But it was the MEC delegates who made the best use of "spheres" of gospel teaching as a way to circumvent the discussion of social equality. Equality as a clearly delimited principle allowed the delegates to push aside the question of social equality without addressing the messy mechanics of how equality in the church would avoid becoming equality in the social sphere. As MEC delegate David G. Downey put it, "social equality" was a matter that would take care of itself. It was "hardly a matter to be considered by thoughtful men who are handling church matters."[29] MEC ministerial delegate and Joint Commission secretary Abram W. Harris agreed that it was not "polite to talk about equality between gentlemen."[30] He suggested that instead they should use the phrase "common social life." Then Harris went on to prove his conservatism in regard to a "common social life" among the races by saying that he would rather see his own daughter in the grave than to see her marry a "colored man." To show that these comments reflected acceptable notions of equality and not blind prejudice, Harris said he hoped that "Dr. Jones and Dr. Penn will understand what I have just said, and if they have the proper spirit of manhood in them I know that they wouldn't want one of their daughters to marry a white man either." The white supremacist views of White were not what Harris liked to hear said out loud, but he had to agree that what Judge White said was true. But, argued Harris, it was possible for limited numbers of "darkies" to participate in the General Conference without endangering the segregated social life of the church. No white men in the Joint Commission, he contended, had been hurt by the presence of Jones and Penn.[31]

Rousseau, Not Christ

As the common terms for the negotiations at Savannah emerged, equality among the races was qualified three ways: spiritual equality, ecclesial equality, and social equality. All the members agreed that spiritually, all races were equal. By "spiritually" they meant that a Christian salvation was equally available to all human beings, no matter what their race or class. It also meant that there was no spiritual hierarchy in a heavenly eternity. A Christian heaven would not be organized according to earthly hierarchies. Spiritual equality was the sphere referred to in the New Testament principle "all are one in Christ."

Ecclesial equality was an altogether different matter. Occasionally called the political sphere, this sphere basically encompassed the relationships in any human organization, including church institutions. This was the sphere in which the commissioners understood themselves to be negotiating. The level of equality in the ecclesial sphere was where agreement in the Joint Commission fell apart.[32]

Social equality, like spiritual equality, was an area they all agreed upon, though they didn't recognize it amongst themselves. As we have seen, the commissioners returned over and over again to this topic, either worrying about the danger and threat of social equality themselves or attempting to reassure other worried commissioners that no one wanted any such thing as social equality. Social equality, it would seem, was a "bogey." As we saw earlier, MEC Bishop Leete delivered one of the more systematic treatments of the "spheres" theory of equality. Several delegates had seized upon a comment made by MEC Bishop McDowell to the effect that French philosopher Jean-Jacques Rousseau, and not Jesus

Christ, was responsible for the "doctrine of social equality." Leete developed this claim more fully. Jesus was not a "leader of society" and did not "mingle much with society," said Leete. Jesus taught a few principles that had some bearing on society, but not any principles that would indicate that all members of society should have equal social footing. Rousseau taught much to consider about the "rights of man, but very little or almost nothing about the higher duties and privileges of man." Christians should think in three different spheres, argued Leete (not to be confused with spheres of equality): first are a Christian's "obligations," then a Christian's place in the "kingdom of Christ," and then the "benefits" of Christian salvation. After this, the question of "mere rights rather takes care of itself" in time if a Christian will only stick to these spheres of thinking and follow the laws of the church and act "in the best interest of society." As proof that an arrangement such as the MEC was proposing could work, Leete read from a letter written by a Protestant Episcopal pastor. That church had integrated its governing bodies, and the writer explained to Leete that the black members had all the same rights and privileges in the church councils that white members had, "save that in social matters, for example, they never show up, though the invitations are general."[33]

The question before the Joint Commission, said Leete, was not a matter of politics or society, but rather a question of the "life of the church," and in that arena he thought that the black MEC membership should not be pressured out of the church. By setting off the question of racial equality as a matter of categories, Leete, like his peers in the MEC, attempted to avoid any debate about social equality entirely. He hoped to convince those opposing equality in the church that just because someone advocated equality in one area of life did not mean he or she advocated it in all areas of life.[34]

If the question was one of politics or society, Leete said he would be in the most conservative camp of the group. Taking this a step further, Leete tried even harder to display his social conservatism and make a sympathetic connection to his counterparts on the MECS commission. Leete delivered a loving honorific to the South and paid homage to his own southern-ness. He had been born and raised in South Carolina, and in his episcopal duties in the MEC he was assigned to work in the South. As to his personal feelings about the matter, Leete said he was raised "with about every prejudice that a Southern man ever had." Because of this, Leete admitted, the position he had just outlined in regard to the new church and its racial makeup was not precisely his own. Rather, he was speaking for his church, but thought he could understand "exactly the feeling of the Commission to which I belong with reference to the negro ."

MEC reserve delegate Charles Pollock was one who did not make much attempt to identify or sympathize with "southern" ways of thinking; instead he tried to show that the Methodists in the North were more strongly set against social equality. For example, he asked the MECS delegates how they understood blacks: "Is he a human being? Has he a soul? Do you expect to meet him in heaven?" But then he differentiated these considerations with questions of social equality:

> I believe it is a fundamental principle with you good people of the South that there cannot be social contact between the two races. But let me tell you sirs, if I rightly interpret the spirit of the North, they are just as strong in their conviction upon that question as you are. The people of the North do not expect—they do not want nor will they permit social contact. I would expect the South to come into social relations with the negro before the people of the North.[35]

This and other exchanges in the transcriptions read as if some members were competing for the most conservative position on social relations between the races.

The State, the Good Samaritan; the Church, the Levite, and Priest

Many MECS delegates struggled to align their personal opinions with their official General Conference position. Robert E. Blackwell was one of those who differed most openly in the meetings.[36] His resistance to the official position seemed to arise from the disjuncture between his own personal discomfort with the idea of working closely on an equal footing with black Methodists in a new church and his perception that he and other whites in the South had woefully wronged black Americans and never even attempted to correct those wrongs. At Savannah, Blackwell responded to the white supremacy speech delivered by H. H. White in an attempt to reassure the MEC delegates that White's pessimistic vision was not the dominant vision.

Blackwell said that White's view of the situation among MECS membership was not accurate. He said what no other MECS delegate had said up to that point: that he and every other white person in the South owed a large debt to black Americans, and they had not even begun to repay it. Unfortunately, the government of the United States had taken more aggressive steps than the MECS, and in that way was the Samaritan, while the MECS, by its inclination to leave "the Negro to develop his own racial destiny," was in danger of becoming the Levite and the Priest.[37] Blackwell's speech was unique in its emphasis on white southern Americans' culpability rather than their victimhood as a culture left with a problem created by powers from outside. Blackwell began with the details of his personal gain from the profits of slavery: "The most pathetic spectacle in history is the negro. He was brought here against his will. We Southern people have profited by him. I stand here as one who has profited by him. . . . I was helped in getting my education with money that was mine through my mother's slaves. I owe him a debt. I have not paid it. Many of my fellow Southerners have not paid the debt they owe the negro."[38]

In particular, said Blackwell, the MECS had not kept up its obligations to the black Methodists who came from their own denomination—those who moved on to become the CME Church. He accused his fellow delegates of a disingenuous reporting of the history of the CME split and their concern for the welfare of its members and the members of the other black Methodist denominations. Other MECS delegates had described the separation of the MECS and CME as a mutual undertaking that benefited both sides. There was also, they said, plenty of support from the MECS for the CME congregations, both financial and otherwise. Blackwell described this history differently. There was an attempt initially to retain an intimacy between the two bodies. The MECS supplied ministers to the new CME churches, but that ended almost immediately in 1870. This situation was, he said, too "socially difficult"—even more so, said Blackwell, than the plans on the table at the Joint Commission. But that was the end of any real engagement with their former slaves and fellow church members, he said, and since then they had done very little but send money because they did not want to run the risk of having their "social relations" with blacks criticized. This situation was not, as his fellow delegates would have it, a plan to which they gave much thought: "The plan we drifted into causes us no qualms of conscience. We have hardly more concern about the Negroes of the Colored M. E. Church than we have about Presbyterians or Episcopalians."[39]

White represented the view of an older and waning generation, said Blackwell. Young whites in the South were finding a "new conscience" for the black community and were working to find solutions other than furthering segregation. It was the complete independence of the CME that allowed the MECS to forget their obligations to that church, and a similar relationship with the black members of the MEC in the new church would result in the same problem. By creating an independent black church they would be, like the Levite and the Priest, going "by on the other side, calling to the man who is down to get up and help himself and cultivate his race consciousness and not rely upon any Samaritan to help him up."[40]

The proposal Blackwell offered was completely different from any offered by another MECS delegate up to that point. Complete racial separation would be his personal preference, he said, but it would not be the right thing to do. He proposed to organize the new church in the way that Robert E. Jones and Irvine G. Penn had proposed: annual conferences separated by race with proportionate representation in a biracial General Conference. Blackwell then made the subtle accusation that some of his fellow delegates were engaging in tactics that were inflaming the fears of MECS membership. They could alarm the membership, he said, by characterizing such an arrangement as a church where "Negroes make laws for white people," but that would not be possible any more than it would be possible for any single white annual conference to make laws for the whole church. The solution to convincing the MECS membership to accept this compromise, argued Blackwell, would be to imagine the black membership of the MEC as "their Negroes," those whom the MECS abandoned "to the North" years ago:

> If we could only consider these Negroes as our Negroes, Southern Negroes, we should have less difficulty; but they have been separated from us by Northern Help and we unconsciously look upon them as Northern Negroes. When we get together, they will become our Negroes, helped by us, and the situation will be quite different. Then all our fear of Negroes making laws for us and many other fears vanish as a bad dream.[41]

Blackwell's call to his fellow delegates was more than just a compromise. His insistence that the proposed arrangement would banish their fears of inappropriate social relations was expressed in the language of a proprietary intimacy. This argument was based on Blackwell's own knowledge of what kind of social relationships white southerners considered acceptable and what kind they considered potentially dangerous. By proprietary intimacy I mean that kind of affection one might hold for a possession—in this case, a slave. By describing the potential racial relationships in the compromise he proposed as a renewal of an antebellum affection between slaves and slaveholders, Blackwell was tapping into a discourse of intimacy that was both familiar and acceptable to the older generation of the MECS. This is abundantly clear in the negotiations. Stories of being coddled in the "heaving bosoms" of "mammies," the loyalty of slaves during the Civil War, and close friendships with ex-slaves were almost a standard introduction to many MECS speeches. Speakers used the stories to prove that their call for racial separation was not the result of race prejudice. The stories also proved that racial segregation was based on the impersonal facts of social science and race history, not on personal racial animosity.

"Not with Whom I Eat, but What I Eat"[42]

The use of the trope of proprietary intimacy to disparage notions of social equality was not limited to the MECS delegates. Penn and Jones were from the South as well, and they participated in the almost ritualistic practice of beginning their speeches by paying homage to intimate relationships born out of human slavery. In his first major speech at Savannah, Penn described his friendship with the man who had owned his mother. He described him as one of the best friends he had ever had. Penn then described a relationship with another white man that illustrated the difference between the apparently acceptable friendship based on proprietary relationships and a relationship built outside of that social structure. MEC bishop McDowell had visited Penn's home church in Virginia, and Penn told how his black church had met McDowell at the train station to welcome him, but then immediately handed him over to a white delegation from the MECS church in that town "for the courtesies that I knew the white people in that city would be glad to give him." What Penn was hoping to prove to his nervous listeners was that even when blacks and whites were members of the same church, blacks would not extrapolate falsely from that ecclesial relationship that somehow they were also entitled to ride in the same car through town or eat lunch with their fellow white Methodists.[43]

Stretching his conservative persona to its full height, Penn told the Joint Commission that "so-called social rights and prerogatives" were not the central issue for blacks in the MEC. At issue was their access to the basic rights accorded them by their membership in the MEC: full conference status and proportionate representation in the General Conference. Penn had heard the rumors circulating among white MECS members about what would happen in the new church when the General Conference met in a southern city such as Atlanta. Would not the black membership, since it was given equal status with whites in the General Conference, demand to stay in the same hotels and eat in the same restaurants as whites? "Foolish" is what Penn called such talk. Twelve black representatives in the General Conference—what he and Jones had agreed to at that point—would "give no more trouble" than he and Jones had at the Joint Commission meetings. Those delegates would do just what he and Jones had done: "they would take care of themselves, and meet you in the General Conference, do their work, get out, and go about their business."[44]

Penn and Jones both went to great lengths to prove their conservative stance. Both also publicly placed themselves in the camp of Booker T. Washington rather than W.E.B. Du Bois in the national debate on the direction black Americans were to take.[45] In his very first speech in Baltimore, Penn's first sentences established this: "I think everybody here knows I am a Booker T. Washington conservative. I have tried never to utter anything rash in the newspapers or on the platform. I have rather belonged to the school of Booker T. Washington than to any other negroes in the country." Penn had a brush with racial activism of the more radical kind early in his career that had convinced him of the more conservative path. The World's Columbian Exposition in 1893 did not include any exhibits by black Americans. Frederick Douglass and Ida B. Wells edited a pamphlet in protest, and asked Penn to write a section of the pamphlet. The pamphlet, titled "The Reason Why the Colored American Is Not in the World's Columbian Exposition," received extensive criticism from both whites and blacks as an act of irresponsible agitation.[46] Penn did not handle the criticism well, and considered the project a complete failure. Attempting to distance himself from the fiasco, Penn, as the commissioner of the section of the Atlanta Exposition in 1895 that dealt with "negro" education, was at least partly responsible for placing Booker T. Washington at the top of the list of speakers. This was the speech that put Washington at the forefront of the national conversation on race. In his speech at Baltimore, Penn reminded his fellow delegates of this, saying he had supported Washington because "a rash word from a colored man could have brought confusion between North and South and made the Exposition absolutely a failure."[47]

Jones, for his part, had always been known as a leader who would rather work within the clear bounds of law and social courtesy to effect change. He was known nationally for his work for "racial uplift" of black Americans and segregated interracial harmony in New Orleans. In the February 1916 issue of *Crisis* magazine, Jones was highlighted in the regular "Men of the Month" feature. The magazine described him as a notable leader of "every big race movement in New Orleans for the past ten years."[48] In 1930 Jones figured prominently in a *Crisis* article about Gulfside. Gulfside was the Mississippi seaside resort for black Americans founded by Jones. The article described Jones as a conservative—at least by *Crisis* standards. He was "neither aggressive nor self-assertive," but because of his strong stance on working within the bounds of common social protocols and his commitment to nonconfrontational methods, Jones had been able to "accomplish many things that a more aggressive or self-conscious Negro could never have done."[49] It seems that the *Crisis* held a grudging respect for Jones and the results of his efforts. With this kind of national awareness of his work and his reputation as an accommodating race activist, one might think that Jones would not have felt the need to prove that he was not an agitator. But this was not so.

This conservative stance was consciously strategic for Jones. He was not a leader without a strong vision, nor was he someone easily walked over. Jones was not afraid to stand his ground publicly, even when he was clearly outnumbered and in danger of offending white men. His conservatism seems to have been a style of carefully choosing battles. What becomes clear in the Joint Commission, though, is that the social equality issue, no matter what Jones might have really felt about it, was not a battle he was going to fight. As we have seen, even before the Joint Commission negotiations Jones had to address the social equality issue publicly. This continued throughout the negotiations, so much so that when he delivered his major address at Savannah, he prefaced all he had to say in regard to the proposals on the table with a long repudiation of racial social equality. He began his speech by admitting that he would rather not be on the Joint Commission at all because it is not his usual way of approaching a problem. His usual method had been to pursue a "policy of aloofness," he said.[50] Then, reflecting a general trend in the Joint Commission conversation, he distanced himself from the language of "race consciousness." He warned his white counterparts: "That is not what you want, brothers. Do you know what race consciousness is? It is human consciousness acute. It is human consciousness resenting discrimination. It is a drawing up. It is becoming self-content and at the same time resenting what you may feel, that others are treating you as something separate and apart."[51] This version of race consciousness characterized the very approach to racial problems that Jones had worked so hard to avoid. His whole approach to race problems entailed coming to terms with separateness by spurning bitterness, resentment, and anger. This kind of race consciousness also led to the kind of radicalism that occasionally called for total equality, including social equality.

To prove himself and the black Methodists he represented on the Joint Commission, Jones tried to be as forceful as possible. He used his own family history and his marriage as proof. Jones told his fellow delegates that his mother was "7/8ths white," and that his father was a "colored man." Despite this heavily white proportion of blood in his mother's veins, she "recoiled and resented it" when Frederick Douglass married a white woman. Among blacks in the South, he boasted, this was such an affront that Douglass, despite strong support before his marriage, nearly "lost caste" because of it. To make it clear that it went both ways, Jones said that any black woman who would "sell her virtue to a white man" should be shunned. To make his disgust with interracial marriage even more clear, he told the delegates that if they really thought that black Methodists wanted social equality he would "underwrite a contract with you and . . . split my veins and sign it in my own blood and we will build a wall so high that no negro can get over it, and so thick that no white man can go through it." As final proof, Jones said he had married a woman "of darker skin than [his] own" because he had "said before God that my children should know who they were."[52]

But there were two sides to this social equality problem. Jones addressed the question of miscegenation first because it was the most contentious issue. This is certainly made clear by the widespread lynching of that era.[53] Yet when discussing social equality, most delegates had a more literal notion of "social" in mind. As MEC delegate J. H. Reynolds suggested, the crux of the debate they were in was more about "social mechanics" than about a well-defined principle.[54] By social mechanics he meant that they did not know how, if they were to work together in the General Conference, black and white Methodists would manage the awkward business of bathrooms, restaurants, hotels, cars, taxis, and sidewalks. By their own admission, the delegates of the Joint Commission did not think that equal institutional footing should lead to equal social footing. But when confronted with the hard reality of such a large public occasion as the General Conference meetings, how would they manage that awkward transition from enclosed meeting hall to public space? How would they know when they were talking business or pleasure? How would they know a business lunch from a social coffee? Jones attempted to reassure his fellow delegates on these issues as well. Jones said he was so sensitive to intruding on the social standing of a white fellow MEC member that he was often, by common standards, downright impolite. He would often simply ignore a white MEC bishop visiting New Orleans if he thought there was the chance that he might impede the "social life" of that bishop or his other white contacts in the city.

This description of his social conduct fits precisely the glowing description that MEC Bishop Leete gave of black MEC members in the South. Leete attempted to convince the Joint Commission that the black members of the MEC were of an entirely different and better "type" than other black Americans. In his experience as bishop of the "Negro work" in the South, he said, he had found that "that kind of negro is not trying to embarrass white men in their social relations." He proudly claimed that in the six years he had worked there in Atlanta not one of the black superintendents of the black conferences had ever come to his house. He has not even had to discuss this with them, he said, because they are "anxious that I should be unimpeded in my social relations. If they had business, they have called up and over the telephone we made arrangements to transact that business in the inside office, not in the corridor. . . . As I understand the social code, it deals with matters of eating and drinking, our private life. We have the right to choose our associates. I think that right is equal on both sides and proper."[55] This short speech by Leete was the most explicit description of how the "social mechanics" of ecclesial equality were supposed to work. His explicit use of the phrase "social code," as if there were a written set of rules somewhere, shows us how the aversion to human social equality was thoroughly engrained in American society, and how these Christian Americans worked fervently to convince those both inside and outside their churches that their Methodist Christianity gave them no cause to think or act differently.

5

The Final Three Meetings

The Problem of Missions
and the Urgency of Patriots

Before we consider in depth the final meetings of the Joint Commission, it will be helpful to step back briefly to 1917, to a celebration of the fiftieth anniversary of the Freedman's Aid Society, that arm of the MEC that reached out to help provide education for former slaves after the Civil War. It had been, by most accounts, a successful venture, founding vocational schools, colleges, and medical schools throughout the southern states. In April 1917, the MEC sponsored a gala, featuring Bishop Quayle, a white senior bishop, as the plenary speaker. His speech marked a generational shift, in that his audience was largely made up of African Americans who had never been slaves. He focused his remarks not so much on their uplift, or the specific gains of the Freedman's Aid Society, but on race itself. His speech was a celebration of race, and it was intended to encourage his mostly black audience to a kind of celebratory race consciousness:

> A Race! What an electrical word that is shot through with light and flame. A race—a huge block of men, a kinsmanship of blood by history, by suffering, by shipwreck, by survival. What a vivid, vital thing a race is, how weighty like a mountain range and like a mountain range cold and bleak and dangerous and high and sunlit and with health and cooling and with its pines and streams. A Great Divide of History and Civilization. A race is a momentous thing, and an august thing. We are here tonight, to look a race in the face and take a race by the hand and give a smile and a word of cheer to a mighty race at march toward what it is to be.[1]

For Quayle, race was the foundation of human identity, a way of telling one's story, the means to understand and to make history, and the primary divide between groups of people. All a race—by way of its individuals—had to do in order to find its apotheosis was to know itself fully, to embrace its place on the map, to endure the hardships inherent to it, and then to stand tall like a mountain and be glorious in itself. Quayle and others were trying to excite black Americans about their race. Black Americans, too, were writing their own race histories that "constructed expanded notions of religious and racial communities that had persevered through time."[2] But the problem with separate race histories, of course, was that there existed in the United States more than one race, and white Americans were convinced that the characteristics and qualities that made the United States the emerging world power that it was came from their race. So Quayle and others who understood U.S. citizenship in a more generous fashion had to work to calm the fears of those who supported a fuller implementation of Jim Crow oppression of black Americans.

In this vein, Quayle offered a list of ten traits of African Americans. The list was intended as comfort for those who feared that black Americans would, through gradual social and economic progression, begin to expect broad social equality along with their equality of citizenship. The list was mostly composed in the negative: "He is not a tramp; He is self-respecting; He does not solicit the bounty of burial; He is not a socialist. He is not discontented. He is never an anarchist. He is social. His bias is religious. He is not bitter. He is an American."[3] Besides providing a good illustration of the prevailing biological determinism that shaped the general grammar of difference, this list tells us a lot about the fears and anxieties that shaped the racism of the era. Six of the items on the list are expressed in the negative. These reflect white fears of the social disorder they expected would follow in the wake of a weakening of Jim Crow. The inversion of these negative traits also illustrates a few characteristics of white identity: naturally self-supporting, independent, self-assured, forward-looking, loyal, etcetera. But the list ends emphatically in one positively constructed declaration: "He is an American." Quayle was trying to make the case not that African Americans deserved good treatment, or that they deserved equal treatment by Methodists, but that they were a race in their own right, and that they needed to embrace that race within their primary identity, as Americans. And as Americans, "Negroes" were happy, not aligned with the foreign-based political radicals. They could be trusted not to hold a grudge against white Americans over slavery.

Quayle's speech is a good illustration of the kind of environment that made the job for Penn and Jones in the Joint Commission so difficult.

The speech was intended as encouragement for black Methodists, but it was encouragement laced with warning, too, especially in the lines about bitterness, socialism, anarchism, and discontent. These were words of counsel, words that admonished black Methodists that they were already being associated with radical elements in the world, and that they needed to fight these assumptions by showing a less aggressive and radical stance. If they were to retain the "American" next to their name, then they needed to reject the politics of agitation and shift to a more conciliatory mode. It was in speeches and articles and books that made arguments like this one that the conflation of whiteness and American-ness could be seen so strongly. A certain kind of racial behavior was commensurate with citizenship, and it was behavior that white men like Quayle warned corresponded with the right to be called "American."

The final three meetings of the Joint Commission, especially the first, were hurried, almost frantic. There had emerged from the Savannah meeting a plan that, while not approved by the Joint Commission as a fully formed proposal, carried over as the framework for debate. This basic plan called for regional conferences comprising all white U.S. congregations, and then other conferences, tentatively called "central" conferences, comprising all other nonwhite or non–U.S. groups. This included Methodists in Europe, South America, Asia, Africa, and the Caribbean, and the African American congregations in the United States. All these would have representation in a General Conference. Several key points were undecided, though: the composition and powers of the white U.S. regional conferences, and the nature of the representation of central conferences. The problem this posed, really, was the question of who was worthy of full membership rights in the new church. The question had been shaped by the Savannah proposal: race and nation, and a clear notion of how the categories of missionary and missionized ought to be defined. During these meetings broader U.S. national concerns—of war and the disillusionment of continued or increased domestic unrest over race and "labor" —directed the commissioners' racial discourse away from the more individually focused language of social equality and consciousness to language shaped by American patriotism, American nationalism, and American Christian manhood. Commissioners competed for ownership of this language, eliding the difference between Methodist and American identities.

Race and the Nation

We have seen that a strictly religious Methodist identity was at odds with racial identity. The language of Methodism common to all the Joint Commission members, in other words, was unable to incorporate satisfactorily the multiple racial identities of the commissioners into a common denominational identity. All members of the Joint Commission agreed that no matter what the level of civilized progress, races needed proper differentiation in order to maintain the social order. By the end of the Savannah meeting, this was all the Joint Commission had agreed upon concerning "the negro problem." A fleshing out of "race consciousness" had not led them anywhere. They had spent a tremendous amount of time discussing whether ecclesial equality would destroy the fabric of American society by leading to social equality of the races. The final arena in which they explored the problem of race was national identity and patriotism; the full rights and privileges of being American were discerned in terms of "Christian manhood." Like all the modes of racial discourse, American nationalism and patriotism appeared and reappeared throughout the negotiations. But it was in the final three meetings that they came more to the fore in light of U.S. involvement in the war in Europe. What destabilized the commissioners' dependence on nationalistic language to sort out their problems were the competing notions of nationalism: civic nationalism and racial nationalism. These competing discourses gave them choices for a moral high ground. Either one carried sufficient cultural weight to lend it authority. In the tension created by their opposing ideals there was enough creative space for the Joint Commission to assemble a morally viable proposal. These broader cultural ideals helped them alleviate the problem of reconciling the conflicting forms of Christian equality with which they had been wrestling. Heightened in the national consciousness because of the focus on the war in Europe, American national identity and the accompanying ideals of patriotism, loyalty, and sacrifice offered a separate public discourse on civilization that the Joint Commission embraced.

In the final meetings, the lines between competing factions blurred considerably. Gone was the strong, explicit white supremacist voice. Gone, too, were the attempts at shaping a "race consciousness" that would dissolve pejorative notions of racial segregation. And gone were the frantic responses to the language of equality. Discussions of race crystallized around American-ness. Two variant uses of American patriotism emerged, and these different positions realigned the factions within the

Joint Commission. Those opposing an integrated church called for black Methodists to sacrifice their "technical" rights and privileges to membership in favor of the greater good of the unity of the majority whites in the two churches. This gesture was patriotic because they all agreed that the union they were working for was for the greater good of the American nation. For black Methodists to stand in the way of (white) union on "mere" rights would show that they had not yet developed into a full "Christian manhood."

Those delegates who were still working for some form of an integrated church were, by the last three meetings, not as willing as they had been to sit quietly, and not as reticent to point out more forcefully the import of the tension between competing nationalisms. Jones and Penn, especially, along with Alexander Simpson, had spent all the time they cared to listening to speakers extol the virtues of America and its principles of freedom and democracy and then argue that access to the privileges of American citizenship was circumscribed by race. They had also tired of the "mass versus the individual" argument that held a "civilized" individual captive to the median level of that individual's race.

The nationalizing dynamics of the war in Europe turned up the emotional thermostat of the final meetings. A sense of urgency pervades the transcripts, and that urgency caused many delegates to push their agendas harder than they had before. It also realigned allegiances and loyalties, as some delegates who supported the position of the other church either privately or behind the scenes proclaimed publicly their opposition to the colleagues of their own church. Some of these apparent switches were undoubtedly political moves as well. On the MEC side, this came most prominently from Bishop Cranston. He openly criticized the black delegates for not performing their "manly" duty and removing themselves as the impediment to union. On the MECS side, Bishop Cannon, one of the strongest and most willful bishops in that church, emboldened the resistance to change among the MECS delegates. His presence seemed to steel the resolve of those who had offered the strongest resistance to compromise.

St. Louis Meeting

The meeting at St. Louis, April 10-13, 1918, was a last-minute effort on the part of the Joint Commission to pass some kind of proposal that would go before the MECS General Conference that summer. They gave themselves only three days to work, in hopes that they would limit their speeches and enter a more deliberate phase of their negotiations. After much debate over procedure, they decided to address the question of regions first. They hoped to decide on other issues before they attempted the question of racial membership, so that if they did not come to some agreement on that, they would have at least some agreement to show their respective denominations.

The argument from most MECS delegates was that they needed a regional design that provided some "protection of minorities" or local interests—"minorities" in this case referring to the smaller number of MECS congregations and members. They worried that their needs would be overlooked if conferences were not organized by regions in such a way as to ensure that former MECS regions would always have at least enough votes to block any offending legislation from the northern-dominated General Conference. As in nearly every phase of the Joint Commission negotiations, it quickly became apparent that the underlying concern was the "status of the Negro." Inadequate protection of "local interests" would leave white southern regional conferences vulnerable to legislation from the General Conference that would open their churches to racially integrated membership, to oversight by a bishop from a black conference or mission conference, or to equal status of black and white bishops. Opponents of this position feared that the creation of powerful regional conferences would produce a church that was nothing more than a loose confederation that would function not very differently from the cooperative arrangement already in place.[4]

On both sides of this regional argument, though, race was the underlying issue. Bishop Hoss, for instance, offered a long speech that celebrated geography and patriotic sectionalism. But his arguments kept returning to racial mixing, especially when it came to the superintendence of black bishops and transfer of membership from black congregations to white congregations.[5]

The Joint Commission also attempted to reach an agreement on the general nature and role of the episcopacy—what bishops would do, what their powers would be, how they would be chosen, over whom they would administer—but they continued to fall into the race discussion. The problem was that most MECS members wanted to return to the "original restrictive rule" on the episcopacy from the 1808 discipline. They wanted a true "itinerant general superintendency," meaning that bishops, like clergy, could be moved or transferred out of the region in which they were elected. But they only wanted this for the white regional conferences. Black bishops of black conferences, they argued, should not be truly itinerant, and thus they would not ever oversee a white conference.[6]

After they had reached tentative agreement on regional conferences, judicial council, and the episcopacy, the delegates moved on to what they were calling, at that point, the central conferences. These included not only the black congregations in the United States, but also the conferences in all other countries. It was at this point that Penn offered his first major proposal. It was this proposal that completely derailed any hope that the Savannah proposal under discussion would work at all. Penn's amendment split the Joint Commission, and badly split the MEC commission.

At Savannah, Penn had offered his support for a plan that put the black MEC membership in a separate conference on the same level as the central conferences. [7] He withdrew his support after he realized that those conferences were to be called or at least treated as "mission" conferences. The primary point of contention for Penn was an automatic limit on membership that would make any central conference a separate General Conference.[8] With this proposed amendment, Penn reinstated his support for a central conference designation, but only with proportionate representation in the General Conference.

This speech was Penn's most forceful and confrontational yet. He was outraged. He accused his white colleagues of commodifying the black membership for the benefit of whites without any real intention of seriously considering their rights:

> It is inconceivable that I should believe that my people are being bartered from Church to Church "as if they were mere chattels and pawns in a game," even the great game of unification of American Methodism; and yet there are not words adequate to express the feeling, which grows deeply with the colored people, that somehow their status in the reorganized Church is not a matter for discussion in the sense that they are to be singled out and deprived of privileges, fellowship, and rights which they now peacefully enjoy in the Church of their choice, when no other people in the home field of either Church are being thus singled out for a deprivation of rights. Unification is to be desired by all right-thinking Methodists, if not purchased by the heart's blood of any portion of the members, parties to the same, for we are living in a day

when we are fighting in the world for the rights of weaker peoples. If, therefore, any people, however weak or dependent, should feel that they had been wronged in the matter, unification would have a scar upon it forever.[9]

One of the appeals Penn made was to the patriotic sensibilities of his colleagues. Penn's style of argument for racial equality had always been the production of quantitative proof that black Americans were "worthy" of equality. From his first major publication in 1890, Penn had compiled lists of accomplishments and virtues of "the Negro." In this speech, Penn made the argument that black Americans were again, in spite of continued social and legal inequities, doing their part and making progress on the path toward civilization. In particular, he argued, they were supporting the war effort. Young black men were serving at the front in Europe; black farmers at home were growing food for the Army; black Americans were buying war bonds and giving money to the Red Cross. He told the story of an old black woman who gave all the money she had saved for the burial of a family member to buy war bonds.

The first delegate to respond in the negative to Penn's proposal was Goucher. It was here that Goucher produced his strongest defense of white supremacy. It was not delivered in the language of H. H. White's white supremacy, but it was the same basic racial ideology of dominant white American Christian civilization. Goucher returned again to the "racial development" view he had pushed in his "race consciousness" arguments in Baltimore. The debate was not about injustice or discrimination, he argued, but about "differentiation" based on the "facts" of racial development. The facts were that American blacks and all the other central (mission) conferences were not yet developed enough to be entrusted with full General Conference responsibilities.[10] With rhetoric that seemed designed to instill panic among his white colleagues, Goucher estimated that with the inevitable influx of black Methodists into a new integrated church, the 315,000 current black members would swell to nearly a million by 1920.[11] Eighty percent of these were illiterate, he said, and not in the "habit of grasping and wrestling with and pondering over great world problems." They were not yet capable of legislating for anything beyond their "local interests."[12] Goucher solidly favored putting all white Americans at the center of the new denomination with the power to control the General Conference. All other conferences were to be mission conferences. Goucher's argument about lack of development extended to all of these, and his images of dark-skinned illiterate hordes clamoring for space on the floor of the General Conference was carefully calculated to jolt the genteel sensibilities of his fellow delegates. And while many delegates expressed agreement or sympathy with Goucher's concerns, several also suggested that there was a difference, both qualitatively and in terms of U.S. citizenship rights, between black Americans and foreign mission peoples.[13]

Jones shared Goucher's view, but at this point in the meeting, when the Joint Commission in general was feeling urgent, Jones was angry. He abandoned his regular habit of hiding his frustration and lashed out. Like Penn, he accused the white commissioners of unseemly political exploitation of the black membership. He was unwilling to accept the "missionary" status that would come with fixed representation. Central to his rejection of this structure was his insistence that American citizenship and the ideals of American national life should not be used and discarded depending on the political needs of the moment. The current plan, he said, was simply a plan for "autocracy," and was "un-American" and "un-Southern" as well. Speaking directly to his white counterparts, Jones warned: "[Y]ou are putting too much stress on my patriotism and . . . denying me entirely too much when you expect me to furnish my quota to help win the war—and you cannot win without us, you simply cannot win without us—you are putting entirely too much stress on my patriotism when you cannot give me a fair deal in a matter like this."[14] Jones's argument was essentially a "separate but equal" argument. He assumed that compromise on his part began with the status quo in the MEC and in the nation generally: races may be separate, but their access to privilege and power must be equitable. Jones and Penn knew better than anyone in the Joint Commission that this equality was juridical only. They had hoped at the beginning of the unification process that the new church they were building would rise above that status quo. At this point late in the negotiations, Jones was fighting for the black membership not to lose "separate but equal" status. When Jones warned about the stress on his patriotism, he was warning that there might be an exodus of black members—and those whites who supported them—from the church if such a plan came to be, which would probably be a national public relations disaster. He was also warning that there might be responses from the black membership that the whites did not want. Jones used a lot of editorial space in the *Southwestern Christian Advocate* cautioning and pleading with the MEC black membership to remain calm in the face of the bad news from the negotiations. He feared "agitation" as a wedge their opponents would use as proof that the black membership was incapable of civilized behavior. Some black MEC leaders were calling for a separate meeting to voice their concern over the Joint Commission proposals that did not give them proportionate representation. Jones warned his fellow white MEC commissioners in a private MEC meeting, as far back as 1916, that if the Joint Commission continued to meet without presenting some unified statement on the black membership question there would be trouble. The black membership would be subjected to "criticism, pressure, and threats in the Church and out of the Church."[15] Even worse, Jones warned, the black membership would respond by holding a meeting and would produce a statement the MEC at large would not accept. This would likely produce "an embarrassing situation."[16] In other words, black MEC loyalty and patriotism was showing itself right then with its silence and willingness to play along and wait. Jones had a clear conception of the kind of pose black Americans needed to strike if they were to remain at the table of American privilege and power.

Jones also used his editorial space to publicly denounce any such meeting or statement. In an editorial in early 1918, Jones pleaded for moderation from the black MEC membership. His plea was formulated in terms of the proper response to the challenges God had put before a beleaguered race. God was challenging black Americans, and God expected them to respond moderately and responsibly. God was looking for a race, wrote Jones, that

> can love and preach human brotherhood; a race that has been tried in the fiery furnace, a race that has withstood oppression without becoming sour or revengeful, a race that can smile when the days are dark and hope when all else is gone. A race that has a forgiving heart, that loves while others hate. A race that soon forgets wrongs and quickly forgives. A race that will take the attitude that no man or men can make it hate others and whatever may be the attitude of others toward that race, it will put all others on the defensive when it comes to prejudice and hate. A race that keeps its heart clean and unmarred by revenge, uncontaminated by bitterness, "shall inherit the earth."[17]

As in most of Jones's public words, this sermon to his fellow black Methodists was also written for the benefit of anxious white Methodists. Those whites, especially in the MECS, were concerned that if the churches were united and racially integrated, they would be forced into close physical proximity with black Methodists, a kind of social intimacy that white Methodists feared would also encourage a fuller sense of general equality of the races. This might encourage confrontations by black fellow Methodists who were angry and resentful and who would demand all manner of restitution from whites. Jones tried to reassure white Methodists that there was no such lurking resentment.

But the message Jones was trying to convey with his anger at the St. Louis meeting was that there were limits to the loyalty of black Methodists. The surprising turn at the St. Louis meeting, though, was that Jones's anger was met full force with the anger and frustration of a commissioner from his own church. Bishop Cranston turned the rhetorical tables on Jones and Penn by inverting their call for respect and patriotism, reframing it as a lack of patriotism for making any demands at all.[18] Cranston's speech began innocently enough, with praise for the diligence and spirit of compromise on both sides of the Joint Commission. The only signal of what was to come was Cranston's use of "we" when he referred to the MEC commissioners. As with nearly every other use of "we" by a white delegate, "we" meant whites. Cranston meant it so fully that his language divided the Joint Commission into three clear factions: twenty-five white MECS delegates, twenty-three white MEC delegates, and two black MEC delegates. He narrated the history of those blocs this way: both blocs of white delegates had made significant "material concessions," including the concession from white MEC delegates of proportionate representation for the black membership. It appeared that Jones and Penn had made this same concession, but they later withdrew it. Instead, accused Cranston, the "colored membership stands absolutely fixed in its demand up to this moment."[19]

Cranston went on to accuse Jones and Penn of greediness in light of their resistance to the inclusion of other black Methodist denominations. It is difficult to imagine how Cranston might have read the black commissioners' position this way, since Penn and Jones had made clear their reasons for resisting this discussion. First, white Methodists merely assumed that there would be widespread desire in the black Methodist churches to join with a rich white Methodist church. Jones and Penn both had tried to make clear that they thought this was an ignorant and offensive assumption. They had done some surveying of leaders in those churches and had found an overwhelming negative response to the idea of joining the new church. Second, the influx of so many black congregations into the new church would favor black political interests, not harm them. Penn and Jones had opposed the black church inclusion because they understood that such a shift in power was a primary concern to the MECS. Jones and Penn assumed, correctly, that any push for such a merger would shut down MECS participation in the Joint Commission.

And yet Cranston managed to turn this against them. Not only did he accuse them of greediness for their attempt to protect their own personal power, but he also extended this to accuse them of disloyalty to their race. Cranston boxed them in from two fronts: the domestic and the foreign. By resisting the formation of one conference of black Methodists in the United States and in Africa they were skirting their responsibility for the evangelization of Africa. Cranston insinuated a "natural" obligation on the part of blacks in the United States to their racial family in Africa.[20] Again, Cranston's attack was twofold. Jones and Penn were hoarding power by resisting a larger conference with Africans. Even more damaging, though, was the implication that this lack of racial solidarity was a sure sign of African Americans' lack of progress toward true "Christian manhood." They had not done these things "willfully," said Cranston; he was only stating them "as a matter of fact." The lesson Cranston wanted his fellow white delegates to learn was that Jones and Penn were only partially developed racial beings, and thus these selfish acts were not willful, but rather the instinctive reactions of their undeveloped racial character. He addressed Jones and Penn directly: "My call is to our colored brethren that are here and to those behind them, and I make it solemnly before God, that they shall be ready to do something better as an expression of their faith in God and Methodism, something better as an expression of their Christian manhood, than to stand squarely and uncompromisingly upon every technical right attaching to their ecclesiastical relations."[21]

What relationship did Cranston insinuate between the "Christian manhood" of black Methodists and their clinging "uncompromisingly" to their rights as full-fledged MEC members? While "taking a stand" on one's principles was often seen as a heroic act, it could also be interpreted as an unsophisticated and naïve gesture. As we saw in speeches by Bishop Mouzon and H. H. White in Savannah, announcing one's intractability could be viewed as a reflection of one's principled and mature Christian manhood. But in this case, Cranston and others who were criticizing Jones and Penn were attempting to turn their stand into an immature fit. Rather than allow that Jones and Penn had reached the limit of their willingness to compromise through a long and arduous process, these critics attempted to undermine their position by accusing them of clinging to "technical rights." The language of "technicalities" insinuated a lack of substantive analysis of the problem and a less than thorough comprehension of the larger issues at stake. Sure, Cranston seemed to be saying, black Methodists have the right to be full members *technically*, but if they had truly reached their full manhood, they would see that one's rights are but the surface of the problem. Jones and Penn were not Christian heroes taking a principled position in the face of fierce opposition; they were unmanly Christian weaklings out of their depth and grasping at mere rights when there were greater issues beyond the limits of their present vision.[22]

With very little time left in their meeting before the MECS General Conference could convene, the Joint Commission put together one more eight-member committee to work out another proposal for the organization of black conferences. MEC lay delegate Alexander Simpson was on this committee, and when they returned a report, Simpson was the lone dissenting vote. The report recommended that the black conference in the United States and all other foreign conferences be given the title of "regional" conferences rather than "central" conferences. It also recommended representation in the General Conference from these conferences that was proportionally lower than white U.S. conferences. They also included fixed caps on that representation. The implications of this plan were that the black Methodist conferences in the United States would be categorized in the same way that foreign mission conferences were, and that none of them would be given equal status with white conferences in the United States. Simpson attacked this plan in a short, passionate speech that made one last attempt to persuade the Joint Commission to treat the black MEC membership equitably. Unless the Joint Commission wanted to pursue some "legal ingenuity" to pry their rights as members away from them, he said, there had been no reasonable argument given besides sheer blind prejudice that would convince him to support the report. Even if he were to accept the argument that black Americans were "backward," the only logical result of that would be the "deprivation of privileges to all who are personally backward, without regard to race."[23] But this line of reasoning had no effect on the deliberations other than to delay any agreement.

With the little time they had left, and after they had fretted about their limited time to work out an agreement, the delegates still took time to end their meeting just as they had begun: with resolutions expressing support for the war effort and for President Woodrow Wilson, and with the reading of a patriotic poem titled "The Blue and the Gray." The poem romantically envisioned the "sons of the North" and the "sons of the South" advancing in the war in France. The voice in the poem hoped that the "spirit of Grant" and the "spirit of Lee" were marching with their respective compatriots. But the last stanza hoped that the "Spirit of God" would be with them all "as the sons of the Flag advance!"[24] As the choice of poem suggests, the disjuncture between the national united front for the war in Europe and the inability of the two largest bodies of American Methodism to find a way to set aside Civil War–era disputes weighed heavily on their minds. The war and the themes of loyalty and duty and manhood shaped their arguments and the way they presented themselves to those watching.

The way the Joint Commission used its time at the end of this meeting gives some sense of where their focus was. The final debate in St. Louis, despite the MECS General Conference looming in just a matter of days, was on how they ought to respond to what the chair of the meeting described as an "unpatriotic interview" in a local newspaper with the President of the German Alliance of Missouri. Some delegates suggested that the Justice Department might be alerted. Some suggested that a letter from the Joint Commission ought to be drafted and sent out to the major press. One delegate suggested that they should find a way of punishing the *St. Louis Post Dispatch* for publishing the interview. The entire discussion, and all the patriotic rhetoric and resolutions before and after the meetings, in light of the gravity and urgency of the task they were actually assigned, only makes sense if we understand it not as disjuncture but as continuity. In other words, delegates' concerns about the German Alliance of Missouri—a group organized for the benefit and support of ethnic Germans in the United States —were of a piece with the very concerns that kept the Joint Commission from finding a solution to their own immediate problem of how to construct a new church. These Methodists were trying to build an authentic Methodist church that was just as authentically American.

The meeting ended with the Joint Commission badly split and no clear proposal on which the MECS General Conference might be asked to vote. They parted hoping only that they would be given permission to keep working. If this happened, they planned to meet in Cleveland, Ohio, July 7–10, 1919.

Cleveland and Louisville: The Problem of Missions and the End of the Joint Commission on Unification

Two major events seemed to shape the language of the final two meetings of the Joint Commission: the celebrations in both churches in 1919 of one hundred years of mission work, and the end of the war in Europe. The celebration of the centennial of missions—called the "Centenary" in both churches—caused the churches to consider their relationships to mission-ized peoples everywhere. This included mission projects in the United States as well, and so as the Joint Commission considered how to organize different groups in a new church, these domestic missions complicated the organization of conferences. How, particularly, were they to define black American Methodists as a mission conference when the white conferences were defined by their national citizenship and their status as missionizers? What made black Americans an object of missions even though they them-selves participated in mission funding and missionary activity to other groups? This is where the Joint Commission had arrived in its delibera-tions: the closest they had come to an agreement was around grouping black Americans with other mission conferences. The problems that re-mained were access to General Conference power for black American Methodists and for foreign conferences, and whether the African Ameri-can conferences were to be designated as mission conferences.

We have seen how the war weighed heavily on the minds of the Joint Commission delegates; in the same way, the war's end shaped their think-ing about the role of the new church and how, as a worldwide organiza-tion, it would function as an American-defined institution. What would be the place of foreigners in the new church? And who, really, were for-eigners? If attaining proper Christian manhood was the benchmark for full access to church power, what qualified a group as properly lifted up by American Christian civilization? And the central question for the Joint Commission—for it seemed a given that black Methodists would not ini-tially be fully members of the new church—was whether a racial group deemed unfit to hold the reins of power would ever be fit to do so.

Methodists in both churches were ambivalent about how the war had changed the world. Like many Americans, they were optimistic that the "Great War" had forever made the world safer and that American-style democracy and international cooperation would control aggressive na-tions. Victory had convinced them of American greatness and reinforced their self-perception as the primary dispensers of Christian civilization. But there remained discomfort in several areas. The political maneuvering, both domestic and foreign, around the issue of the League of Nations muted the idealism of the war. At the beginning of the Louisville meeting the Joint Commission approved a public statement urging the U.S. government to set aside politics and approve the League. The statement argued that the war had been supported wholeheartedly by both Methodist bodies, that the only way this was possible was because they had understood it to be a sacred cause, and that to pull back from international cooperation was to betray the trust given by the churches and their people:

> [T]he war ideals . . . were sanctioned and enthusiastically supported by the Christian Churches as consonant with the Christian conception of the unity and brotherhood relationship of all races and people; that under any other inspiration the Churches of Jesus Christ could not have sent forth their young men as to a holy crusade; that without this religious factor so large an army could not have been peaceably mobilized by conscription, nor could our soldiers have fought with such utter abandonment of self for any less object than that lofty declaration was echoed over the world as America's assurance and prophecy of liberty and just government for all men.[25]

Besides the problem of cooperation among the allied victors in the war, there was the continuing problem of racial strife at home. The race riots and the recurrence of lynching, even of black veterans, were reminders to those white Methodists who wanted world influence and also to maintain American white supremacy in the denomination that a segregated church could look much more like a cause of racial strife than like part of the promotion of national unity. And the hopes of black Methodists, including Jones and Penn, that the efforts made by black Americans to support the war would bring about a new era of racial mutuality at least in the church, were deflated by the lack of change. As the war was winding down in September 1918, Jones was writing in his editorials that because of all that black Americans had done for the war effort, America would never again be so "narrow" for them. But by November 14, just three days after the war officially ended, Jones was cautioning his readers to temper their celebrations. He warned that although some good changes would undoubtedly come, black Americans needed to be wary of expecting too much too soon, and careful not to demand too much too loudly:

"There was never a period which demanded so much of self restraint and self control and good common sense on the part of the Negro as the period of reconstruction just ahead of us," he wrote.

> Let us not be deceived. Our ultimate and full emancipation is assured. No one can delay it but ourselves and we only can delay it by irresponsive and unnecessary remarks and attitudes that will promote opposition rather than progress. This will require restraint, but restraint we have. This will require poise, but poise we have. This will require silence and silence we may have. It will even require endurance. We have learned full well this lesson and it has been of inestimable value to us in our progress. Let us not cast it aside.[26]

While addressing black Americans at large, Jones could just as well have been addressing his fellow black Methodists concerning their expectations of the Joint Commission. Jones seemed, all through the Joint Commission negotiations, to have a nagging sense that the Joint Commission would fail. And as we will see from their final actions and words at the Louisville meeting, both Jones and Penn seemed to be throwing up their hands in frustration after having given up everything they thought possible to make unification happen. This sacrifice included their dignity as well.

For a while, anyway, optimism reigned in the Joint Commission at the Cleveland meeting. In particular, the MECS came to Cleveland prepared to move to the position taken by the MEC at the St. Louis meeting.[27] But they were surprised to find that the MEC had also shifted its stance— *away* from the MECS position. While the churches had joined hands to celebrate the mission Centenary, the MEC seemed to be more affected by it. The New York *Christian Advocate* gave much greater coverage to the Centenary events in the MEC than did the Nashville *Christian Advocate* to the events of its church.[28] When the MEC commission presented its stance at the Cleveland meeting, the Centenary was mentioned as a primary reason for the change in the proposal to which it had agreed in St. Louis. The focus on missions had pushed the MEC commission to realize that by segregating the black membership in the United States it was endangering missions work overseas.

Bishop McDowell tried to explain the shift in the MEC stance. Four main factors shaped their new position: "legal rights and standing" of the black membership; a sense of historic inevitability, what he called "our historic attitude and our sense of moral obligation in view of our history"; the desire on the part of the MEC not to contribute to a perceived growing chasm between "the white race and the black race" in America, especially in light of continuing migration of black Americans to northern cities; and the growing realization among MEC membership and leadership, in light of the Centenary, that the MEC mission endeavors were extremely important to them and that they did not want to jeopardize those relationships by agreeing to a compromised racial relationship in the United States.[29] That the black membership had "legal rights and standing" was nothing new to the discussion. Neither was the notion that the MEC had a history of working toward more progressive race relations. But the last two reasons were new, even if they did not reflect any real change in how the MEC delegates understood race. Both of these reasons were based on concerns about how those outside the elite white leadership of the MEC would perceive a new church in which its longstanding black membership was relegated to a less-than-full membership status. After the war, the MEC, more so than the MECS, considered itself the flagship of a "World Christian Democracy," and it was finally too much of a compromise, even for the sake of the unification dream, to agree to disproportionate representation for blacks in the General Conference and to push them toward an independent Associate General Conference in the future. The failure of unification meant the failure of American unity, but so did a compromise on racial representation. In the end the MEC decided that to abandon their own membership could be perceived as the greater of the two evils.

It was for many of the same reasons that the MECS had decided to agree to the mission conference proposal that had been left on the table at St. Louis. But there was too much to be lost yet for them in a compromise that treated black Methodists the same as white Methodists. This is apparent in the presentation by Bishop James Cannon Jr. at the Cleveland meeting.[30] He expounded again the "mass versus the individual" arguments about race. The "Negro is an immature race . . . a child race . . . he should be dealt with from the missionary viewpoint—not every individual, not every single Church, but as a mass."[31] It was a white racial distinctiveness, tied up with regional identity, that remained the barrier beyond which the MECS would not go in its compromise.

Frank M. Thomas, in his ornate and dramatic style, described this need for a white racial identity. He argued that if the Joint Commission did not achieve unification, the MEC, which was the "mightiest evangelistic Church on the earth," would nevertheless be without a great resource from the MECS: "the most potential homogeneous body on the earth." That homogeneity was "Anglo-Saxon." In its racial and ethnic diversity, the larger and more powerful MEC would be much more powerful if it had the MECS with it, as it represented the most "virile, potential, splendid body of Anglo-Saxon virility."[32]

Thomas was concerned that most of his fellow commissioners considered the two proposals submitted at Cleveland to be essentially the same. The difference was only that the MECS proposal would have the black membership in a conference set up the same way as other mission conferences. Their representation would be limited to only 5 percent of the General Conference. The MEC proposal did not limit the representation of the black membership, but they argued that there would still only be 5 percent representation. But Thomas did not see it this way. "Brethren, in my judgment (and I have thought through this matter for many years), there is a difference between these two reports almost as deep as life itself."[33] For Thomas and his other more conservative colleagues, it was extraordinarily important that the racial differences be marked overtly. There could be no eliding of this difference, no compromise on an "essentially" similar distinction. An erasure of the lines of difference of the sort the MEC was arguing for—vague nomenclature, blurring of institutional hierarchies—was only asking for trouble. Racial division had to be clear and unquestioned. To hide behind such dissembling in order to please those watching was not the kind of "Anglo-Saxon virility" Thomas cherished. It was a sign of weakness.

MEC members tried to reassure Thomas that his fears were unfounded. MEC ministerial delegate Claudius B. Spencer also used the language of Anglo-Saxonism. Spencer, like most MEC delegates, still defended segregation in the church, but not unequal representation. Spencer went so far as to defend the use of "race prejudice": "Race prejudice is not of necessity a bad word . . . it may mean race feeling, race consciousness, race pride, race protection. If it means a prejudice in favor of race purity and race protection and keen help all the way round, it may be a source of uplift, of solidarity, and mutual help, all the way round."[34] This is the way the MEC delegates understood the segregated conferences. Spencer argued that such an organization would promote not a world church but a "new world order" that was beginning after the war: "we are in the Second Series of the Year of our Lord—Anno Domini, Second

Series, Year One!" The MEC plan, with proportionate representation for black Methodists, would be a first step in the new order, while still maintaining the purity and dignity of each race. Rather than causing the kind of "racial intermixtures" that Thomas was worried about, the MEC plan would instead "place the Methodist Church, the reorganized Methodist Church, as a daysman [sic] or mediator between that giant white god of the Anglo-Saxon race and that immature race . . . of the colored membership of this Church."[35] Calling the black American Methodists a "mission field," warned Spencer, would bring upon the new Methodist body their anger. He compared the possible outcomes to the Russian revolution of 1917.

The meeting at Cleveland was brief, and it ended with another impasse. At one point the two commissions thought they were almost in agreement, and then they realized there were different assumptions being made about the powers of the black conference. The meeting nearly fell apart, and the commissions separated to talk it over. When they returned, Bishop Cannon presented his view of the situation. He argued that the MEC, by proposing that there be a separate jurisdiction but with the same powers as the white conferences, was proposing a system based entirely on color. This was truly racist, he argued, because there were no qualitative reasons given for the racial segregation. The MECS proposal, on the other hand, proposed that the black conference be separate and also have powers and representation based on the ability of the race to govern itself. This was not racist but discriminating according to qualitative judgments.[36] They parted ways with no proposal in hand. Instead, they authorized a committee to meet separately in Richmond, Virginia, in the fall of that year to reconsider the "whole question of unification."[37] The full Joint Commission would convene again January 15-20, 1920, for its final meeting.

Besides the unification proposal the Joint Commission agreed upon but submitted without recommendation, the Louisville meeting was notable for several moments of candid discussion about motives. Primarily, several MECS members admitted that they resisted on several points that did not directly deal with the black conference because they were trying to assure the folks they represented that they were protected from black members joining their local congregation or from black bishops administering over their conference. Early in the meeting, the MEC recommended that the language describing the powers of the white regional conferences be changed from "legislative" to "administrative." MECS commissioners immediately protested that their counterparts had just "eviscerated" the entire proposal. MECS ministerial delegate Paul H. Linn openly admitted that the language of "legislative" power was "cardinal" because it was distinctly tied to their problem with black membership of any kind. Their fear about non-legislative or semi-autonomous regional white conferences was that once the new church body was in place, the regional conferences in the South would be unable to stop the larger northern conferences from upgrading the status of black membership.[38] This fear of racial intermingling in local congregations and at conference had some impact on nearly every aspect of the negotiations. Black, white, North, South, all commissioners calculated the level of racial interaction that would result, even remotely, from any organizational structure.

Both Penn and Jones agreed, though only because they felt it was the last resort, to a fixed General Conference representation for the black conferences. Penn agreed to it first, saying that as long as the language of the proposal showed that the fixed proportion was roughly equal to the proportion of black membership at the time, he would go along with it.[39] Jones agreed shortly after. Having given in on the representation issue, Jones must have felt he had a little more leverage, and he pushed on several more issues right up to the end of the meeting. The most pressing issue was the matter of Associate General Conferences that the central conferences could "request" when their numbers reached a certain level. Jones belittled the entire idea, calling them an open invitation for the central conferences to leave. The existence of the entire clause was insulting:

> I grant you that there is enough pressure put upon us to keep us from being particularly enthusiastic about getting men into the kingdom. . . . If you think that I am going to an Associate General Conference, you are wrong. . . .Why do we have this sort of trapdoor that might spring sometime when we are not quite conscious of it! You cannot put that in there without its being interpreted as the ultimate hope of the Church.[40]

Jones was not finished. After more debate between white delegates over the relative merits of the Associate General Conference, he stood again and gave the most impassioned plea for unity. In this speech Jones described the thin line between accommodation and agitation that he had walked throughout his career in the MEC, and especially in the Joint Commission where they were negotiating his right to remain in the

church to which he had given his life and career. Jones warned that "radicals" and "agitators" were already seeking black Americans and gaining
their sympathy. Any further divisions created in the new church would
only push black Methodists further and further out of the mainstream of
civil life. As he had before, he warned that talk of race consciousness was
dangerous. Race consciousness was the language of agitation and radicalism. He had just the day before seen in a newspaper a "call for those
people"—meaning those who "thrive upon race consciousness and race
independency"—"to join in with the radicals and agitators, saying that
these would welcome them, and that the negro would get freedom and
liberty by joining in with them." Jones was hoping to tap into the fear of
the "Red Scare." Several white commissioners had already said in the
Joint Commission that they feared that black Americans would turn to
such political movements if they were not welcomed fully by such groups
as the Methodists. Jones was adding personal testimony to that fear.

And then Jones laid himself open in a particularly vulnerable way. The
worst thing for America would be for the twelve million black citizens to
be "solidly a race in themselves." Jones admitted his own struggle with
his place in the church, and that he was always conscious that there were
easy opportunities and welcoming arms in the black Methodist churches
if he chose to go.

> Don't you suppose I know and measure every step I take here? Don't
> you know that I know that the larger part of my people are in Churches
> that are thriving in large measure by what you call race consciousness
> and racial solidarity, and that I have given myself to opposition to all
> that? God deliver us from the day when white men and black men shall
> be arrayed over against each other!

The Associate General Conference was predicated on the very idea of race
consciousness, he said, and would come back to haunt them. Race consciousness is easy:

> I have it now! I can walk out of the MEC tomorrow. I resist that, in the
> interests of peace and good will and the larger life of my country. Do
> you think we want to stay in the Church for the philanthropy of it? The
> Negro does not want that; he wants not charity, but a chance. He wants
> to associate himself with the believers in the fellowship of saints, that he
> may grow.

As a final word, Jones reminded his fellow commissioners that the black man they had in their minds as "docile, kind, charitable, tractable" was not always so. Whites did not own all the prejudice and hate. Because of this, Jones said, it would be the "easiest thing in the world to champion some sort of disassociation from you men," and his choice to go the difficult way of engagement with whites rather than separation came with some sacrifice of his "self-respect."[41]

Despite Jones's personal pleas, the delegates approved the proposal to create a new church with white conferences organized by region and black conferences together in an "Associate General Conference." And while there was, for the first time in the life of the Joint Commission, a single proposal put forth, they decided not to put it to a vote, but rather recommend it as "the best that we have been able to agree upon under the circumstances, and in accord with the instructions given us, and submit the same for their consideration and decision."[42]

Epilogue

The General Conferences in both churches received the proposal to create the new church just as unenthusiastically as it was presented. Rather than act directly on it, the MEC General Conference of 1920 suggested that the two churches hold a special "Joint General Convention" to discuss it. This was widely interpreted in the MECS as opposition to the proposal. The 1922 General Conference of the MECS approved it in principle, and then rejected the idea of a joint session, instead approving a new commission authorized to continue negotiations with the MEC. The MEC also put together a new commission. In this way the negotiations for union basically started all over again. The new Commission met and proposed a two-jurisdiction plan. The idea was something like a federation, with one jurisdiction consisting of all the former MEC conferences, and the other consisting of all the former MECS conferences. The new plan passed the 1924 MEC General Conference by an overwhelming majority. The MECS called a special General Conference for later that same year to vote on the new proposal—much to the dismay of the opponents of unification, led by Bishop Denny and Andrew J. Lamar. The special Conference approved the proposal, but the vote among the Annual Conferences did not meet the required two-thirds majority. This effectively ended the life of the Joint Commission.

Further official negotiations for union were nonexistent until 1935, when the Methodist Protestants started the discussion again, and a new Commission was formed. This new Commission, in which there were several prominent members from the original Joint Commission—including, notably, Bishop Robert E. Jones—adopted the basic form of the Joint Commission proposal from 1920 that had called for a racially segregated Central Jurisdiction. While there were black members of the MEC who thought (or at least expressed publicly) that a separate jurisdiction would, temporarily, provide a beneficial opportunity for black

Methodists to develop leaders and gain experience, it is safe to say most thought the plan tragic. This general feeling was evident at the General Conference of 1939—the "Uniting Conference" with which we began this book—about which we read of the protest and the tears of the black delegates while the rest sang joyously of Christian unity. Thus the Methodist Church, one of the largest, wealthiest, and most powerful religious institutions in America, was born as a fully racialized Christian institution. Even as some annual conferences desegregated over the next three decades, the segregated Central Jurisdiction existed until the church merged with the Evangelical United Brethren in 1968 to become the United Methodist Church.

Identity was the defining element of this long-term denominational power-struggle. The protest at the "Uniting Conference" was symbolic of disagreement with their fellow Methodists; the protesters did not, however, leave. They could have removed themselves to a doctrinally matching, and certainly more welcoming, church at any time. But remaining Methodist in the Methodist church they were already in—not the AME, for instance, where they could have gone—was what those black Methodists wanted. There was more to being Methodist than the particular doctrinal emphases or polity or history that defined it. As so many black Methodists said at the time, they considered it *their* church as much as anyone else's. To leave their Methodist church meant leaving the church of their families, the church where generations of their ancestors had worshipped, been baptized, and married. It would have meant abandoning the buildings they had built, paid for, and maintained, and with the buildings would go financial investments, emotional ties, long memories, and often the graves of their loved ones. Their Methodist church was their spiritual home and the center of so many black communities. To leave it would be to leave parts of themselves. And why, they wondered, should they be the ones to leave? If white people didn't want to be in the church they had all inherited, then why didn't the white people leave? But the white Methodists did not want to leave their Methodist church either, and they held most of the reins of power.

But holding all the power did not mean they could use it indiscriminately, because the power had to be wielded in ways that could be explained in terms of some kind of acceptable Christian discourse. If the exercise of power were not framed carefully that way, then much of the power could be lost in the resulting sway of public opinion. It is how the dynamics of this power struggle were worked out in detail in the Joint

Commission conversation that has concerned us most in this book. In trying to understand what drove these commissioners and the Methodist supporters of union they represented, it is perhaps too easy to recognize and name as a cause the desire for greater national political power. It was part of the public argument—not a guarded back-room secret—that a merger would greatly increase the political and cultural influence of American Methodism. And attending to the national public perception outside the Methodist churches of divided regional Methodisms in a nation just recovering from the acrimony of Reconstruction was critical to arguments for the necessity of a merger. Without the positive public opinion that these Methodists had enjoyed for decades, they would no longer hold their place as the epitome of American Christian civilization. In this light, the failure of the Joint Commission—its inability to solve the problem of racial membership—shows us clearly the relationship between racial membership and concerns about political and national influence. The fear that white Americans outside Methodism would perceive the church to be endorsing inappropriate racial equality was greater than the opportunities inherent in becoming the largest and first mainline church in America to embrace full racial equality. Broad national authority was at stake, and the Methodists who won the fight over racial membership held the view that moral authority in American culture would be supported more by segregation in the church than by integration. A significant percentage of white Methodists, like so many white Americans in general, believed outright that racial integration and the inevitable social equality and miscegenation that would follow would be the downfall of Christian civilization. But even those who might have believed, in an idealistic sense, that the new Methodist church would better reflect Christian values if it were integrated, were willing to forgo that spiritual ideal for one they wanted more—that of a large, powerful, internationally influential church that would lead the world's greatest Christian civilization.

We have also seen that the central feature of racial identity in these negotiations was, as Martha Hodes has put it, its "mercurial nature."[1] The shifts in the discussion in the Joint Commission—from "race consciousness" to various types and varying degrees of scientific theorizing, to racial nationalism—reflect the amorphous quality of race itself. Not only did the Joint Commission delegates fail to agree on any specific racial theory, they also failed to settle into a common racial discourse in which they might debate racial church membership. Like mercury in their hands, when they tried to tighten their hold on race in order to understand it, it slipped through their fingers. As in any particular incidence of race-making, the combination of differing interests and ideas exploded any grip on race the group tried to muster.

Some—perhaps most—observers of the cultural and historical process of the social and cultural construction of race have argued that this picture of race as baseless, floating, malleable, indeterminate, *not real*, is intended to undermine the power of that process. I would share that hope. But rather than intend this study as primarily a genealogical dis-closure of a phantom epiphenomenon, I have tried to keep in mind that to write the "vicissitudes of race" (Jacobson) into the light is to show that race is phenomenally real. Hodes's claim is that the malleability of race is its "abiding power," not its greatest flaw.[2]

And the particular racial discourse of the Joint Commission, as a very local setting, demonstrates the power of race well. As the delegates chased race around the table, as it were, the power of race as the principal impediment to their shared goal of unification never wavered. It may in fact have become even more powerful because of its maddening inscrutability. As we observed in chapter 2, many delegates, and a large portion of the Methodist public in general, were disappointed and surprised by the lack of any visible progress at the first meeting. Perhaps at that point many delegates were blissfully ignorant of the distance between particular constructions of race that individual commissioners held, and so for the moment agreement seemed possible.

What was revealed through the delegates' shifting racial discourse was the depth to which race was embedded in their ostensibly separate concerns about American Christian civilization and Methodists' self-conception as the primary carriers of that civilization. As the explicit language of race failed to inscribe any common ground, the language of American Christian civilization, an implicitly racialized discourse of whiteness, emerged as a rickety platform on which they were able to build an equally unstable proposal. For it was only after they were immersed in the (relatively) more comfortable moral terrain of the critical structures of moral discrimination that they found some way to work. And thus race, in its characteristic malleability, became stronger in its shift to the silence of whiteness. If race were not so malleable, so mercurial, perhaps the Joint Commission would never have found a mutually acceptable plan that segregated the Methodist conference racially. If race were a fixed phenomenon, perhaps the Joint Commission would have abandoned their project earlier for want of common ground, and national racial segregation among Methodists would not have prevailed. If race were as simple as disproving a weak scientific theory, perhaps that would have been accomplished and segregation would have fallen away with it. Instead, race shifted again and provided a racially silent and morally viable discourse of racial division upon which to promote institutional unity.

We set out in this book to explore the religious culture of Methodism during the Jim Crow era, and particularly to see how it participated in and contributed to the further strengthening of Jim Crow. After the Civil War and the emancipation of the slaves, the MEC made strides, only briefly, to begin a large-scale work of desegregation in the church, holding out some hope that the church would serve as an example to the rest of the nation. This lasted only until the 1870s, when whites in the South began to take back political control of southern states, and whites in the North declined to intervene. Indeed, the MEC leadership, similar to the way it shut down the debates over abolition of slavery in the 1830's, attempted to silence debates over racial matters. The perception that Robert E. Jones was a moderate on issues of "social equality," for example, contributed in part to his receiving enough white support to make him editor of the *Southwestern Christian Advocate*. Northern whites, especially in the churches like the MEC, failed to step in or even voice much criticism as the tangle of laws that became known as Jim Crow wound around and through the lives of black Americans. But beyond the failure of silence on issues of racial justice, the debates of the Joint Commission, watched so closely by the nation, and eventually leading to the creation of a nationally segregated church, directly contributed to the strength and reach of Jim Crow. The churches were considered the arbiters of morality and critical for the national conscience—they were almost single-handedly responsible for national prohibition of alcohol during this period—and thus the nation looked to its most successful churches to sense what might be amiss. The Joint Commission clearly conveyed two things: that racial integration was not necessary for the Christian nation of the United States to maintain its claim to moral authority, and that the further progress of American Christian civilization was impossible without the separation of the races.

The ascendancy of the United States as a global power in the latter third of the nineteenth century and especially with its new position in world politics after World War I was accompanied by a renewed national narrative of divine calling to that success and power. This invigorated sense of manifest destiny that firmly anchored so many Americans' national identity was the product of a strongly reciprocal relationship between Christian churches and broader secular American culture; the conflation of nation and church was not solely the product of ambitious Christian churches. America's rise to power and the perceived affirmation of divine calling was accompanied by the quick rise and fearsome extension of Jim Crow. In that era, just as the broader national narrative of power was more explicitly tied to the language of divine destiny, so was the consolidation of white power articulated in Christian terms. As broad forms of increasing American economic and military power were interpreted as signs of God's approval, so too did those white Americans who wielded most of that power come to describe its acquisition in terms of divine destiny. Whiteness emerged more concretely into American culture as the primary marker of the pinnacle of human progress—American Christian Civilization—and the Christian churches, in both North and South, played a central role in that emergence. In the church and in the rest of America, Christian civilization was nationalized and racialized.

Appendix

List of Delegates to the Joint Commission with Biographical Notes

Delegates from the Methodist Episcopal Church

Bishops

Richard J. Cooke (1853–1931), Helena, Mont. Cooke was one of the least parochial, at least in experience, of the Joint Commission members. Born into a first-generation Irish Roman Catholic family in New York City, Cooke moved to Tennessee as a young man to work on the railroad. He began his ministerial work in the Tennessee Conference, then served in the Holston and Georgia Conferences. In 1889 he began fifteen years as a professor at U.S. Grant Memorial University (University of Chattanooga). He served as editor of the *Methodist Advocate Journal,* and as Book Editor for the Church from 1904 to 1912.

Earl Cranston (1840–1932), Washington, D.C. Cranston was a native of Ohio and graduated from Ohio University in 1861, after which he joined the Union Army. He served three years during the war and left with the rank of captain. He began serving pastorates in 1867 in Ohio and Colorado. In 1884 he was elected a church publishing agent, and he spent twelve years in Cincinnati in that capacity. He was elected to the episcopacy in 1896, and was assigned to the Northwest region. In 1904 he was assigned to Washington, D.C., to supervise mission work. Cranston was one of the strongest voices for union on the Joint Commission. His conception of Methodist union as a high spiritual ideal shaped the conversations about race and the means of treating it in a church.

John W. Hamilton (1845–1934), Washington, D.C. Though he was born in West Virginia, and served in California, Hamilton took on the identity of the region he served for most of his career—New England. Hamilton served major churches in Boston, especially, and he became famous for his campaigns against class and race discrimination. Hamilton was elected to the episcopacy in 1900 and retired in 1916, before his involvement in the Joint Commission. He served as chancellor of American University after his retirement. Hamilton was the strongest voice—and one of only two, including lay commissioner Alexander Simpson Jr. —for a racially integrated Methodist church. Hamilton was forceful, lively, and combative in his frequent interventions on the Joint Commission floor.

Frederick Deland Leete (1866–1958), Atlanta, Ga. Leete was born and educated in New York state, and graduated from Syracuse University. He served pastorates in the Northern New York Conference beginning in 1888, and also served in Detroit, Michigan. He was active in the ecumenical movement, serving as a member of three of the Ecumenical Methodist Conferences and as president of the Ecumenical Council of the Americas and Orient (1931–1934). Leete's episcopal election was at the 1912 General Conference, and his first assignment, in Atlanta, proved formative for his role on the Joint Commission as a sympathetic voice for MECS concerns about an integrated church. He was an active and influential member of the Joint Commission. Leete is perhaps best known for his collection of historical materials on Methodist bishops, which formed the basis for his book of biographies of bishops, *Methodist Bishops* (1948).

William F. McDowell (1858–1937), Washington, D.C. McDowell was an Ohio native, and graduated from Ohio Wesleyan in 1879. He served pastorates in Ohio from 1882 until 1890, when he moved to Denver to serve as chancellor of the University of Denver. McDowell was elected bishop in 1904, and was assigned to the Chicago area until 1916, when he became resident bishop of Washington, D.C., where he remained until his retirement in 1932. McDowell was the most prominent leader from the MEC on the floor of the Joint Commission negotiations. He spent a lot of time attempting to soothe hurt feelings and restating, in more moderate language, the immoderate words of other commissioners. McDowell was also one of the few commissioners who openly changed their stance on the "status of the negro."

Ministers

Edgar Blake (1869–1943), Chicago, Ill. Blake grew up in New England. He attended the school of theology at Boston University from 1895 to

1898, and then he began serving pastorates in New Hampshire until he was made corresponding secretary of Sunday Schools of the MEC. He was elected to the episcopacy at the General Conference of 1920. His first assignment was in Paris, France, where he served until he received the first of his assignments in the midwestern United States in 1932. From 1932 to 1936 he was president of the MEC Board of Education. Blake was one of the most active members of the Joint Commission. He and David Downey were perhaps the most active in articulating specific and detailed compromises throughout the meetings. Blake also wrote in the church papers concerning union, and proposed in that medium that the black membership of the MEC ought to remove itself as the impediment to union.

David G. Downey (1858–1935), New York, N.Y. Born in Ireland, Downey served as Book Editor for the Methodist Episcopal publishing house. Downey held several pastorates in Connecticut. His last was in Brooklyn, New York. He was one of the more active and vocal ministerial delegates in the meetings.

John Franklin Goucher (1845–1922), Baltimore, Md. Goucher served pastorates in the Baltimore Conference from 1869 to 1891. He was on the founding board of the Women's College of Baltimore, later renamed Goucher College in honor of generous donations from him and his wife. He was president of the College from 1890 to 1908. Goucher was very active in the Board of Missions, and traveled extensively, especially in Asia.

Robert Elijah Jones (1872–1960), New Orleans, La. Jones was born in North Carolina, and served his first pastorates there before he was made assistant editor of the *Southwestern Christian Advocate* in New Orleans in 1897. He was editor from 1904 to 1920, when he was elected bishop. He and Matthew W. Clair were the first African American bishops in the MEC. Under Jones's leadership the Gulfside Assembly, in Waveland, Mississippi, was purchased and established as the first major MEC retreat center for black members. It would be difficult to overstate Jones's influence on the Joint Commission. His presence was formative and his carefully chosen interventions were influential.

Albert J. Nast (n.d.), Cincinnati, Ohio. Nast came from a family influential among German-speaking Methodists in the MEC. He was editor, after his father, of *Der Christlicke Apolegete*.

Frank Neff (n.d.–1936), Hutchinson, Kans. Neff represented the difficult rural circuits of the Plains states. He was not an active participant in the Joint Commission discussions.

Edwin M. Randall (1862–1839), Everett, Wash. Randall served various pastorates in the Puget Sound Conference. In 1903 he was elected president of the University of Puget Sound. He served as general secretary of the Epworth League from 1904 to 1912. He was elected delegate to the General Conference in 1904 and 1908.

Claudius B. Spencer (1856–1933), Kansas City, Mo. Spencer was a Michigan native who served in the Detroit Conference and the Colorado Conference. While there he edited the Rocky Mountain *Christian Advocate* from 1892 to 1900. He was a graduate of Northwestern University (1881), and was active in the Epworth League. Spencer published a book advocating union, *That They May Be One*, just before the Joint Commission meetings began. He was a frequent participant in the Joint Commission meetings, and was clearly sympathetic to the desires of black Methodists.

Joseph W. Van Cleve (1859–1926), Chicago, Ill. Van Cleve filled pastorates in the Southern Illinois Conference and the Illinois Conference. He was elected delegate to the General Conference six times, and was involved in numerous committees and boards for his annual conference.

John J. Wallace (1857–1933), Pittsburgh, Pa. Wallace served pastorates in the East Ohio Conference until he became editor of the *Pittsburgh Christian Advocate*, a post he held from 1908 to 1928. He was elected as General Conference delegate from 1904 to 1928, and was a delegate to the Ecumenical Conference in London in 1921.

Laymen

George Warren Brown (1853–1921), St. Louis, Mo. Brown was born in New York state, and moved to St. Louis to work in his brother's shoe business. He started his own company in 1878, and it grew into the nationally recognized Brown Shoe Company. Brown was an active and generous lay member of the MEC. He was not an active participant in the Joint Commission.

Charles W. Fairbanks (1852–1918), Indianapolis, Ind. Fairbanks was Republican Vice President of the United States under President Theodore Roosevelt, 1904–1912. He made his reputation as a lawyer in Indiana, and entered politics there. He served as senator from Indiana from 1897 to 1909, but left that office when elected vice president. While a public supporter of union and a person of great influence, Fairbanks was not a vocal participant in the Joint Commission negotiations.

Abram W. Harris (1858–1935), MEC Commission Secretary, New York, N.Y. Harris spent his entire career as an educator and an active church layman. Born in Philadelphia, he received degrees from Wesleyan, Bowdoin, and the Universities of Maine and New Brunswick. He taught at Dickinson Seminary in Pennsylvania, and at Wesleyan, and also taught for the U.S. Department of Agriculture. He was president of the University of Maine from 1893 to 1901, and president of Northwestern University from 1906 to 1916. Harris served as both corresponding secretary and secretary of the MEC Board of Education. He also chaired the executive board of the Religious Education Association. He was a trustee of Drew University. Harris's was an active and moderate voice in the meetings of the Joint Commission.

Charles W. Kinne (1852–1933), Jacksonville, Fla. An active lay member in the St. John's River Conference, Kinne was a businessman in real estate and insurance. He served as a lay delegate to General Conference three times. Kinne was not a vocal participant in the meetings.

Irvine G. Penn (1867–1930), Cincinnati, Ohio. Born in Virginia, Penn spent most of his early career as a teacher and author. He spent a tremendous amount of energy writing about the accomplishments of black Americans. His first major publication was a volume of biographies of African American newspaper editors and journalists. He was the director and organizer for the "Negro" exhibits at the 1895 Atlanta Exposition, and he played a significant part in the decision to place Booker T. Washington in the leading role there that launched Washington into the national spotlight. In the MEC, Penn was the deputy secretary of the Freedman's Aid Society. The details of Penn's death have been difficult to track down, but there is some speculation that he died as the result of injuries sustained while being thrown off a segregated train car in South Carolina.

Ira E. Robinson (1869–n.d.), Charleston, W.Va. Robinson was a federal district judge in West Virginia, and had been a judge on the West Virginia Supreme Court of Appeals.

Henry Wade Rogers (1853-1926), New York, N.Y. Rogers was a judge in the Federal Circuit Court (U.S. Court of Appeals, 2nd Circuit, 1913–1926) in New York state.

William Rule (1839–1928), Knoxville, Tenn. Rule was the publisher of the daily *Knoxville Journal*. He had been a pioneering journalist in the southern states, serving as writer for the *Knoxville Whig* before the Civil War. After serving in the Union Army during the war, Rule returned to the *Whig* and served as the editor until 1870, when the paper was discontinued. Rule then set up a new Republican newspaper, *The Knoxville Chronicle*. He owned and edited that paper until 1882, when he was elected mayor of Knoxville. He was reelected in 1885, the same year he started the *Knoxville Journal*.

Alexander Simpson Jr. (1855–1935), Philadelphia, Pa. Simpson was a lawyer and judge in Philadelphia. He was appointed for life to the Pennsylvania Supreme Court in 1918, and later served as Chief Justice. He was a founding member of the Pennsylvania Bar Association. Simpson and Bishop Hamilton were the most proactive supporters of racial integration.

Rolla V. Watt (1868–1925), San Francisco, Calif. Born in Ohio, Watt moved early in his life to California and became wealthy in the insurance business. He was an active layman and generous philanthropist to Methodist institutions. The California Conference elected him to seven General Conferences. Though not a frequent vocal contributor in the Joint Commission meetings, Watt was an opponent of an all-white union.

Alternates

Bishop Luther B. Wilson (1856–n.d.), New York, N.Y. Wilson completed his studies to become a medical doctor, but pursued church ministry instead. He began serving churches in the Baltimore Conference in 1878,

and remained there for sixteen years until his appointment as superinten-
dent of the Washington, D.C. district. He was elected bishop at the 1904
General Conference.

Rev. Frank M. North (1850–1935), New York, N.Y. (Cleveland and
Louisville meetings). North was one of the better-known ministerial delegates from the MEC. After many years of pastoral work in New York
annual conferences, he served in city missions to immigrants, and was
made chair of the Board of Foreign Missions in 1912. He was influential
in founding the Federal Council of Churches in Christ in America, and
served as its president. North is perhaps best known for composing the
Methodist Social Creed, which became a standard for many denominations and ecumenical organizations. He was also an author and hymn-
writer.

Rev. Charles M. Stuart (1853–1932), Evanston, Ill. Stuart was president
of Garrett Biblical Institute from 1911 to 1924. Born in Scotland, Stuart
served pastorates in the River Forest and Rock River conferences, and
later served as editor of the *Michigan Christian Advocate* and the *Northwestern Christian Advocate*. He taught at Garrett beginning in 1896.

James R. Joy (1860–1957), New York, N.Y. Joy was the editor of the
New York *Christian Advocate* from 1915 to 1936, and, like his prede-
cessor at the weekly paper, was sometimes called "the Bishop-maker."
When he retired from the paper, circulation was over 170,000. Joy was
born in Massachusetts, and graduated from Yale in 1885. He spent almost his entire career in Methodist work, beginning in 1891 on the editorial staff of the Methodist Book Concern and joining the *Christian Advocate* in 1904. Joy's influence on the union negotiations extended to his
broad public influence as the editor of the MEC's primary newspaper, but
he was an active participant in the Joint Commission negotiations as well.

Elmer L. Kidney (n.d.), Pittsburgh, Pa. (Cleveland and Louisville meetings).

Charles Andrew Pollock (1853–1928), Fargo, N.D. Born in New York
state, Pollock studied law at the University of Iowa, and opened a law office in Fargo, North Dakota, in 1881. He was appointed a lecturer in law
at the University of North Dakota. He served as district attorney in the
Territory of Dakota before his appointment as a judge in 1889.

Delegates from the Methodist Episcopal Church, South

Bishops

Warren Akin Candler (1857–1941), Atlanta, Ga. Chair, Baltimore meeting. Candler was an outspoken opponent of union, and rarely inserted himself into the discussions of the Joint Commission. He is perhaps known best as chancellor of Emory University and Candler School of Theology. He battled there as an opponent of "modernism."

James Cannon Jr. (1864–1944), San Antonio, Tex. (Cleveland and Louisville meetings). Cannon was another of the more colorful figures on the Joint Commission. He was known widely among Methodists, in international church circles, and on the national political scene in the United States. Cannon was educated at Randolph-Macon (Va.) and Princeton Universities, and served as president of Blackstone Female Institute from 1904 to 1918, during which time he was also editor of the *Baltimore and Richmond Christian Advocate.* He was elected bishop in 1918, and was in charge of several mission areas. His fame arose from his passionate devotion to the cause of prohibition. During the U.S. presidential election of 1928, when Alfred Smith was the democratic nominee running on an anti-prohibition platform, Cannon led the group known as the "Anti-Smith Democrats" which broke the party's solid hold on the southern states and probably lost it the election. Cannon was later investigated for campaign fund indiscretions, during which he publicly defied the Senate committee responsible for the charges. In the Joint Commission, Cannon was a strong voice for those resisting racial integration.

Collins Denny (1854–1943), Richmond, Va. Denny was a lawyer before he became a minister in 1880. Educated at Princeton and the University of Virginia, Denny later taught philosophy at Vanderbilt; he left when Vanderbilt separated from the MECS in 1910. That same year he was elected bishop. Denny was a staunch opponent of a racially integrated church of any kind, and argued against it throughout the Joint Commission meetings, though after it became apparent that some form of an integrated church was going to be proposed, his participation was largely in the form of strict parliamentary procedure from the chair. When the Methodist Church was formed in the 1939 merger, Denny refused to shift his episcopal status to the new church.

Elijah Embree Hoss (1849–1919), Muskogee, Okla. (Baltimore through St. Louis meetings). Hoss was an active participant in the Joint Commission meetings, with a combative style. While he favored union, he had, early in his career, spoken out against MEC expansion in the southern United States. He served pastorates in Tennessee, California, and finally Asheville, N.C. He was a professor and later president at Martha Washington College in Virginia, beginning in 1879, and also served in both of those positions at Emory and Henry College, beginning in 1881. From 1885 to 1890 he taught at Vanderbilt University, after which he was made editor of the Nashville *Christian Advocate*.

Edwin Du Bose Mouzon (1869–1937), Dallas, Tex. Mouzon grew up in South Carolina, graduated from Wofford College, and then began serving pastorates in Texas and Missouri. He left the pastorate to teach, and after he was elected bishop in 1910 he was instrumental in the establishment of Southern Methodist University in Dallas. He later became Dean of the Perkins School of Theology. Mouzon was active as a bishop in the Board of Missions and presided over several mission conferences. He was the presiding bishop during the establishment of the Brazil Methodist Church in 1930. His earlier experiences in Brazil shaped the views of race and the church that he advocated in the Joint Commission. He was an ardent proponent of segregated union.

William Benton Murrah (1851–1925), Memphis, Tenn. Murrah was born and raised in Alabama, and graduated from Southern University in Greensboro in 1874. He began his pastoral ministry in 1876 in the North Mississippi Conference. In 1892 he was elected president of Millsaps College (Miss.). He was elected bishop at the 1910 General Conference, after which he lived in Jackson, Miss., and finally Memphis.

Ministers

William N. Ainsworth (1872–1942), Savannah, Ga. Ainsworth lived and worked in Georgia most of his life. After graduating from Emory College, he began serving pastorates in 1891. Beginning in 1909 he served three years as president of Wesleyan College (Ga.). He was elected bishop at the General Conference of 1918. His episcopal areas included several states as well as Cuba, China, Japan, and Korea. He was also active in the temperance movement, and served as the president of the Anti-Saloon League of America.

Charles McTeiyre Bishop (1862–1949), Georgetown, Tex. Bishop filled pastorates in North Carolina and Missouri, and beginning in 1911 was president of Southwestern University in Georgetown. In 1925 he was appointed head of the New Testament Department at Southern Methodist University.

Edwin Barfield Chappell (1853–1936), Nashville, Tenn. Chappell was born in Tennessee, and attended Vanderbilt, graduating in 1879. He began his ministry in 1879 in the Memphis Conference, at which time he was appointed president of McKenzie College. Four years later, he moved to the Texas Conference, then in 1891 to the St. Louis Conference, and in 1898 to the Tennessee Conference. In 1906 he was made Sunday School editor and secretary, a capacity he filled until his retirement in 1930. He was the author of several books on religious education.

James E. Dickey (1864–1928), Atlanta, Ga. (Cleveland and Louisville meetings). Dickey was born and educated in Georgia, and worked and lived there most of this life. He graduated from Emory College and was a professor there. He served as pastor at Grace Church in Atlanta for three years, after which he was appointed president of Emory. He left there in 1915 to pastor First Church in Atlanta, and then was elected to the episcopacy at the 1922 General Conference.

Horace Mellard Du Bose (1858–1941), Nashville, Tenn. (alternate at Cleveland and Louisville meetings). Du Bose was born in Alabama and served pastorates in the Mississippi Conference, Texas Conference, Georgia Conference, and in Los Angeles, California. He also served as the editor of the *Pacific Methodist Advocate*. He was executive secretary of the Epworth League, and became Book Editor for the church and editor of the *Methodist Quarterly Review*. He held these posts from 1915 until his episcopal election in 1918. Du Bose is also known for his published histories of Methodism and biographies of Methodist bishops.

Thomas Neal Ivey (1860–1923), Nashville, Tenn. Ivey was best known for his work as editor of the Nashville *Christian Advocate*. Born in South Carolina, he graduated from Trinity College (later Duke University) in 1879, spent a few years as a teacher, and then joined the North Carolina Conference in 1886. After nine years as a pastor, Ivey was elected joint editor of the North Carolina *Christian Advocate*. Three years later he was elected editor of the Raleigh *Christian Advocate*, and finally he moved up to the central MECS publication published in Nashville. Ivey's participation in the Joint Commission discussions was moderate, but it stood out for its evenhandedness. Ivey was one of the few Joint Commission members to publicly change his mind about questions of racial segregation. He took the highly unusual step of announcing his shift away from strong segregation in his editorial column.

Andrew Jackson Lamar (1847–1933), Nashville, Tenn. Lamar was a vocal and combative participant in the Joint Commission. He was strongly against any racially integrated proposal, and was relentless in his attempts to convince his fellow commissioners that the MECS was not ready for union. He had perhaps the most colorful past of any member of the Joint Commission. He was a student at the University of Georgia when the Civil War began, and he fought as a member of a student regiment, and later as a member of another artillery regiment from Virginia. After the war he returned home to Georgia, and then moved to Alabama, where he had inherited a plantation. In 1872 he entered law school at the University of Georgia, and returned to Alabama in 1873 to practice law. He was converted at a revival meeting, and was licensed to preach in 1874. He was ordained in 1876 in the Alabama Conference. He was elected publishing agent of the Methodist Publishing House in Nashville in 1903. He remained there until his retirement in 1932.

Paul Hinkle Linn (1873–1924), Fayette, Mo. (Cleveland and Louisville meetings). Linn began his career as a lawyer in Missouri, but entered ministry in 1897. In 1910 Linn began an appointment as a Missionary Evangelist. In that assignment he traveled to foreign mission fields. In 1913 he was elected president of Central College (St. Louis).

John Monroe Moore (1867–1948), Nashville, Tenn. (Moore served as an episcopal delegate after he became bishop in 1918). Moore was an active and vocal proponent of union during his years on the Joint Commission and through the merger in 1939. He undertook graduate study at Yale, Leipzig, and Heidelberg, and finished a Ph.D. at Yale in 1895. He served pastorates in St. Louis, San Antonio, and Dallas. He was editor of the Nashville *Christian Advocate*, served on the Joint Hymnal Commission, and was secretary of the Home Department and the Board of Missions. His first episcopal assignment was to Brazil.

Charles Claude Selecman (n.d.–1958), Los Angeles, Calif. (Cleveland and Louisville meetings). As a pastor, Selecman served in Missouri, Louisiana, and Los Angeles. He served on the War Work Commission in France during World War I. He became president of Southern Methodist University in 1932, and was consecrated bishop in 1938. His episcopal areas were in Arkansas, Oklahoma, and Dallas.

Frank Morehead Thomas (1868–1921) (MECS Secretary), Louisville, Ky. Thomas grew up in Kentucky, spent some time in the western United States as a young man, and returned to Kentucky to become a minister. He graduated from Vanderbilt in 1892 and began his ministry in the Louisville Conference the next year. He served churches in the conference until he was named book editor and editor of the *Methodist Quarterly Review* in 1918. Thomas also served in the Kentucky National Guard during the Spanish-American War and spent a year in Cuba. Thomas was a strong proponent of segregated union, and, by his own count, had served on more committees and commissions considering the problem than any other member of the Joint Commission.

Alexander Farrar Watkins (1856–1929), Jackson, Miss. Watkins was president of Millsaps College during the Joint Commission meetings.

William James Young (1859–1936), Atlanta, Ga. Young was born in Baltimore, and educated at Vanderbilt. He received his license to preach in 1876, later joined the Texas Conference, and served churches in the Virginia Conference as well. In 1914 he began teaching homiletics and missions at the new Candler School of Theology at Emory.

Laymen

Robert Emory Blackwell (1854–1938), Ashland, Va. Blackwell graduated from Randolph-Macon College (Va.), became professor of English there in 1876, was appointed vice president in 1900, and president in 1902. He was active not only in MECS-related educational ventures, but also on national educational boards and institutions. He was the founder of the Virginia Commission on Interracial Cooperation, and this extra-church involvement apparently influenced his thinking. Blackwell was one of the most moderate members of the MECS commission, and certainly one of the most willing to compromise on the racial integration.

Robert Stewart Hyer (1860–1929), Dallas, Tex. Hyer was trained in physics at Emory College and went on to teach at Southwestern University (Georgetown, Tex.), where he also served as regent from 1897 to 1911. He then moved on to assist in the founding of Southern Methodist University, and he was its first president from 1911 to 1920. He continued there as professor of physics until his death. Hyer was also active in the ecumenical movement, and was a frequent delegate to General Conference. Hyer was not a vocal participant in the Joint Commission.

P. D. Maddin (n.d.), Nashville, Tenn. Maddin was a lawyer and a judge.

J. G. McGowan (n.d.), Water Valley, Miss. (Cleveland and Louisville meetings).

John R. Pepper (n.d.–1931), Memphis, Tenn. (Baltimore through St. Louis meetings). Pepper was a banker. He was active in organizing lay participation in his church, and was instrumental in establishing the Board of Lay Activities. He was one of the more conservative members of the MECS commission, and shared the white supremacist race theories (though not to the same degree) of H. H. White. Pepper participated moderately in the Joint Commission's debates.

E. C. Reeves (n.d.–1929), Johnson City, Tenn. Reeves was a lawyer.

John Hugh Reynolds (1869–n.d.), Searcy, Ark. Reynolds was a prominent educator in Arkansas. After graduate work in history and political science at the University of Chicago, he taught at the University of Arkansas. He then began a long connection to Hendrix College, having already graduated from there, and he served as its president from 1913 to 1945. He was one of only a few members of his commission to serve on all the different commissions and committees regarding union. Reynolds was one of the few MECS delegates willing to accept some form of a racially integrated proposal.

Thomas Drake Samford (1868–1947), Opelika, Ala. Samford was an attorney, and was the U.S. district attorney in Alabama for much of his career. Samford also served on the board of trustees of Alabama Polytechnic Institute, and sat on the board of directors of the *Alabama Christian Advocate* for forty-two years.

Henry Nelson Snyder (1865–1949), Spartanburg, S.C. Snyder was an English professor at Wofford College for twelve years before he was elected president of the college in 1902. He retired from that position in 1942. Snyder served as chair of the Board of Education for the South Carolina Conference, and was elected a delegate to every General Conference from 1906 to 1940.

Moses Lauck Walton (n.d.), Woodstock, Va. Walton was an attorney and state senator in Virginia. He was a General Conference delegate. While a state senator he authored a literacy poll test that he argued was not racist because it made no color distinction. His participation in the Joint Commission discussions was minimal.

H. H. White (n.d.), Alexandria, La.. White was a lawyer and judge.

Alternates

Bishop W. N. Ainsworth, Savannah, GA (Cleveland and Louisville meetings) See his listing above under ministerial delegates.

Bishop James Atkins (1850–1923), Waynesville, N.C. (Baltimore through St. Louis meetings). Atkins served pastorates in the Holston Conference from 1872 to 1879, when he was appointed president of Asheville Female College (N.C.). In 1889 he was elected president of Emory and Henry College, and in 1896 he was elected editor of Sunday School materials for the church Book Committee. He was elected to the episcopacy at the 1906 General Conference. Atkins was influential in the founding of Southern Methodist University, and was the chair of the MECS Centenary Commission.

Rev. William D. Bradfield (1866–1947), Dallas, Tex. (Cleveland and Louisville meetings). Bradfield pastored in the North Texas Conference for all but three years of his career; for those three years he served in St. Louis. He was editor of the Texas *Christian Advocate* from 1915 to 1918. He was professor of Christian Doctrine at the School of Theology at Southern Methodist University from 1922 to 1937. He replaced John M. Moore as a ministerial delegate on the Joint Commission in both meetings for which he was an alternate.

Rev. Corona Hibbard Briggs (1849–1932), Sedalia, Mo. (Baltimore through St. Louis meetings). Briggs began his ministerial service in 1870 and served in Missouri for the next fifty-five years. He was also heavily involved in the Freemasons, and achieved high standing in its regional leadership.

Rev. William Asbury Christian (1866–1936), Richmond, Va. (Baltimore through St. Louis meetings). Christian attended Randolph-Macon College and graduated from Vanderbilt in 1890, after which he began serving pastorates in the Virginia Conference. He was also president of Blackstone College for Girls (Va.) for six years. He was known for his advocacy of prohibition, and was the president of the Virginia Anti-Saloon League.

Rev. Isaac Cheney Jenkins (1874–1949), Jacksonville, Fla. (Cleveland and Louisville meetings). Jenkins served first in the North Alabama Conference and transferred to the Florida Conference in 1901. He was editor of the *Florida Christian Advocate*, and served as the vice president of Florida Southern College.

Rev. D. H. Kern (1866–1924), Roanoke, Va. (Cleveland and Louisville meetings). Kern served pastorates in the Baltimore Conference from 1896 to 1920. He was also a trustee of Randolph Macon College.

Rev. Eldridge Vetch Regester (1862–1949), Alexandria, Va. (Baltimore through St. Louis meetings). He served pastorates in the Baltimore Conference for forty-one years. He was at one time editor of the *Baltimore Southern Methodist*.

Rev. Luther Edward Todd (1874–1937), St. Louis, Mo. (Cleveland and Louisville meetings). Todd served pastorates in the Fulton Circuit in Missouri after seminary training at Vanderbilt. The MECS General Conference in 1918 created the General Board of Finance, to which Todd was appointed the executive secretary, a position he held until his death.

William Patterson Few (1867–1940), Durham, N.C. (Cleveland and Louisville meetings). A life-long educator, Few taught at Wofford and later at Trinity College, where he became dean in 1902. When Trinity was reorganized as Duke University, Few became the new university's first president. He was active in lay work and administration, serving as the chair of the General Board of Lay Activities for ten years.

C. M. Hay (n.d.), St. Louis, Mo. (Cleveland and Louisville meetings).

Edward W. Hines (n.d.), Louisville, Ky.

G. T. Fitzhugh (n.d.), Memphis, Tenn.

Notes

Notes to the Introduction

1. William B. McClain, *Black People in the Methodist Church: Whither Thou Goest?* (Cambridge, Mass.: Schenkman Publishing Co., 1984), 85. Like McClain and other scholars of race and Christianity, I have chosen to use language that reflects current usage rather than repeat the specific terms used in earlier eras. For instance, the terms "Negro" and "colored" or "Anglo Saxon" were commonly used in the early twentieth century, and while I often quote those terms, I have more often substituted the more current "black" or "African American" and "white."

2. Russell E. Richey, *The Methodist Conference in America: A History* (Nashville, Tenn.: Kingswood Books, 1996), 33-34.

3. Nathan Hatch and Jonathan Wigger make a strong case for the significance of this growth for American culture more broadly in their introduction to *Methodism and the Shaping of American Culture*, ed. Nathan O. Hatch and Jonathan H. Wigger (Nashville, Tenn.: Kingswood Books, 2001). Hatch also wonders why American historians have not recognized more fully the centrality of Methodists in his essay in that collection, "The Puzzle of American Methodism," 23-40.

4. Richard Carwardine repeats this story as well, and in the same essay argues that not only were Methodists politically influential, but prior to the Civil War, their religious culture shaped the language and form of democratic politics in the United States, while also pulling the nation toward war with the gravity of the North-South regional split in the 1840s. Carwardine, "Methodists, Politics, and the Coming of the American Civil War," 309-42, in *Methodism and the Shaping of American Culture*.

5. Catherine Brekus, "Female Evangelism in the Early Methodist Movement, 1784-1845," in *Methodists and the Shaping of American Culture*, 137. For a thorough study of women in early Methodism, with more detailed portraits of individuals, see Jean Miller Schmidt's *Grace Sufficient: A History of Women in American Methodism* (Nashville, Tenn.: Abingdon Press, 1999).

6. See Carol V. R. George, *Segregated Sabbaths: Richard Allen and the Rise of Independent Black Churches, 1760–1840* (New York: Oxford University Press, 1973).

7. For the fullest account of this struggle over slavery, see Donald G. Mathews, *Slavery and Methodism: A Chapter in American Morality, 1780–1845* (Princeton, N.J.: Princeton University Press, 1965).

8. McClain, *Black People in the Methodist Church*, 65–67.

9. The Methodist Protestant Church withdrew from official negotiations after the Chattanooga meeting after it became evident that major disagreements existed between the two much larger churches.

10. Several white and black conferences merged prior to 1968, and a few also remained segregated until 1973.

11. I assume throughout the book the language of the Methodists I am studying in regard to what constituted "Christian." Because it is outside the scope of this project, I will not spend the space necessary to more fully explore the use of "Christian" in the way they meant it, which means to say they did not include Roman Catholics in that designation.

12. One recent collection of essays, *Reimagining Denominationalism*, addresses the need for a reevaluation of the role of denominations and denominationalism in the study of American religion. The essays range from a harsh appraisal of denominational historians by Henry Bowden to one by Charles Long in which he says the lack of work on denominations has seriously hampered the study of American religion. Richey argues that the study of denominations has been so disdained that many scholars hide their work under different language and analytical categories. Robert Bruce Mullin and Russell E. Richey, eds., *Reimagining Denominationalism: Interpretive Essays* (New York: Oxford University Press, 1994). In a 1995 article, John Wilson wonders if the rejection of denominational church history as the paradigm for American religious history has gone too far. He writes that if denominations are not fully integrated into the "broader field of religious reality and activity that we now routinely recognize," they become artificial. He predicts a cultural studies–enhanced denominational historiography will emerge. This book fits that description. John Wilson, "A New Denominational Historiography?" *Religion and American Culture* 5, no. 2 (1995): 249–63.

13. Russell E. Richey, *Early American Methodism* (Bloomington: Indiana University Press, 1991), particularly Chapter 6, "The Four Languages of Early American Methodism."

14. Ibid., 96.

15. Ibid., 89.

16. J. Douglas Green, "Africa Rediviva: Northern Methodism and the Task of African Redemption, 1885–1910," Ph.D. dissertation, Kent State University, 1998.

17. Eddie Glaude, *Exodus! Religion, Race and Nation in Early Nineteenth-Century Black America* (Chicago: University of Chicago Press, 2000).

18. Ibid., 16–17.

19. Will Gravely, "'Playing in the Dark'—Methodist Style: The Fate of the Early African American Presence in Denominational Memory, 1807–1974," in *The People(s) Called Methodists: Forms and Reforms of Their Life*, ed. Dennis M. Campbell, William B. Lawrence, and Russell E. Richey (Nashville, Tenn.: Abingdon Press, 1998), 178.

20. Martha Hodes, "The Mercurial Nature and Abiding Power of Race: A Transnational Family Story," *American Historical Review* 108, no. 1 (February 2003): 84–119.

21. For thorough discussions of the breakdown of scientific race theories see Henry Louis Gates, *"Race," Writing, and Difference* (Chicago: University of Chicago Press, 1985); Ashley Montagu, *Man's Most Dangerous Myth* (New York: Columbia University Press, 1942), which was republished six times, and his edited volume on race and intelligence, *Race and IQ* (New York: Oxford University Press, 1999); for a regional study see Edward J. Larson, *Sex, Race, and Science: Eugenics in the Deep South* (Baltimore, Md.: Johns Hopkins University Press, 1996); for an early synthetic treatment see Thomas F. Gossett, *Race: The History of an Idea in America* (New York: Schocken Books, 1965).

22. Matthew Frye Jacobson's book, *Whiteness of a Different Color: European Immigrants and the Alchemy of Race* (Cambridge, Mass.: Harvard University Press, 1998), covers this story, especially in the "Epilogue," 274–82.

23. Barbara J. Fields, "Ideology and Race in American History," in *Region, Race, and Reconstruction: Essays in Honor of C. Vann Woodward*, ed. J. Morgan Kousser and James M. McPherson (New York: Oxford University Press, 1982).

24. Toni Morrison, "Romancing the Shadow," in *Playing in the Dark: Whiteness and the Literary Imagination* (Cambridge, Mass.: Harvard University Press, 1992), 44.

25. See for example, Robert T. Handy, "Negro Christianity and American Church Historiography," in *Reinterpretation in American Church History*, ed. Jerald C. Brauer (Chicago: University of Chicago Press, 1968). Lewis V. Baldwin, adding to a conversation about new ways of approaching the study of Methodism, suggests that scholars need to spend more time "filling in" the picture of Methodism with more historical detail about black Methodists. Lewis V. Baldwin, "New Directions for the Study of Blacks in Methodism," in *Rethinking Methodist History: A Bicentennial Historical Consultation*, ed. Russell Richey and Ken Rowe (Nashville, Tenn.: Kingswood Books, 1985), 185–93.

26. Ruth Frankenberg, *White Women, Race Matters: The Social Construction of Whiteness* (Minneapolis: University of Minnesota Press, 1993), 1.

27. Kevin Gaines, *Uplifting the Race: Black Leadership, Politics, and Culture in the Twentieth Century* (Chapel Hill: University of North Carolina Press, 1996).

28. Jacobson, *Whiteness of a Different Color*. Prior to Jacobson's book, both John Higham's *Strangers in the Land: Patterns of American Nativism, 1860–1925* (New York: Atheneum, 1963) and Reginald Horsman's *Race and Manifest Destiny: The Origins of American Racial Anglo-Saxonism* (Cambridge, Mass.: Harvard University Press, 1981) were the standard works on the history of race in the United States, and remain a fuller account in some areas—especially on the history of Anglo-Saxonism—than Jacobson's work.

29. Jacobson, *Whiteness of a Different Color*, 7.

30. For detailed accounts, see especially Noel Ignatiev, *How the Irish Became White* (New York: Routledge, 1995), and Karen Brodkin, *How Jews Became White Folks & What That Says about Race in America* (New Brunswick, N.J.: Rutgers University Press, 1994).

31. Grace Elizabeth Hale, *Making Whiteness: The Culture of Segregation in the South, 1890–1940* (New York: Pantheon, 1998). As I will articulate more fully in later chapters, I differ with Hale and others on the centrality of "the South" in the construction of silent narratives of whiteness. It is "the North" that most fully erases its explicit whiteness and merges it quietly with American-ness.

32. Gary Gerstle, *American Crucible: Race and Nation in the Twentieth Century* (Princeton, N.J.: Princeton University Press, 2001).

33. Gail Bederman, *Manliness and Civilization: A Cultural History of Gender and Race in the United States, 1880–1917* (Chicago: University of Chicago Press, 1995).

34. Ibid., 25.

35. Ibid. Bederman argues that the higher the degree of sexual difference achieved by a race/civilization, the higher the level of progress by that race/civilization.

36. The role of gender in this race discussion—especially in light of the all-male membership on the Joint Commission, their use of the discourse of manhood, and their preoccupation with the "bogey of social equality"—could bear greater scrutiny than I give it here.

37. Fields, "Ideology and Race," 159.

38. Edward J. Blum, *Reforging the White Republic: Race, Religion, and American Nationalism, 1865–1898* (Baton Rouge: Louisiana State University Press, 2005).

39. Ibid., 9.

40. James B. Bennett, *Religion and the Rise of Jim Crow in New Orleans* (Princeton, N.J.: Princeton University Press, 2005).

41. Joint Commission on Unification, *The Proceedings of the Joint Commission on Unification of the Methodist Episcopal Church, and Methodist Episcopal Church, South*, 3 vols. (New York: Methodist Book Concern, 1918–1920; Nashville, Tenn.: Smith and Lamar for the Publishing House of the Methodist Episcopal Church, South, 1918–1920).

42. All of the secondary source material that addresses the Commission is found in studies of the larger narrative culminating in the 1939 merger that created The Methodist Church (1939–1968). A broader denominational context for the story is told best by Dwight Culver's *Negro Segregation in the Methodist Church* (New Haven, Conn.: Yale University Press, 1953) and Harry V. Richardson's *Dark Salvation: The Story of Methodism as It Developed among Blacks in America* (Garden City, N.Y.: Anchor Press, 1976). Culver's is the earliest and most thorough work to address segregation within the mixed-race Methodist Church, while Richardson's work is considered by many to be the classic overview of African American Methodism. Richardson's book is crucial to understanding the complex variety of African American Methodist institutions and how they have related to each other. The most detailed accounts of the Joint Commission deliberations can be found in Frederick E. Maser's essay "The Story of Unification, 1874–1939," in *The History of American Methodism III*, ed. Emory Stevens Bucke (Nashville, Tenn.: Abingdon Press, 1964), 407–78; Henry Nathaniel Oakes's Ph.D. dissertation, "The Struggle for Racial Equality in the Methodist Episcopal Church: The Career of Robert E. Jones, 1904–1944" (University of Iowa, 1973), 158–226; and Richey, *The Methodist Conference in America*, 175–84.

The most complete and recent narrative of the rise, life, and dissolution of the Central Jurisdiction is Peter Murray's *Methodists and the Crucible of Race, 1930–1975* (Columbia: University of Missouri Press, 2004). An early example is Paul A. Carter's 1958 essay "The Negro and Methodist Union," in *Politics, Religion, and Rockets: Essays in Twentieth-Century American History* (Tucson: University of Arizona Press, 1991), 89–106. James P. Brawley, R. N. Brooks, Matthew W. Clair Jr., and Willis J. King were all African American leaders in the Methodist Episcopal Church who participated in the negotiations (those after the Joint Commission) and/or in the Jurisdiction itself and then went on to write about it. All of these are in either denominational journals or denominationally published reference works. James P. Brawley, "The Methodist Church from 1939," *Central Christian Advocate*, October 15, 1967, 3–10; R. N. Brooks, "Methodism and the Negro," *Christian Advocate* (New York), May 19, 1938, 461–62; Matthew W. Clair Jr., "Methodism and the Negro," in *Methodism*, ed. William K. Anderson (Nashville: Methodist Publishing House, 1947), 240–50; Willis J. King, "The Central Jurisdiction," in *The History of American Methodism III*, ed. Emory Stevens Bucke (Nashville, Tenn.: Abingdon, 1964), 485–95. James S. Thomas has published one of only a handful of full-length studies, *Methodism's Racial Dilemma: The Story of the Central Jurisdiction* (Nashville, Tenn.: Abingdon Press, 1992). Thomas was a young minister in the Central Jurisdiction from its formation in 1939, and was eventually one of the "Committee of Five" assigned to study the elimination of the Jurisdiction in the 1960s. Two Ph.D. dissertations also address segregation in Methodism: Karen Young Collier,

"An Examination of Varied Aspects of Race and Episcopacy in American Methodism, 1844–1939" (Duke University, 1984), and Peter C. Murray, "Christ and Caste in Conflict: Creating a Racially Inclusive Methodist Church" (Indiana University, 1985). Collier's study attempts to "bracket" questions of motive or racial bias in order to discern more clearly whether the institutional structures of Methodist churches lend themselves to biased exclusion as the Central Jurisdiction did. Murray's is a narrative of the struggle between 1939 and 1968 for the dissolution of official racial segregation in the Methodist Church. The full-length history most important to this study is John M. Moore's *The Long Road to Methodist Union* (Nashville, Tenn.: Methodist Publishing House, 1943). Moore was the only member of the Joint Commission to reflect so thoroughly in print on the negotiations. His anecdotes as well as his synthesis of some of the bureaucratic history have been invaluable to the background of this history.

The monograph that most closely examines the MECS in this time period is Robert Sledge's *Hands on the Ark: The Struggle for Change in the Methodist Episcopal Church, South, 1914–1939* (Lake Junaluska, N.C.: Commission on Archives and History, The United Methodist Church, 1975). While the scope of his book is much broader than the Joint Commission, which he covers from the MECS perspective, Sledge's work has filled in many gaps in the research that were beyond my reach and beyond the scope of the book. Sledge has skillfully composed a broader narrative of shift and disorder in MECS culture that clarifies much about the motives of Joint Commission members as well as the actions of their respective General Conferences.

43. Susan Friend Harding, *The Book of Jerry Falwell: Fundamentalist Language and Politics* (Princeton, N.J.: Princeton University Press, 2000).

NOTES TO CHAPTER 1

1. John M. Moore, *The Long Road to Methodist Union* (Nashville, Tenn.: Methodist Publishing House, 1943), 42.

2. See chapter 11, "Fratricide and Business," in Russell E. Richey, ed., *The Methodist Conference in America: A History* (Nashville, Tenn.: Kingswood Books, 1996), 109–19.

3. Ibid., 147–52.

4. For a general overview focusing on Presbyterians see Milton J. Coalter, John M. Moulder, and Louis B. Weeks, eds., *The Organizational Revolution: Presbyterians and American Denominationalism* (Louisville, Ky.: Westminster/John Knox Press, 1992). Russell Richey also addresses this phenomenon in his essay on the morphology of denominations and denominationalism, noting that many Protestant leaders responded in the "interest of ideals—missions reform, order, unity—and in the recognition that the existing system posed knotty theological, particularly ecclesiological, issues." In Robert Bruce Mullin and Russell E.

Richey, eds., *Reimagining Denominationalism: Interpretive Essays* (New York: Oxford University Press, 1994), 85.

5. It is worth noting here that three members of the Joint Commission on Unification of 1916 were a part of this earlier Commission on Federation: Bishop Hoss from the MECS, and John F. Goucher and Richard Cooke of the MEC.

6. This body was sometimes called "Joint Committee on Federation," and sometimes "Joint Commission (or Committee) on Federation of Methodism."

7. For a reprint of this recommendation see Moore, *Long Road*, 112.

8. For partial transcriptions of the speeches from the Chattanooga meeting see "Addresses Delivered by the Joint Commission on Methodist Federation in Chattanooga, Tenn., 1911." General Conference Collection, United Methodist Archives, Madison, New Jersey.

9. Some confusion arose after the 1912 MEC General Conference, since the Conference took no specific action on the report, but merely expressed its support of the progress toward unity. This meant that the MEC commissioners had to report again to the 1916 General Conference and seek more specific responses and instructions before serious joint negotiations could begin. See "Report of the Commission on Federation," 1916. General Conference Collection, United Methodist Church Archives, Madison, New Jersey.

10. Prior to the Joint Commission meetings, the main *Christian Advocates* of each Church declined to publish commentary on the issues of unification. Many of the conference *Advocates*, meanwhile, battled it out ferociously. The Nashville *Christian Advocate* would occasionally reprint or summarize these positions, but they were criticized by the New York *Christian Advocate* for doing so. See *The Christian Advocate* (Nashville), June 30, 1916, 21 and 24, for the summaries. For the New York *Christian Advocate* response see August 10, p. 7. The New York editors held themselves to short notes on activities such as "union services" in towns in which there were both MEC and MECS congregations. See August 24, p. 6.

11. The John Howard Lindgren Foundation for the Promotion of Peace and International Unity, *A Working Conference on the Union of American Methodism* (New York: Methodist Book Concern, 1916).

12. Roy W. Trueblood, "Union Negotiations between Black Methodists in America," *Methodist History* 8, no. 4 (July 1970): 18–29.

13. "An Epochal Meeting," *Southwestern Christian Advocate* (New Orleans, La.: Methodist Book Concern, 1916), 1. This was the leading church paper among black members of the MEC. Jones (1872–1960) was a nationally recognized leader in the African American community in New Orleans. Jones and Matthew W. Clair were elected the first black bishops in the MEC in 1920. As we will see, Jones was one of the most influential members of the Joint Commission, probably only because of his studied and very public Booker T. Washington

conservatism. For a full biography, see Nathaniel Oakes's dissertation, "The Struggle for Racial Equality in the Methodist Episcopal Church: The Career of Robert E. Jones, 1904–1944" (University of Iowa, 1973).

14. John Howard Lindgren Foundation, *A Working Conference*, 224.

15. Ibid., 224–25.

16. Ibid., 233.

17. Ibid., 229.

18. Ibid., 231.

19. Years later Jones would often refer to his presentation at the Working Conference on Methodist Union in Evanston, Illinois, as his "Evanston speech." It became important as the first public articulation of his position on reunification, especially when he would later be accused of inconsistency and of changing his position to suit shifting church politics.

20. John Howard Lindgren Foundation, *A Working Conference*, 234.

21. We will take up this theological problem in greater detail as it appeared in the Joint Commission in chapter 3, but it is worth taking time now to see the ways race history was being formulated in the larger discussions of Methodist union. For overviews of this topic see in particular J. Albert Harrill, "The Uses of the New Testament in the American Slave Controversy: A Case History in the Hermeneutical Tension between Biblical Criticism and Christian Moral Debate," *Religion and American Culture: A Journal of Interpretation* 10, no. 2 (summer 2000): 149–86. For general overviews see Donald G. Mathews, *Religion in the Old South* (Chicago: University of Chicago Press, 1977), and Christine Leigh Heyrman, *Southern Cross: The Beginnings of the Bible Belt* (New York: Knopf, 1997).

22. Thirkield was not on the Joint Commission, probably because Bishop John Hamilton, who held similar integrationist views, was already representing that position there. Like Hamilton, Thirkield was a well-known advocate of racial integration in the MEC. He served as president of black schools—Gammon Theological and Howard University—and was assigned in his episcopal duties to the MEC churches in the New Orleans area.

23. John Howard Lindgren Foundation, *A Working Conference*, 260.

24. Henry Nelson Snyder (1865–1949), besides his work as a college professor and president, was highly active in lay activities and was a perennial General Conference delegate.

25. John Howard Lindgren Foundation, *A Working Conference*, 242.

26. Jay Douglas Green, "Africa Rediviva: Northern Methodism and the Task of African Redemption, 1885–1910," Ph.D. dissertation, Kent State University, 1998.

27. The Civil War was difficult to explain in this logic, but this was usually accomplished in a sort of Darwinian fashion: America had learned from its mistake, and had progressed in its civilization past such internecine bloodshed.

28. *Christian Advocate* (New York), July 20, 1916: 1. Also see John Franklin Goucher, *Christianity and the United States* (New York: Eaton and Mains, 1908) for an earlier unflinching portrait of the United States as the chosen nation of God. Once the United States entered the war in Europe, MEC publications on this theme multiplied. For a good example of the smaller chapbook and pamphlet publications, see *Methodism and the Flag* (New York: Methodist Book Concern, 1917), published by the New York Conference, which included an essay expressing enthusiastic support for the U.S. declaration of war—as well as derisive condemnation for Christian pacifists—and a much-publicized and often-reprinted poem by Bishop Luther B. Wilson entitled "Wave, Flag of Freedom, Wave."

29. Earl Cranston, *Breaking Down the Walls: A Contribution to Methodist Unification* (New York: Methodist Book Concern, 1915). His other publications and printed addresses included topics from anti-Roman Catholicism to missions in Korea. Cranston (1840–1932) was a highly respected and influential member of the Joint Commission. His spiritualizing of the concept of unity was one of the key maneuvers in the negotiation of race and Methodism.

30. John M. Moore, *The South Today* (New York: Missionary Education Movement of the United States and Canada, 1943). Moore (1867–1948) was born in Kentucky, and was one of the MECS leaders that led the transition to a "New South." He was elected to the episcopacy in the MECS in 1918, and was a bishop in the new Methodist Church. He was a key player in the eventual merger in 1939.

Other significant publications by Joint Commissioners include Claudius B. Spencer's *That They May Become One: In Behalf of the Organic Union of American Methodism* (New York: The Methodist Book Concern, 1915); Elijah Embree Hoss, *Methodist Fraternity and Federation, Being Several Addresses and Other Papers on the General Subject* (Nashville, Tenn.: Publishing House, Methodist Episcopal Church, South, 1913).

31. Cranston, like most of his white counterparts, argued for a new constitution that resembled that of the MEC in which congregations and annual conferences were racially segregated.

32. The "idea of the South" is a complex and multilayered problem, and has been the subject of a great deal of study since C. Vann Woodward's famous work. See for instance a recent forum in the *American Historical Review* on regionalism and "sub-national places," especially Michael O'Brien's "On Observing the Quicksand," *American Historical Review* 104, no. 5 (1999): 1202.

33. Nina Silber has argued that Americans in the northern states played a part in creating the myths of a paradisal South destroyed by the war. Gilded Age white northerners, in their anxiety about collapsing Victorian ideals, looked for lost civilizations such as the antebellum plantation days as ideals on which to rebuild. This mythmaking extended to the spheres of gender and race and class. It

was in sharing this romanticized memory with the MECS that the MEC tried to take the hard political edge off of the negotiations. As Silber puts it, the idea of a reunion between North and South was gendered feminine, so that the ideal of "Dixie" served as a common metaphor for the goal of a rescued Victorian-style womanhood. This shared ideal helped to depoliticize sectional divisions. Nina Silber, *The Romance of Reunion: Northerners and the South 1865–1900* (Chapel Hill: University of North Carolina Press, 1993).

34. Cranston, *Breaking Down the Walls*, 142–43.

35. Moore, *The South Today*, xiv. There was a growing generational division within the MECS that manifested itself in many ways. The degree of emphasis on regional identity was one way. The struggle for the character and shape of the church Robert W. Sledge describes often came down to matters of regional identity. The older generation who identified with the days of civil war and the Reconstruction era in the South battled younger leaders of the church who were hoping to move the church toward a less regional and more national outlook. Moore represented a moderate younger voice in this internal debate.

36. John Higham and Alexander Saxton have both argued that in the early twentieth century the worship of the Anglo-Saxon tradition was widespread and was part of the national public discourse on race and nationality. Moore assumed this in his abbreviated description of Anglo-Saxons. John Higham, *Strangers in the Land: Patterns of American Nativism, 1860–1925* (New York: Atheneum, 1967); Alexander Saxton, *The Rise and Fall of the White Republic: Class Politics and Mass Culture in Nineteenth-Century America* (New York: Verso Books, 1990).

37. Moore, *The South Today*, 111.

38. Ibid., 136.

39. Ibid., 112.

40. Ibid., 114. The euphemism for segregation should also be noted here: "turning much of the Negro patronage to the professional men of the Negro race."

41. Ibid., 116.

42. Ibid., 124.

43. Ibid., 125.

44. Ibid., 180.

45. Ibid., 122.

46. Ibid., 123.

NOTES TO CHAPTER 2

1. These items and many more can be found in the collections of the Drew University Methodist Library, and the General Commission on Archives and History of the United Methodist Church, both in the United Methodist Archives at Drew University, Madison, New Jersey. Many are on permanent display.

2. Thomas A. Tweed, "John Wesley Slept Here: American Shrines and American Methodists," *Numen* 47, no. 1 (2000): 41–68.

3. Russell E. Richey, "History as a Bearer of Denominational Identity: Methodism as a Case Study," in *Perspectives on American Methodism*, ed. Russell E. Richey, Kenneth E. Rowe, and Jean Miller Schmidt (Nashville, Tenn.: Kingswood Books, 1993), 480–98.

4. My thinking on ritual and institutional memory is influenced primarily by Paul Connerton's work in *How Societies Remember* (Cambridge: Cambridge University Press, 1989).

5. Joint Commission, *Proceedings*, vol. I, 35.

6. Ibid., 12–13.

7. Ibid., 14.

8. Donald B. Marti, "Rich Methodists: The Rise and Consequences of Lay Philanthropy in the Mid-19th Century," in *Rethinking Methodist History: A Bicentennial Historical Consultation*, ed. Russell E. Richey and Kenneth E. Rowe (Nashville, Tenn.: Kingswood Books, 1983), 159–66.

9. For a good overview of the history of these narratives see Alden T. Vaughan and Edward W. Clark, "Cups of Common Calamity: Puritan Captivity Narratives as Literature and History," in *Puritans among the Indians: Accounts of Captivity and Redemption, 1676-1724*, ed. Alden T. Vaughan and Edward W. Clark (Cambridge: Belknap Press, 1981), 1–28. For an analysis of captivity narratives involving women see David T. Haberly, "Women and Indians: *The Last of the Mohicans* and the Captivity Tradition," *American Quarterly* 28 (1976): 431–41.

10. See a discussion of this by Toni Morrison as this pertains to American literature in *Playing in the Dark: Whiteness and the Literary Imagination* (Cambridge: Harvard University Press, 1992), 44–45. A "constituted Africanism" is what animates the major concerns of American literature, even in the absence of an obvious Africanist character. "It was this Africanism," says Morrison, "deployed as a rawness and savagery, that provided the staging ground and arena for the elaboration of the quintessential American identity."

11. *Proceedings*, v. I, 20.

12. Candler (1857–1941) was one of the more colorful bishops of the MECS, even entering national politics at one point. He was a member of the Joint Commission only out of a sense of duty, because he was strongly against a merger. Candler believed that any merger would only serve to destroy the distinctiveness of Methodism among whites in the southern United States. Thus his participation in the meetings was minimal, as his sense of honor would not allow him to interject a contrarian's voice into a process that was intended to produce a merger.

13. This sermon, probably because of its length, was not included in the published version of the *Proceedings*, but was published separately as an extended

pamphlet. Warren A. Candler, "The Church: The Fullness of Christ and the Hope of the Universe: A Sermon Preached at the Opening Session of the Joint Commission on Unification in the First Methodist Episcopal Church, Baltimore, Maryland, Dec. 26, 1916" (n.p., 1916).

14. Bishop William F. McDowell (1858–1937) was the primary spokesperson (and commission chair) for the MEC delegation for the life of the Joint Commission. McDowell was strongly in favor of union and was, for a time, willing to consider a compromise on black membership in order to attain that goal. As we will see in later chapters, though, McDowell experienced a change of heart on this issue, and withdrew his position of compromise. McDowell was well suited to his role, as he constantly attempted to restate other commissioners' positions—both MEC and MECS—when he thought they sounded too intransigent. On more than one occasion he called for a break in a meeting and suggested that the Joint Commission separate into separate church commissions to cool off and re-evaluate their direction.

15. *Proceedings*, v. I, 162.

16. *Proceedings*, v. II, 656.

17. Collins Denny (1854–1943) was thoroughly against union, even a racially segregated one. Denny was of the opinion that the MECS was better off retaining its regional distinctiveness, and that it would not be improved by a merger with the larger MEC. Denny and others like him feared that the MEC would overwhelm their church and one of the last and best representatives of (white) southern culture would be lost. Denny rarely spoke in the meetings.

18. *Proceedings*, v. I, 184.

19. *Proceedings*, v. II, 608. This is rather an odd comment coming from a preacher.

20. Ibid., 373.

21. Ibid., 375.

22. *Proceedings*, v. III, 213.

23. *Proceedings*, v. II, 655.

24. Cranston added that it wasn't their fault because their "first lessons in politics were corrupting and degrading, and it is no great wonder that his conceptions of humanity [*sic*] rights revolve about a ballot box or in the Church around the bishopric. He learned that from white men." Ibid., 655.

25. Ibid., 655–56. The notion of "self-direction" and the need of a "sphere of influence" for an "immature" race is addressed in greater detail in chapter 3.

26. MEC ministerial delegate Claudius B. Spencer (1856–1933), speaking at the Cleveland meeting. *Proceedings*, v. III, 319. Claudius was a passionate proponent of the separate racial jurisdiction within the new church, and felt strongly that the black jurisdiction should not be called a "mission" of any kind.

27. Frank M. Thomas (1868–1921), MECS ministerial delegate, had just been named the editor of the *Methodist Quarterly Review* at the 1918 General

Conference. Thomas held strong views about the necessity of racial segregation. He also tended to the melodramatic, often reading from prepared speeches that spiritualized and dramatized the possibilities of (white) union. At one point, as he attempted to convince his fellow commissioners of his passion for union, he said that he wanted unification so dearly that, while burdened with this problem and unable to sleep a few nights earlier, he had prayed and vowed to God that he would be willing to die that night if it meant bringing about a "wise" solution to the unification problem. He said he would forgo seeing his home, his mother, his wife, and children again if he could find the answer. *Proceedings*, v. III, 315.

28. Ibid., 208.

29. Richard Cooke (1853–1931) was not a frequent contributor, and seemed to take on the role of mediating observer. As in this example, he often attempted to synthesize what had been said by others and to show how apparently insuperable differences could be overcome.

30. *Proceedings*, v. II, 193.

31. Frederick Deland Leete (1866–1958) was an influential bishop who had spent many years in Atlanta overseeing MEC work in the southern states. Leete used his experience in Atlanta to try to convince his MECS counterparts on the Joint Commission that at least some of the MEC commissioners understood their position. Leete was one of the MEC commissioners openly willing to compromise with the MECS on a segregated racial membership.

32. Alexander Simpson Jr. (1855–1935) was a successful lawyer in Philadelphia who was appointed for life to the Pennsylvania Supreme Court in 1918. Simpson and Hamilton were the lone champions on the Joint Commission for full racial integration. Simpson was articulate and passionate and openly questioned the Christian integrity of those who would accept racial inequality for the sake of white institutional union.

33. See especially Simpson's speech at Savannah. It was one of his most sustained arguments that those in favor of a separate organization for black members were wrong in Christian terms. He accused them of ignoring "their own humanity." *Proceedings*, v. II, 607–8.

34. Ira E. Robinson (1869–n.d.) was a federal judge from West Virginia. He was a rare contributor to the discussion on the floor. When he did, he attempted, as he does in this example, to turn the discussion away from "expedient" solutions.

35. At several points during the meetings, white delegates advocating for a white church discussed the legal implications of the loss of membership rights of the black Methodists currently in the MEC. H. H. White argued that there was legal precedent for lawmaking bodies of churches to rescind rights in the same way they could grant them *Proceedings*, v. III, 286–97. Henry Wade Rogers (MEC) made a similar argument in Savannah (*Proceedings*, v. II, 339–40).

36. *Proceedings*, v. III, 300.

37. It is worth remarking that though the black delegates on the Commission often made good use of arguments by their white counterparts from both sides, I have not encountered them using this kind of theological claim about slavery.

38. *Proceedings*, v. II, 431.

Notes to Chapter 3

1. *Passing of the Great Race* (New York: Scribner's Sons, 1916), vii.

2. Ibid., xx–xxi.

3. Ibid., 4, 57.

4. An excellent distillation of this moment is Jeffrey Stewart's introduction to the collection of Alain Locke's lectures, *Race Contacts and Interracial Relations: Lectures on the Theory and Practice of Race* (Cambridge: Harvard University Press, 1992), xix–lix, especially xxi–xxxiv.

5. "The Theoretical and Scientific Conceptions of Race," in Stewart, ed., *Race Contacts and Interracial Relations*, 5–8.

6. Stewart, "Introduction," in *Race Contacts and Interracial Relations*, xxv.

7. "The Theoretical and Scientific Conceptions of Race," 96–97.

8. *Syllabus to an Extension Course of Lectures on Race Contacts and Interracial Relations* (Washington, D.C.: R. L. Pendleton, 1916).

9. Many commissioners commonly used images of black Americans as wild and intemperate crowds. In this case, Alexander Farrar Watkins (1856–1929), MECS ministerial delegate, was arguing that the more common "type" of "negroes"—unlike the "type" represented by Penn and Jones—were too backward and "undeveloped intellectually, morally, socially, industrially" to be trusted with solving their own problems. *Proceedings*, v. I, 167.

10. One of the best sources on the fluidity and uses of regions in American history is Edward L. Ayers, ed., *All over the Map: Rethinking American Regions* (Baltimore, Md.: Johns Hopkins University Press, 1996), with essays by the editor, Patricia Nelson Limerick, Stephen Nussenbaum, and Peter S. Onuf.

11. I have discussed in some detail the rise of histories of and encomiums to Anglo-Saxonism. There was a corresponding increase of histories of African Americans and Africans. For a description of some of the more important contributions to that body of work and an analysis of the reception of them see Laurie Maffly-Kipp, "Mapping the World, Mapping the Race: The Negro Race History, 1874–1915," *Church History* 64 (December 1995): 610–26.

12. Elijah Embree Hoss (1849–1919), was from Oklahoma. He was an active participant, and tended to dramatic and colorful rhetorical flourishes. He had been a vocal supporter of union for years before the Joint Commission was formed. Like many of the MECS leaders of his generation, Hoss was known for

his fights against theological "modernism" and his assessment that contemporary America was in moral decline. In his book *Methodist Fraternity and Federation* he laments the "serious decay in the purity of family life." He perceived a state of "sexual morality that would scandalize a Hottentot and put an Australian Bushman to the blush" (61).

13. *Proceedings*, v. I, 95.

14. More on Goucher's speech below.

15. *Proceedings*, v. I, 95.

16. Ibid.

17. Ibid., 96.

18. Ibid., 164. Chapell (1853–1936) was an infrequent contributor to the discussion. He remained opposed to a racially integrated proposal throughout the meetings.

19. Horace M. Du Bose (1858–1941) lived in Nashville, Tennessee, and was book editor for the MECS and editor of the *Methodist Quarterly Review* during the Joint Commission meetings. Du Bose was a frequent and lively speaker, with great rhetorical powers and the confidence, though he was not a bishop, to debate anyone else in the Joint Commission. Only a few commissioners who were not bishops felt as free to openly challenge the senior leadership from either church as Du Bose did. He became a bishop at the 1918 General Conference. At the Savannah meeting Du Bose described in romantic terms his passion for Methodist union. He described several natural disasters he had experienced personally: an earthquake, an astronomical "vision," a forest fire, and a North Dakota blizzard. He compared the way they changed him to the way the prospect of Methodist unification had changed him: "I can never any more be the same man I was before into our midst was flung, like a burning star, this great concrete suggestion of the unification of American Methodism. It has become a fire in my bones, a sword driven through my cranial bone. It has become iron in my blood and a fire in my brain. . . . I affirm a new sense of universal brotherhood and sympathy, and I have been led to the largest conclusion by most careful personal reflection and analysis of this world thought, this great age-thought," *Proceedings*, v. II, 118.

20. Ibid., 131–32.

21. Edwin Du Bose Mouzon (1869–1937), who lived in Texas at the time of the Joint Commission meetings, was another strong MECS proponent of union, and had worked on several prior committees on the question of union. Like Du Bose, Mouzon was a frequent contributor to the discussions and was a strong advocate of preserving a distinctive southern identity and racial segregation in the union proposal. Mouzon had a good bit of experience supervising Methodist mission conferences in South America, and was convinced that they were good models for dealing with the "negro problem" in the United States.

22. *Proceedings*, v. I, 105.

23. Ibid., 134–35.

24. This assumes, of course, an emphasis on the "nurture" side of the classic developmental debate. But following that thread is not of concern here.

25. This is the sort of classic and even stereotypical model of Progressive-era patronage, usually associated with "the North." It was strongly resonant with Progressive political and social theories of the time. It was, I think, a most natural and effortless position for many in the MEC. Jay Douglas Green describes MEC race views in a similar way, arguing that this racial view was part of a "larger providential scheme to perfect all of humanity by revamping the environmental structure of the entire social order." Green, "Africa Rediviva: Northern Methodism and the Task of African Redemption, 1885–1910" (Ph.D. dissertation, Kent State University, 1998), 129.

26. There were exceptions to the "mass vs. individual" arguments. At Savannah, Abram W. Harris explained that northern whites and southern whites have a distinctly different type of love for blacks. Northern love is "communistic" and southern is "individualistic." He tells the story of a black southerner who was stranded in Boston and tried to find help by going from door to door. He was turned away without any help from everyone until he finally happened upon the house of a southern white man. This expatriate spoke to him harshly and without dignity but was the only one to feed him. Harris summarized this way: "No matter what the manner of expression, [the black southerner] understood it. It seemed like home, because he knew that in and through and dominating his manner was the personal interest to see that he should not starve." *Proceedings*, v. II, 334.

27. The MEC did not want to create a new church structure that formed regional voting blocks. This issue did, however, serve as the MEC's best compromise position, which most likely explains their reluctance to offer it too early in the negotiations.

28. *Proceedings*, v. I, 175–76.

29. William N. Ainsworth (1872–1942), a ministerial delegate, lived in Savannah, Georgia, at the time. He was elected bishop at the 1918 General Conference. Ainsworth's participation was sporadic.

30. *Proceedings*, v. I, 149–50.

31. Ibid., 149.

32. Ibid., 170. William James Young (1859–1936), a minister, was a professor at Candler School of Theology at the time.

33. Ibid.

34. *Proceedings*, v. I, 181. P. D. Maddin (n.d.) was a lawyer and judge in Tennessee. He was not a frequent participant on the floor, but he was a strong opponent of a racially integrated church.

35. June 27–30, 1917.

36. *Proceedings*, v. I, 435–36.

37. The composition of the Associate General Conferences was inconsistent at best. Along with the conflation of U.S. Negro conferences with African mission conferences, "Latin American" conferences in the United States were to be paired with their counterparts in South America. But there was no such conflation of the old German-speaking conferences in the MEC with German national conferences in Europe, or Chinese congregations in the United States paired with Chinese missions, etcetera. Most telling in this scheme is the lack of connection between whites in the United States and whites in Europe. Whites in the United States were just "Americans," and whites in Europe were also organized according to national affiliations. White Americans were true Americans. Black Americans and Hispanic Americans were not. This view was not, of course, held this clearly by all delegates. Strangely, many MECS delegates were insistent that Mexicans living in the United States be undifferentiated from white conferences in the United States. In an exchange on this at Savannah, Abram W. Harris argues that Caribbean nations be included in white regional conferences. Edgar Blake points out the inconsistency of this position, but Du Bose later explains that the "issues" that "divide us here" are not a problem outside the United States. *Proceedings*, v. II, 530–32.

38. H. H. White (n.d.), from Alexandria, Louisiana, was a lay MECS commissioner and staunch opponent of union. He was a lawyer and judge, and boasted of his involvement in Louisiana politics in the Reconstruction era, during which he helped institute "Jim Crow" laws that returned that state's governments to white control. In the next chapter I spend time analyzing his advocacy of a white supremacist position. White was the only commissioner who openly advocated a white or Caucasian supremacy position in such stark terms.

39. For the full Traverse City statement, see ibid., 473.

NOTES TO CHAPTER 4

1. For writing on lynching, see especially Stewart E. Tolnay and E. M. Beck, *A Festival of Violence: An Analysis of Southern Lynchings, 1882-1930* (Urbana, IL: University of Illinois Press, 1995); Orlando Patterson, *Rituals of Blood: Consequences of Slavery in Two American Centuries* (Washington, D.C.: Civitas/CounterPoint, 1998); Donald G. Mathews, "The Southern Rite of Human Sacrifice," *Journal of Southern Religion* (Online) 3 (2000): http://jsr.as.wvu.edu/mathews.htm (accessed June 2006); James Allen, ed., *Without Sanctuary: Lynching Photography in America* (Santa Fe, NM: Twin Palms, 2000); Robert L. Zangrando, *The NAACP Crusade against Lynching, 1909-1950* (Philadelphia: Temple University Press, 1980); Jacquelyn Dowd Hall, *Revolt Against Chivalry: Jessie Daniel Ames and the Campaign against Lynching* (New York: Columbia University Press, 1979); William Fitzhugh Brundage, *Under Sentence of Death: Lynching in the South* (Chapel Hill: University of

North Carolina Press, 1996). For a compilation of scholarly work on lynching, see Norton Moses, *Lynching and Vigilantism in the United States: An Annotated Bibliography* (Westport, Conn.: Greenwood Press, 1997).

2. W.E.B. Du Bois was so concerned about the treatment of the tens of thousands of black American soldiers in Europe that he traveled there after the Armistice to monitor their treatment as they returned to the command of white American forces. What he found was not only a repeat of Jim Crow separation, but a widespread attempt to discredit any positive accounts of their performance in the war. See Du Bois, "The Negro Soldier in Service Abroad during the First World War," in *The Journal of Negro Education* 12, no. 3, "The American Negro in World War I and World War II" (summer 1943): 324–34.

3. See in particular Mathews, "The Southern Rite of Human Sacrifice." Mathews's essay is the most in-depth consideration of what we have missed for many years in the story of lynching—its religious underpinning. His arguments flow naturally out of his earlier essays on the role of "purity" for white Christian culture in this time period.

4. *Rope and Faggot: A Biography of Judge Lynch* (New York: Alfred A. Knopf, 1929; reprint, Notre Dame, Ind.: University of Notre Dame, 2001).

5. White, *Rope and Faggot*, 51–52.

6. James C. Scott, *Domination and the Arts of Resistance* (New Haven, Conn.: Yale University Press, 1990).

7. Irvine Garland Penn (1867–1930) worked in Cincinnati, Ohio, at the time. Penn was born in Virginia. He spent most of his early career as a teacher and author. He spent a tremendous amount of energy writing about the accomplishments of black Americans. His first major publication was a volume of biographies of African American newspaper editors and journalists. He was the director and organizer for the "Negro" exhibits at the 1895 Atlanta Exposition, and he played a significant part in the decision to place Booker T. Washington in the leading role there that launched Washington into the national spotlight. In the MEC, Penn was the Deputy Secretary of the Freedman's Aid Society. The details of Penn's death have been difficult to track down, but there is some speculation that he died as the result of injuries sustained while being thrown off a segregated train car in South Carolina.

8. Penn said: "The white people have not drawn the color line in the MEC without our consent. I want that distinctly understood. I have written certain pages in the discipline myself which drew the color line . . ." *Proceedings*, v. I, 149.

9. Donald G. Mathews, "'Christianizing the South'—Sketching a Synthesis," in *New Directions in American Religious History*, ed. D. G. Hart and Harry S. Stout (New York: Oxford University Press, 1997), 95. See also Mathews's "Religion and the South: Authenticity and Purity—Pulling Us Together, Tearing Us

Apart," in *Religious Diversity and American Religious History: Studies in Traditions and Cultures*, ed. Walter H. Conser Jr. and Sumner B. Twiss (Athens: University of Georgia Press, 1997), 72–101.

10. Mathews, "Christianizing the South," 94.

11. For an analysis of the ways in which black Americans in this era performed particular racial ideologies in public arenas such as the Joint Commission, see Alessandra Lorini, *Rituals of Race: American Public Culture and the Search for Racial Democracy* (Charlottesville: University of Virginia Press, 1999).

12. White, from Alexandria, Louisiana, was a lawyer and judge. Despite his role as the resident extreme conservative, White—along with E. C. Reeves (n.d.), also a lawyer–was often surprisingly flexible on other issues. For instance, he was one of the few MECS delegates to openly declare his desire to "change with the times" and accept women's suffrage in the new church and at the national level as well. Reeves was the only delegate on the MECS commission to openly oppose the creation of regional conferences.

13. For example, in a long discussion about designations of regional conferences, Alexander Farrar Watkins (1856–1929), then president of Millsaps College in Jackson, Mississippi, reminded his colleagues at one point that they could not compromise too far on the names of a "negro" conference without thinking ahead to "that hard fight that we may have to make with conservative constituencies in order that we may induce them to bring about this thing that we believe for the glory of God." *Proceedings*, v. II, 520.

14. This took place in the last meeting at Louisville, Kentucky. Jones demanded that someone explain the presence of a "trapdoor" suggestion in the final compromise that after a certain number of black members was reached, the black membership would have the option to vote to form their own Associate General Conference. After days of dissembling on the purpose of that section of the proposal, Cannon admitted its purpose under this pressure from Jones. *Proceedings*, v. III, 475–76.

15. *Proceedings*, v. II, 137.

16. Ibid.

17. During a long debate about whether a proposed black jurisdiction "shall" or "may" become a separate Associate General Conference, Mouzon said that the MECS insisted on "shall." He punctuated that with "There we shall stand." In his eyes, this was a noble stand. Later, as we will see in chapter 5, such principled immobility on the part of Penn and Jones was called intransigent and small-minded; their own colleagues accused Penn and Jones of displaying a lack of "Christian manhood." It is a good example of how these kinds of tropes and discourses can be swallowed by different ideological stances.

18. Ibid., 139.

19. Hamilton (1845–1934) had been retired by the 1916 MEC General Conference. While he had always been known as an outspoken advocate of more liberal

or progressive views, his retired status may have freed him even more to take on the combative role he played in the Joint Commission.

20. As we will see more clearly in later sections, "agitation" was something akin to anarchy.

21. Ibid., 111–16.

22. Andrew Jackson Lamar (1847–1933) was a ministerial delegate, and influential in the MECS as one of the church publishing agents and one of its most outspoken and revered elder statesmen. Lamar felt free to challenge anyone on the Joint Commission with whom he disagreed, and on many occasions chastised the entire group for wasting time on an issue—the "status of the negro"—that could not be resolved. He did not think the MECS was prepared for an integrated church, and was frustrated more and more as the meetings stretched out and focused more and more on the racial issue.

23. *Proceedings*, v. II, 186.

24. In his opening remarks, and in several other speeches, Hamilton began by reassuring his listeners that he would not, despite their expectations, argue for social equality. He complained throughout the meetings, almost incessantly, about his outsider position on the Joint Commission.

25. Ibid., 191.

26. Ibid., 261.

27. Ibid., 262. To get a sense of the sensitivity of many in the MECS to discussions of racial equality, it is worth revisiting what Ainsworth was referring to. A report on the negotiations in one of the MECS serials quoted Hamilton: "All the negro needs is a spelling book and the Good Book and the pocketbook to make him as good as any white man." Hamilton said the quote was taken out of context, and that he was merely "encouraging a bunch of black boys to be good."

28. *Proceedings*, v. II, 178–79.

29. Ibid., 128.

30. Abram W. Harris (1858–1935) was an active lay member from New York City.

31. Ibid., 314.

32. This distinction was not new. The distinction between racial equality in the political sphere and in the social sphere was made among abolitionists in the early nineteenth century. Struggles among abolitionists for direction of the movement often came down to this distinction, as in the example of Francis Wright. A radical activist, her detractors in the movement branded her "priestess of Beelzebub" because she advocated interracial marriage. See Rachel F. Moran, *Interracial Intimacy: The Regulation of Race and Romance* (Chicago: University of Chicago Press, 2001), 26, and John D'Emilio and Estelle B. Freedman, eds., *Intimate Matters: A History of Sexuality in America* (New York: Harper and Rowe, 1988), 113–14.

33. *Proceedings*, v. II, 226.

34. Ibid., 228.

35. Ibid., 157. Charles M. Pollack (1853–1928), reserve lay delegate, was a judge from North Dakota.

36. Robert E. Blackwell (1854–1938) was a well-known and highly regarded educator. He was president of Randolph Macon College in Virginia. Blackwell was one of the few vocal proponents of a compromise with the MEC on racial integration.

37. Ibid., 141–42.

38. Ibid., 140.

39. Ibid.

40. Ibid., 141.

41. Ibid., 142–43.

42. I. G. Penn, ibid., 245.

43. Ibid., 242–43. Penn also added that at a joint service between the two churches, they had sung lots of "old plantation melodies."

44. Ibid., 252–53.

45. For a good overview of this topic see Louis Harlan's essay, "Booker T. Washington and the Politics of Accommodation," in *Black Leaders of the Twentieth Century*, ed. John Hope Franklin and August Meier (Urbana: University of Illinois Press, 1982), 1–18.

46. Frederick Douglass and Ida B. Wells, eds., "The Reason Why the Colored American Is Not in the World's Columbian Exposition" (published originally with private funds, 1893; reprint, ed. Robert W. Rydell, Chicago: University of Illinois Press, 1999). Penn wrote a section titled "The Progress of the Afro-American since Emancipation." The essay was basically a list of accomplishments by black Americans. The essay was reused in a book co-authored by Penn, Henry Davenport Northrup, and Joseph R. Gay, titled *The College of Life or Practical Self-Education: A Manual of Self-Improvement for the Colored Race, Forming an Educational Emancipator and a Guide to Success* (Horace C. Fry), 1895. For a more detailed description of Penn's role in the Atlanta Exposition and his relationship with Washington, see Lorini, *Rituals of Race*.

47. *Proceedings*, v. I, 146.

48. *Crisis* 11, no. 4 (February 1916): 169. *Crisis* was the journal of the NAACP and was edited by W.E.B. Du Bois.

49. "A Southern Seaside Resort," *Crisis* 37, no. 7 (July 1930): 228–29.

50. *Proceedings*, v. II, 163.

51. Ibid.

52. Ibid., 165. Jones's complexion was so light that he "passed" as white. It was rumored that he was nearly arrested in a Southern city for walking down the street with a black woman—probably his wife. In my own search for information about Jones, I looked past many photographs of Jones because his image

did not match the racial profile I was looking for. The article in *Crisis* on Gulf-side Assembly commented early in the piece that Jones was "quite white." I have heard speculation among Methodist scholars who know more about this than I do that Jones was able to purchase the property for the resort from whites because of his light complexion.

We can only speculate as to just what Jones meant by his desire that his children "know who they were." Did this reflect some personal, lifelong struggle with an unstable racial identity? Was his marriage to a woman with darker skin an attempt to ensure that he did not father children who would have the same struggles as he? Did he believe that he was *truly* of a particular race and only suffered the curse of a confusing complexion, or did he believe there was a social reality that superseded the illogic of his mixed-blood status?

53. Several delegates pointed to lynching as one sign that their new church ought not to contribute to further racial divisiveness. A good bit of space was filled in the *Christian Advocates* on this issue as well, though they were certainly not preoccupied with it.

54. *Proceedings*, v. II, 222.

55. *Proceedings*, v. III, 189–90.

NOTES TO CHAPTER 5

1. New York *Christian Advocate* 46, no. 15 (April 12, 1917): 6.

2. Laurie Maffly-Kipp, "Mapping the World, Mapping the Race: The Negro Race History, 1874–1915," *Church History* 64, no. 4 (December 1995): 613.

3. *New York Christian Advocate* 46, no. 15 (April 12, 1917): 6.

4. It is difficult to ignore the resonance these arguments have with the "state's rights" debates on the national political level.

5. *Proceedings*, v. III, 53. Though I could find no direct evidence, it appears that alliances were made between the more conservative group from the MECS and some members of the MEC delegation, particularly Goucher. They seemed to be maneuvering for a regional arrangement that would allow the white regional conferences in the South to vote themselves completely free from the possibility of falling under black leadership and integration at the congregational level without interference from the General Conference.

6. The problem with this argument, as several MEC delegates eagerly pointed out, was that it was in opposition to the arguments made by MECS leaders during the split of 1844. One of the compromises proposed during that debate was that the southern slaveholding bishop whose status was in question be restricted only to those districts in which he was welcome. Southerners objected that this would destroy the basic nature of the Methodist Episcopal system of itinerant general superintendency.

7. The term "central" was used in these proposals (and later in the Methodist Church) to designate church conferences other than the white U.S. regional conferences with representation in the General Conference. In several versions of the proposal, including the final proposal, the central conferences also had either limited representation in the General Conference or administrative and legislative powers more limited than the white U.S. regional conferences.

8. For Penn's retraction speech at Savannah see *Proceedings*, v. II, 624.

9. *Proceedings*, v. III, 183. The quoted section of Penn's speech is from Woodrow Wilson's description of German political and military maneuvering: "peoples and provinces are not to be bartered about from sovereignty to sovereignty, as if they were mere chattels and pawns in a game, even the great game, now forever discredited, of the balance of power." Penn's comparison of the white delegates' actions with the German Kaiser was undoubtedly purposeful.

10. Though they rarely mentioned it, this did include Europeans. Hamilton made this clear, for instance, in his support for Penn's amendment. He favored Penn's amendment not because it discriminated against American blacks alone, but because all "mission peoples" were set apart. Yet no one but Hamilton was willing, at that point, to examine the possibility of eliminating the concept of "mission" in a church hierarchy. Ibid., 186–87.

11. Despite the advice of Jones and Penn to the contrary, Goucher continued to assume that the members of the AME, AMEZ, and CME churches would naturally desire to join the new church the Joint Commission was forming. Ibid., 187–88.

12. No one pointed out the obvious here: that those delegates favoring regional white conferences in the United States were primarily concerned about "local interests."

13. Bishop Leete (MEC), for example, denigrated "Asiatic illiterates" in favor of the "illiterate groups in this country." Rolla V. Watt (MEC) suggested that admitting India in particular on an equal basis would be "an extremely dangerous thing." Watt and Claudius B. Spencer (MEC) proposed that Penn's amendment be changed to exclude the foreign central conferences from proportionate representation. Ibid., 189, 192.

14. Ibid., 191. In an editorial in the *Southwestern Christian Advocate* (October 5, 1916), Jones called for Christian patriotism from all races and for recognition of only "one kind of American." Jones did not support the use of labels such as "Afro American" because he thought it divisive of a unified national identity. Such labels, he said, only created "hyphenated Americans."

15. These predictions all came true. In this same meeting, Jones also laid out the proposal that he thought would work. It was almost precisely what the Joint Commission agreed to three years later, and was the basic framework that eventually came to be the structure of the Methodist Church in 1939.

16. MEC Commission to the Joint Commission, minutes of separate meeting, Traverse City, Michigan, July 17, in "Minutes Commission on Unification Methodist Episcopal Church and Executive Committee [*sic*]," General Conference Collection, General Commission on Archives and History of the United Methodist Church, Madison, New Jersey.

17. "God's Supreme Challenge to the Negro Race" (January 2, 1918), 1. He urged restraint again later that year in a lead editorial entitled "Keep Cool" (April 4, 1918), 1.

18. Cranston's speech was not just a blow to Penn and Jones personally. His speech broke down the deliberations entirely, and the commissions had to part and meet separately, and then convene yet another committee to cobble together another plan.

19. *Proceedings*, v. III, 214–15. Penn had withdrawn his support at Savannah after it became clear that the MECS was demanding Associate General Conferences in return. See note 5 above.

20. He went so far as to say, "Africa must be evangelized by Africans," alienating black Methodists further by openly disregarding their birthplace and citizenship. Ibid., 215.

21. Ibid., 216. At Savannah, Cranston had made a similar point more explicitly. Black Methodists were preoccupied with the trappings of political power, he said, but with good reason, because they learned it from whites: "His first lessons in politics were corrupting and degrading, and it is no great wonder that his conceptions of humanity [sic] rights revolve about a ballot box or in the Church around the bishopric. He learned that from white men." By way of arguing that black Methodists did not really need access to positions of power, he added that too much "Church materialism" and "persistent coddling" would make them weak. Rather, black Methodists could use more "self-direction" instead of "the stimulation of unrealized ambitions and the encouragement of the natural human passion for superficial distinctions and barren recognitions." *Proceedings*, v. II, 655–56.

22. Cranston's speech elicited an immediate response from Jones. He asked for the floor by the right of "personal privilege" to defend himself against Cranston's accusations. This privilege was, throughout the Joint Commission meetings, nearly always granted, especially when a member had been singled out for criticism and that member wanted the opportunity to rebut. But this time the chair, MECS Bishop Denny, denied Jones the right, and was uncharacteristically ungenerous with Jones. As Jones began to explain his "question of personal privilege," Denny interrupted him to urge him to move on, and then told him "as a matter of law this is not a question of personal privilege." A vote was taken and Jones was allowed to speak. As soon as he completed his short defense, MEC Bishop McDowell, as he did at several crucial junctures when he sensed the meetings were getting out of control, requested that the two commissions move to separate meetings. *Proceedings*, v. III, 217–18.

23. *Proceedings*, v. III, 230. Hamilton shouted "Hear! Hear!" in support.

24. Ibid., 241.

25. Ibid., v. III, 390.

26. Robert E. Jones, "To the Negroes of America a Word of Caution," *Southwestern Christian Advocate* (November 14, 1918): 1.

27. In his book on the MECS during this period, Sledge argues that the 1918 MECS General Conference that preceded the Cleveland meeting was significant in many ways for that church, but for the purposes of this chapter it is important to note only the general shift to a more moderate stance on several main issues: the status of women in the church leadership, more support for the educational programs of the church, and a more moderate stance on unification. The effects of this were seen in the Joint Commission because several members were replaced. The most significant change was the replacement of Bishop Hoss, who died in the interim, by the newly elected James Cannon Jr. Cannon became a central actor in the last two meetings. John Moore was elected to the episcopacy, and his replacement in the ministerial group was William D. Bradfield. Bradfield was placed on the committee that drafted a new proposal on the status of the black membership, and his lone dissenting vote gave momentum to the MEC view. This general moderating effect was part of the impetus for the MECS commission to offer a more generous compromise than they had at St. Louis. Sledge, *Hands on the Ark*, 55–58.

28. The Exposition was held June 20 through July 13, 1919. For an overview of the Exposition see the *Christian Advocate* (New York), July 31, 1919.

29. *Proceedings*, v. III, 286.

30. Bishop James Cannon Jr. (1847–1933) had just been elected to the episcopacy at the previous MECS General Conference, and he entered the Joint Commission meetings with that weight of authority paired with a good bit of respect and notoriety he already had in general Methodist circles. He was immediately deferred to by members of both church commissions, and was asked to give his opinion of the general state of MECS opinion. While Sledge argues that Cannon was a moderate in the MECS political spectrum, he was a little less than moderate in his brief two-meeting appearance on the Joint Commission. Cannon struck a confident and uncompromising pose as he argued that he saw little hope in an approval from the MECS for a racially integrated proposal.

31. *Proceedings*, v. III, 290.

32. Ibid., 313–14.

33. Ibid., 313.

34. Ibid., 319.

35. Ibid., 320.

36. Ibid., 351–52.

37. Ibid., 363. The document submitted from the Richmond meeting can be found at ibid., 561–67.

38. Ibid., 415. Bishop Cannon also admitted that the Associate General Conference clause was there to placate conservative factions in the MECS.

39. Ibid., 433.

40. Ibid., 475–76. Penn, expressing his derision for the Associate General Conference clause, said, "I will not take the hint." Ibid., 480.

41. Ibid., 485–86.

42. Ibid., 552.

Notes to the Epilogue

1. Martha Hodes, "The Mercurial Nature and Abiding Power of Race: A Transnational Family Story," *American Historical Review* 108, no. 1 (February 2003): 84–119.

2. Ibid., 84–86.

Selected Bibliography

Primary Sources

General Conference Collection. General Commission on Archives and History, the United Methodist Church, Madison, New Jersey.

Joint Commission on Unification. *The Proceedings of the Joint Commission on Unification of the Methodist Episcopal Church, and Methodist Episcopal Church, South,* 3 vols. New York: Methodist Book Concern, 1918–1920; Nashville, Tenn.: Smith and Lamar for the Publishing House of the Methodist Episcopal Church, South, 1918–1920.

Newspapers and Journals

The Christian Advocate (MEC, New York), 1915–1924.
The Christian Advocate (MECS, Nashville), 1915–1924.
The Southwestern Christian Advocate (MEC, New Orleans), 1915–1924.
Crisis (Journal of the NAACP), 1915–1930.
Opportunity (Journal of the Urban League), 1923–1930.
Methodist Quarterly Review (MEC, New York), 1915–1924.
Methodist Quarterly Review (MECS, Louisville and Nashville), 1915–1924.

Books and Articles

Bowen, J.W.E. *An Appeal for Negro Bishops But No Separation.* New York: Eaton and Mains, 1912.

———, and I. Garland Penn. *The United Negro: His Problems and Progress.* Atlanta, Ga.: D. E. Luther Publishing Co., 1902.

Berry, Joseph F., Frank M. Bristol, Frederick D. Leete, and Henry Wade Rogers. *Francis Asbury: Centennial Addresses.* New York: Methodist Book Concern, 1917.

Brooks, Charles A. *Christian Americanization, a Task for the Churches.* New York: Missionary Education Movement and Council of Women for Home Missions, 1919.

Cranston, Earl. *Breaking Down the Walls: A Contribution to Methodist Unification.* New York: Methodist Book Concern, 1915.

Foster, Randolph, S. *Union of Episcopal Methodisms.* New York: Hunt and Eaton, 1892.

Goucher, John Franklin. *Christianity and the United States.* New York: Eaton and Mains, 1908.

Hartzell, Jacob C. "Methodism and the Negro in the U.S.," *Journal of Negro History* 8 (July 1923): 301–15.

Hoss, Elijah Embree. *Methodist Fraternity and Federation, Being Several Addresses and Papers on the General Subject.* Nashville, Tenn.: Publishing House of the MECS, Smith and Lamar, Agents, 1913.

John Richard Lindgren Foundation. *A Working Conference on the Union of American Methodism.* New York: Methodist Book Concern, 1916.

Moore, John M. *The South Today.* New York: Missionary Education Movement of the United States and Canada, 1916.

————. *The Long Road to Methodist Union.* Nashville, Tenn.: Methodist Publishing House, 1943.

Mouzon, Edwin D. *Fundamentals of Methodism.* Nashville, Tenn.: Publishing House, MECS, 1923.

Neely, Thomas B. *American Methodism: Its Divisions and Unification.* New York: Fleming H. Revell Co., 1915.

New York Conference of the MEC. *Methodism and the Flag.* New York: Methodist Book Concern, 1917.

Reed, John Hamilton. *Racial Adjustments in the MEC.* New York: Neal Publishing Co., 1914.

Shannon, Alexander Harvey. *Racial Integrity and Other Features of the Negro Problem.* Nashville, Tenn.: Publishing House of the MECS, 1907.

Spencer, Claudius B. *That They May Become One: In Behalf of the Organic Union of American Methodism.* New York: Methodist Book Concern, 1915.

Stowell, Jay Samuel. *Methodist Adventures in Negro Education.* New York: Methodist Book Concern, 1922.

Sweet, William Warren. "Negro Churches in the South; A Phase of Reconstruction," *Methodist Review* 104 (May 1921): 405–18.

Thomas, Isaac L. *Separation or Continuity, Which? A Colored Man's Reply to Bishop Foster's Book, "Union of Episcopal Methodisms."* Baltimore, Md.: H. H. Smith, 1893.

Wilson, Luther B. *America - Here and Over There.* New York: Abingdon Press, 1918.

Secondary Sources

Ahlstrom, Sydney E. "Annuit Coeptis: America as the Elect Nation: The Rise and Decline of a Patriotic Tradition." In *Continuity and Discontinuity in Church History*, ed. Forrester Church and Timothy George, 315–37. Leiden: E. J. Brill, 1979.

Allen, James, ed. *Without Sanctuary: Lynching Photography in America*. Santa Fe, N.M.: Twin Palms, 2000.

Allen, Theodore. *The Invention of the White Race: Racial Oppression and Social Control*. New York: Verso, 1994.

Anderson, Benedict. *Imagined Communities: Reflections on the Origin and Spread of Nationalism*. New York: Verso, 1993.

Anderson, Christopher J. "The World Is Our Parish: Displaying Home and Foreign Missions at the 1919 Methodist World's Fair." Ph.D. dissertation, Drew University, 2006.

Anderson, Victor. *Beyond Ontological Blackness*. New York: Continuum, 1995.

Appiah, Anthony. "The Conservation of 'Race.'" *Black American Literature* 23 (1989): 36.

Arendt, Hannah. *Origins of Totalitarianism*. New York: Harcourt, Brace, and World, 1951.

Ayers, Edward. *The Promise of the New South: Life after Reconstruction*. New York: Oxford University Press, 1992.

Ayers, Edward, ed. *All over the Map: Rethinking American Regions*. Baltimore: Johns Hopkins University Press, 1996.

Baldwin, Lewis V. "New Directions for the Study of Blacks in Methodism" In *Rethinking Methodist History: A Bicentennial Historical Consultation*, ed. Russell Richey and Ken Rowe, 185–93. Nashville, Tenn.: Kingswood Books, 1985.

Banner, Lois. "Religious Benevolence as Social Control: A Critique of an Interpretation." *Journal of American History* 60 (June 1973): 23–41.

Baum, Bruce. *The Rise and Fall of the Caucasian Race*. New York: New York University Press, 2005.

Bederman, Gail. "Civilization, the Decline of Middle-Class Manliness, and Ida B. Wells's Antilynching Campaign (1892–1894)." *Radical History Review* 52 (1992): 5–30.

———. *Manliness and Civilization: A Cultural History of Gender and Race in the United States, 1880–1917*. Chicago: University of Chicago Press, 1995.

Bennett, James B. *Religion and the Rise of Jim Crow in New Orleans*. Princeton, N.J.: Princeton University Press, 2005.

Bennett, Tony. *The Birth of the Museum: History, Theory, Politics*. New York: Routledge, 1995.

Berzen, Judith R. *Neither White nor Black: The Mulatto Character in American Fiction*. New York: New York University Press, 1978.

Blankenship, Paul F. "History of Negotiations for Union Between Methodists and Non-Methodists in the U.S." Ph.D. dissertation, Northwestern University, 1965.

Blight, David W. *Race and Reunion: The Civil War in American Memory.* Cambridge, Mass.: Harvard University Press, 2001.

Blum, Edward J. *Reforging the White Republic: Race, Religion, and American Nationalism, 1865–1898.* Baton Rouge: Louisiana State University Press, 2005.

Blum, Edward J., and W. Scott Poole, eds. *Vale of Tears: New Essays on Religion and Reconstruction.* Macon, Ga.: Mercer University Press, 2005.

Boles, John B., ed. *Masters and Slaves in the House of the Lord: Race and Religion in the American South, 1740–1870.* Lexington: University of Kentucky Press, 1988.

Bonnet, Alastair. "'Whiteness Studies': The Problems and Projects of a New Research Agenda." *Theory, Culture and Society* 13 (1996): 145.

Bradley, David H. "Francis Asbury and the Development of African Churches in America." *Methodist History* 10 (1971): 3–29.

Brawley, James P. "The Methodist Church from 1939." *Central Christian Advocate* (October 15, 1967): 3–10.

Brekus, Catherine. "Female Evangelism in the Early Methodist Movement, 1784–1845." In *Methodism and the Shaping of American Culture*, ed. Nathan O. Hatch and Jonathan H. Wigger. Nashville, Tenn.: Kingswood Books, 2001.

Brodkin, Karen. *How Jews Became White Folks & What That Says about Race in America.* New Brunswick, N.J.: Rutgers University Press, 1994.

Brooks, R. N. "Methodism and the Negro." *Christian Advocate* (New York) (May 19, 1938): 461–62.

Brown, Elsa Barkley. "Negotiating and Transforming the Public Sphere: African-American Political Life in the Transition from Slavery to Freedom." *Public Culture* 7 (1994): 107–46.

Brubaker, Rogers, and Frederick Cooper. "Beyond 'Identity.'" *Theory and Society* (February 2000): 1–47.

Brundage, William Fitzhugh. *Under Sentence of Death: Lynching in the South.* Chapel Hill: University of North Carolina Press, 1996.

Carnes, Mark C., and Clyde Griffen, eds. *Meanings for Manhood: Constructions of Masculinity in Victorian America.* Chicago: University of Chicago Press, 1990.

Carter, Paul A. "The Negro and Methodist Union." In *Politics, Religion, and Rockets: Essays in Twentieth-Century American History*, 89–106. Tucson: University of Arizona Press, 1991.

Carwardine, Richard. "Methodists, Politics, and the Coming of the American Civil War." In *Methodism and the Shaping of American Culture*, ed. Nathan

O. Hatch and Jonathan H. Wigger, 309–42. Nashville, Tenn.: Kingswood Books, 2001.

Cash, Wilbur J. *The Mind of the South*. New York: Alfred A. Knopf, 1941.

Cassirer, Ernst. *The Myth of the State*. New Haven, Conn.: Yale University Press, 1946.

Chappell, David L. *Stone of Hope: Prophetic Religion and the Death of Jim Crow*. Chapel Hill: University of North Carolina Press, 2004.

Christensen, Torben, and William R. Hutchison, eds. *Missionary Ideologies in the Imperialist Era: Papers from the Durham Consultation, 1981*. Forlaget Aros, Denmark: Christensens Bogtrykkeri, 1982 (1980).

Clair, Matthew W. Jr. "Methodism and the Negro." In *Methodism*, ed. William K. Anderson, 240–50. Nashville, Tenn.: Methodist Publishing House, 1947.

Coalter, Milton J., John M. Moulder, and Louis B. Weeks, eds. *The Organizational Revolution: Presbyterians and American Denominationalism*. Louisville, Ky.: Westminster/John Knox Press, 1992.

Connerton, Paul. *How Societies Remember*. Cambridge: Cambridge University Press, 1989.

Conrad, Earl. *The Invention of the Negro*. New York: Paul Eriksson, 1966.

Conser, Walter H. Jr., and Sumner B. Twiss, eds. *Religious Diversity and American Religious History: Studies in Traditions and Cultures*. Athens: University of Georgia Press, 1997.

Collier, Karen Young. "An Examination of Varied Aspects of Race and Episcopacy in American Methodism, 1844–1939." Ph.D. dissertation, Duke University, 1984.

Copplestone, J. Tramayne. *Twentieth-Century Perspectives: The Methodist Episcopal Church, 1896–1939*. New York: The Board of Global Missions of the United Methodist Church, 1973.

Crum, Mason. *The Negro in the Methodist Church*. New York: Board of Missions and Church Extension, The Methodist Church, 1951.

Culver, Dwight. *Negro Segregation in the Methodist Church*. New Haven, Conn.: Yale University Press, 1953.

Davenport, F. Garvin Jr. "Thomas Dixon's Mythology of Southern History." *Journal of Southern History* 36 (1970): 350–67.

Davey, Cyril J. *The March of Methodism: The Story of Methodist Missionary Work Overseas*. New York: Philosophical Library, 1951.

Delgado, Richard, and Jean Stefancic, eds. *Critical White Studies: Looking behind the Mirror*. Philadelphia: Temple University Press, 1997.

D'Emilio, John, and Estelle B. Freedman, eds. *Intimate Matters: A History of Sexuality in America*. New York: Harper and Rowe, 1988.

Doraisamy, Theodore R. *What God Hath Wrought: Motives of Mission in Methodism from Wesley to Thoburn*. Singapore: Methodist Book Room, 1983.

Douglas, Ann. *The Feminization of American Culture*. New York: Doubleday, 1988.

Du Bois, W. E. B. *Black Reconstruction in America*. 1935. Reprint, New York: Atheneum, 1962.

Dyer, Thomas. *Theodore Roosevelt and the Idea of Race*. Baton Rouge: Louisiana State University Press, 1980.

Edwards, Lyford P. "Religious Sectarianism and Race Prejudice." *American Journal of Sociology* 41 (September 1935): 167–79.

Ferber, Abby L. *White Man Falling: Race, Gender, and White Supremacy*. New York: Rowan & Littlefield Publishers, 1998.

Fields, Barbara J. "Ideology and Race in American History." In *Region, Race, and Reconstruction: Essays in Honor of C. Vann Woodward*, ed. J. Morgan Kousser and James M. McPherson. New York: Oxford University Press, 1982.

———. "Slavery, Race, and Ideology in the U.S.A." *New Left Review* 181 (May/June 1990): 95–118.

Fishkin, Shelley Fisher. "Interrogating 'Whiteness,' Complicating 'Blackness': Remapping American Culture." *American Quarterly* 47 (September 1995): 428–66.

Fossett, Judith Jackson, and Jeffrey A. Tucker, eds. *Race Consciousness: African-American Studies for the New Century*. New York: New York University Press, 1997.

Foster, Gaines M. *The Ghosts of the Confederacy: Defeat, the Lost Cause, and the Emergence of the New South, 1865–1913*. New York: Oxford University Press, 1987.

Frankenberg, Ruth. *White Women, Race Matters: The Social Construction of Whiteness*. Minneapolis: University of Minnesota Press, 1993.

———. *The Inner Civil War: Northern Intellectuals and the Crisis of the Union*. Urbana: University of Illinois Press, 1963.

———. *Black Image in the White Mind: The Debate on Afro-American Character and Destiny*. Middletown, Conn.: Wesleyan University Press, 1971.

Frederickson, George. *The Arrogance of Race: Historical Perspectives on Slavery, Racism, and Social Inequality*. Middletown, Conn.: Wesleyan University Press, 1988.

Gaines, Kevin K. *Uplifting the Race: Black Leadership, Politics, and Culture in the Twentieth Century*. Chapel Hill: University of North Carolina Press, 1996.

Gates, Henry Louis Jr. *"Race," Writing, and Difference*. Chicago: University of Chicago Press, 1985.

———. "The Trope of the New Negro and the Reconstruction of the Image of the Black." *Representations* 24 (fall 1988): 129–55.

Gatewood, Willard B. *Aristocrats of Color: The Black Elite, 1880–1920*. Bloomington: Indiana University Press, 1990.

George, Carol V. R. *Segregated Sabbaths: Richard Allen and the Rise of Independent Black Churches, 1760–1840.* New York: Oxford University Press, 1973.

Gerstle, Gary. *American Crucible: Race and Nation in the Twentieth Century.* Princeton, N.J.: Princeton University Press, 2001.

Gilbert, James. "Imagining the City." In *The Mythmaking Frame of Mind: Social Imagination and American Culture,* ed. James Gilbert et al. Belmont, Calif.: Wadsworth Publishing Co., 1993.

Gilman, Sander L., and Nancy Leys Stepan. *Difference and Pathology: Stereotypes of Sexuality, Race, and Madness.* Ithaca, N.Y.: Cornell University Press, 1985.

———. "Appropriating the Idioms of Science: The Rejection of Scientific Racism." In *The Bounds of Race,* ed. Dominick Lacapra. Ithaca, N.Y.: Cornell University Press, 1991.

Ginsberg, Elaine K. *Passing and the Fictions of Identity.* Durham, N.C.: Duke University Press, 1996.

Glaude, Eddie. *Exodus! Religion, Race and Nation in Early Nineteenth-Century Black America.* Chicago: University of Chicago Press, 2000.

Gleason, Philip, Martin Marty, and Robert Wuthnow. "Sources of Personal Identity: Religion, Ethnicity, and the American Cultural Situation." Forum in *Religion and American Culture: A Journal of Interpretation* 2, no. 1 (winter 1992): 1–22.

Goen, C. C. *Broken Churches, Broken Nation: Denominational Schisms and the Coming of the American Civil War.* Macon, Ga.: Mercer University Press, 1985.

Goldberg, David Theo. *Racial Subjects: Writing on Race in America.* New York: Routledge, 1997.

Gorrell, Donald K. *The Age of Social Responsibility: The Social Gospel in the Progressive Era, 1900–1920.* Macon, Ga.: Mercer University Press, 1988.

Gossett, Thomas F. *Race: The History of an Idea in America.* New York: Schocken Books, 1965.

Gould, Stephen Jay. *The Mismeasure of Man.* New York: W. W. Norton, 1981.

Grant, Madison. *The Passing of the Great Race.* New York: 1916.

Gravely, Will. "Sydney E. Ahlstrom's *A Religious History of the American People.*" *Journal of Religious Thought* 33 (1976): 106–8.

———. "'Playing in the Dark'—Methodist Style: The Fate of the Early African American Presence in Denominational Memory, 1807–1974." In *The People(s) Called Methodist: Forms and Reforms of Their Life,* ed. Dennis M. Campbell, William B. Lawrence, and Russell E. Richey, vol. 2, 175–90. Nashville, Tenn.: Abingdon Press, 1998.

Green, Jay Douglas. "Africa Rediviva: Northern Methodism and the Task of African Redemption, 1885–1910." Ph.D. dissertation, Kent State University, 1998.

Griffin, John Howard. *Black Like Me.* Boston: Houghton Mifflin, 1960.

Gutmann, Amy, ed. *Multiculturalism: Examining the Politics of Recognition.* Princeton, N.J.: Princeton University Press, 1994.

Haberly, David T. "Women and Indians: *The Last of the Mohicans* and the Captivity Tradition." *American Quarterly* 28 (1976): 431–41.

Hale, Grace Elizabeth. *Making Whiteness: The Culture of Segregation in the South, 1890–1940.* New York: Pantheon, 1998.

Handlin, Oscar. *Race and Nationality in American Life.* Boston: Little, Brown, 1957.

Handy, Robert T. "Negro Christianity and American Church Historiography." In *Reinterpretation in American Church History*, ed. Jerald C. Brauer. Chicago: University of Chicago Press, 1968.

———. *A Christian America: Protestant Hopes and Historical Realities.* New York: Oxford University Press, 1971.

Harding, Susan Friend. *The Book of Jerry Falwell: Fundamentalist Language and Politics.* Princeton, N.J.: Princeton University Press, 2000.

Harlan, Louis. "Booker T. Washington and the Politics of Accommodation." In *Black Leaders of the Twentieth Century*, ed. John Hope Franklin and August Meier. Urbana: University of Illinois Press, 1982.

Harrill, J. Albert. "The Use of the New Testament in the American Slave Controversy: A Case History in the Hermeneutical Tension between Biblical Criticism and Christian Moral Debate." *Religion and American Culture: A Journal of Interpretation* 10, no. 2 (summer 2000): 148–86.

Harrison, Joanne K. *The Life and Times of Irvine Garland Penn.* Philadelphia, Pa.: Xlibris, 2000.

Hart, D. G., and Harry S. Stout, eds. *New Directions in American Religious History.* New York: Oxford University Press, 1997.

Harvey, Paul. "Religion in the American South since the Civil War." In *A Companion to the American South*, ed. John B. Boles, 387–406. Malden, Mass.: Blackwell Publishers, 2002.

Hatch, Nathan O. "The Puzzle of American Methodism." *Church History* 63 (June 1994): 175–89.

Hatch, Nathan O., and Jonathan H. Wigger, eds. *Methodism and the Shaping of American Culture.* Nashville, Tenn.: Kingswood Books, 2001.

Haynes, Carolyn A. *Divine Destiny: Gender and Race in Nineteenth-Century Protestantism.* Jackson: University Press of Mississippi, 1998.

Hempton, David. *Methodism: Empire of the Spirit.* New Haven, Conn.: Yale University Press, 2005.

Heyrman, Christine Leigh. *Southern Cross: The Beginnings of the Bible Belt.* New York: Knopf, 1997.

Hickey, Dennis, and Kenneth C. Wylie. *An Enchanting Darkness: The American Vision of Africa in the Twentieth Century.* East Lansing: Michigan State University Press, 1993.

Higginbotham, A. Leon Jr., and Barbara K. Kopytoff. "Racial Purity and Inter-racial Sex in the Law of Colonial and Antebellum Virginia." *Georgetown Law Journal* 77 (1989).

Higham, John. *Strangers in the Land: Patterns of American Nativism, 1860–1925.* New York: Atheneum, 1963.

Hill, Samuel S. Jr. *The South and the North in American Religion.* Athens: University of Georgia Press, 1980.

Hodes, Martha. "The Mercurial Nature and Abiding Power of Race: A Transnational Family Story." *American Historical Review* 108, no. 1 (February 2003): 84–119.

hooks, bell. *Killing Race, Ending Racism.* New York: Henry Holt, 1995.

Horsman, Reginald. *Race and Manifest Destiny: The Origins of American Racial Anglo-Saxonism.* Cambridge, Mass.: Harvard University Press, 1981.

Hutchison, William R. *The Modernist Impulse in American Protestantism.* Cambridge, Mass.: Harvard University Press, 1976.

———. "A Moral Equivalent for Imperialism: Americans and the Promotion of 'Christian Civilization,' 1880–1910." In *Missionary Ideologies in the Imperialist Era: 1880–1920,* ed. William R. Hutchison and Torben Christensen. Aarhus, Denmark: Christensens Bogtrykkeri, 1982.

———. *Errand to the World: American Protestant Thought and Foreign Missions.* Chicago: University of Chicago Press, 1987.

Ignatiev, Noel. *How the Irish Became White.* New York: Routledge, 1995.

Jacobson, Mathew Frye. *Whiteness of a Different Color: European Immigrants and the Alchemy of Race.* Cambridge, Mass.: Harvard University Press, 1998.

Johnson, Charles S. *The Negro in American Civilization: A Study of Negro Life and Race Relations in the Light of Social Research.* New York: Henry Holt and Co., 1930.

Johnson, Guion Griffis. "The Ideology of White Supremacy, 1876–1910." In *Essays in Southern History,* ed. Fletcher Melvin Green, 124–56. Westport, Conn.: Greenwood Press, 1949.

Jones, Donald G. *The Sectional Crisis and Northern Methodism: A Study in Piety, Political Ethics, and Civil Religion.* Metuchen, N.J.: The Scarecrow Press, 1979.

Juster, Susan, and Lisa MacFarlane, eds. *A Mighty Baptism: Race, Gender, and the Creation of American Protestantism.* Ithaca, N.Y.: Cornell University Press, 1996.

Keita, Maghan. *Race and the Writing of History.* New York: Oxford University Press, 2000.

King, William McGuire. "Denominational Modernization and Religious Identity: The Case of the Methodist Episcopal Church." *Methodist History* 20 (January 1982): 75–89.

King, Willis J. "The Central Jurisdiction." In *The History of American Methodism III*, ed. Emory Stevens Bucke, 485–95. Nashville, Tenn.: Abingdon, 1964.

Kirschner, Don S. "The Ambiguous Legacy: Social Justice and Social Control in the Progressive Era." *Historical Reflections* 2 (summer 1975): 69–88.

Knotts, Alice G. "Race Relations in the 1920's: A Challenge to Southern Methodist Women." *Methodist History* (July 1988).

Hall, Jacquelyn Dowd. *Revolt against Chivalry: Jessie Daniel Ames and the Campaign against Lynching.* New York: Columbia University Press, 1979.

LaCapra, Dominick, ed. *The Bounds of Race: Perspectives on Hegemony and Race.* Ithaca, N.Y.: Cornell University Press, 1991.

Larson, Edward J. *Sex, Race, and Science: Eugenics in the Deep South.* Baltimore, Md.: John Hopkins University Press, 1996.

Leete, Frederick DeLand, ed. *Methodist Bishops: Personal Notes and Bibliography, with Quotations from Unpublished Writings and Reminiscences.* Nashville, Tenn.: Parthenon Press, 1948.

Lehman, Silke. "Exodus, Ethiopia, and Racial Messianism: Texts and Contexts of African American Chosenness: A Response to Albert J. Raboteau." In *Many Are Chosen: Divine Election and Western Nationalism*, ed. William R. Hutchison and Hartmut Lehmann, 167–74. Minneapolis: Augsburg Fortress Press, 1994.

Lemire, Elise. *"Miscegenation": Making Race in America.* Philadelphia: University of Pennsylvania Press, 2002.

Lipsitz, George. *The Possessive Investment in Whiteness: How White People Profit from Identity Politics.* Philadelphia, Pa.: Temple University Press, 1998.

Litwack, Leon. *Been in the Storm So Long: The Aftermath of Slavery.* New York: Vintage Books, 1979.

Loescher, Frank S. *The Protestant Church and the Negro.* New York: Association Press, 1948.

Lorini, Allessandra. *Rituals of Race: American Public Culture and the Search for Racial Democracy.* Charlottesville: University of Virginia Press, 1999.

Luker, Ralph. *The Social Gospel in Black and White: American Racial Reform, 1885–1912.* Chapel Hill: University of North Carolina Press, 1991.

Lyerly, Cynthia Lynn. *Methodism and the Southern Mind, 1770–1810.* New York: Oxford University Press, 1998.

MacKenzie, Kenneth M. *The Robe and the Sword: The Methodist Church and the Rise of American Imperialism.* Washington, D.C.: Public Affairs Press, 1961.

Maffly-Kipp, Laurie F. "Mapping the World, Mapping the Race: The Negro Race History, 1874–1915." *Church History* 64 (fall 1995): 610–26.

Marti, Donald B. "Rich Methodists: The Rise and Consequences of Lay Philanthropy in the Mid-19th Century." In *Rethinking Methodist History: A Bicentennial Historical Consultation*, ed. Russell Richey and Kenneth Rowe, 159–66. Nashville, Tenn.: Kingswood Books, 1985.

Marty, Martin. *Righteous Empire: The Protestant Experience in America*. New York: Harper and Row, 1970.

Maser, Frederick E. "The Story of Unification, 1874–1939." In *The History of American Methodism III*, ed. Emory Stevens Bucke, 407–78. Nashville, Tenn.: Abingdon Press, 1964.

Mathews, Donald G. *Slavery and Methodism: A Chapter in American Morality, 1780–1845*. Princeton, N.J.: Princeton University Press, 1965.

———. *Religion in the Old South*. Chicago: University of Chicago Press, 1977.

———. "Evangelical America—The Methodist Ideology." In *Rethinking Methodist History: A Bicentennial Historical Consultation*, ed. Russell Richey and Kenneth Rowe, 91–99. Nashville, Tenn.: Kingswood Books, 1985.

———. "'Christianizing the South'—Sketching a Synthesis." In *New Directions in American Religious History*, ed. Harry S. Stout and Jon Butler, 84–15. New York: Oxford University Press, 1997.

———. "Religion and the South: Authenticity and Purity—Pulling Us Together, Tearing Us Apart." In *Religious Diversity and American Religious History: Studies in Traditions and Cultures*, ed. Walter H. Conser Jr. and Sumner B. Twiss, 72–101. Athens: University of Georgia Press, 1997.

———. "The Southern Rite of Human Sacrifice." *Journal of Southern Religion* (Online) 3 (2000): http://jsr.as.wvu.edu/mathews.htm (accessed June 2006).

———. "Lynching Is Part of the Religion of Our People: Faith in the Christian South." In *Religion in the American South: Protestants and Others in History and Culture*, ed. Donald G. Mathews and Beth Barton Schweiger, 153–94. Chapel Hill: University of North Carolina Press, 2005.

McClain, William B. *Black People in the Methodist Church: Whither Thou Goest?* Cambridge, Mass.: Schenkman Publishing Co., 1984.

McDannell, Colleen. *Material Christianity: Religion and Popular Culture in America*. New Haven, Conn.: Yale University Press, 1995.

McDowell, John Patrick. *The Social Gospel in the South: The Women's Home Mission Movement in the Methodist Episcopal Church, South, 1886–1939*. Baton Rouge: Louisiana State University Press, 1982.

Minus, Paul M., ed. *Methodism's Destiny in an Ecumenical Age*. New York: Abingdon, 1969.

Montagu, Ashley. *Man's Most Dangerous Myth*. New York: Columbia University Press, 1942.

———, ed. *Race and IQ*. New York: Oxford University Press, 1999.

Moore, R. Laurence. *Selling God: American Religion in the Marketplace of Culture*. New York: Oxford University Press, 1994.

Moran, Rachel F. *Interracial Intimacy: The Regulation of Race and Romance*. Chicago: University of Chicago Press, 2001.

Morrison, Toni. *Playing in the Dark: Whiteness and the Literary Imagination*. Cambridge, Mass.: Harvard University Press, 1992.

Morrow, Ralph. *Northern Methodism and Reconstruction*. East Lansing: Michigan State University Press, 1956.

Moses, Norton. *Lynching and Vigilantism in the United States: An Annotated Bibliography*. Westport, Conn.: Greenwood Press, 1997.

Mullin, Robert Bruce, and Russell E. Richey, eds. *Reimagining Denominationalism: Interpretive Essays*. New York: Oxford University Press, 1994.

Murray, Peter C. "Christ and Caste in Conflict: Creating a Racially Inclusive Methodist Church." Ph.D. dissertation, Indiana University, 1985.

———. *Methodists and the Crucible of Race, 1930–1975*. Columbia: University of Missouri Press, 2004.

Myrdal, Gunnar. *An American Dilemma: The Negro Problem and Modern Democracy*. New York: Harper and Brothers, 1944.

Niebhur, H. Richard. *The Kingdom of God in America*. New York: Harper and Brothers, 1937.

Nisbet, R. *History of the Idea of Progress*. New York: Basic Books, 1980.

Numbers, Ronald L. *Darwinism Comes to America*. Cambridge, Mass.: Harvard University Press, 1998.

Oakes, Henry Nathaniel. "The Struggle for Racial Equality in the Methodist Episcopal Church: The Career of Robert Elijah Jones, 1904–1944." Ph.D. dissertation, University of Iowa, 1973.

O'Brien, Michael. "On Observing the Quicksand." *American Historical Review* 104, no. 5 (1999): 1202.

Owen, Christopher H. *The Sacred Flame of Love: Methodism in Nineteenth-Century Georgia*. Athens: University of Georgia Press, 1998.

Patterson, Orlando. *Rituals of Blood: Consequences of Slavery in Two American Centuries*. Washington, D.C.: Civitas/CounterPoint, 1998.

Rasmussen, Brigit Bander, Eric Klinenberg, Irene J. Nexica, and Matt Wray, eds. *The Making and Unmaking of Whiteness*. Durham, N.C.: Duke University Press, 2001.

Reed, James E. "American Foreign Policy, the Politics of Missions and Josiah Strong, 1890–1900." *Church History* 41 (June 1972): 230–45.

Richardson, Harry V. *Dark Salvation: The Story of Methodism as It Developed among Blacks in America*. Garden City, N.Y.: Anchor Press, 1976.

Richey, Russell E. *Early American Methodism*. Bloomington: Indiana University Press, 1991.

———. "History as a Bearer of Denominational Identity: Methodism as a Case Study," in *Perspectives on American Methodism*, ed. Russell E. Richey, Kenneth E. Rowe, and Jean Miller Schmidt, 480–98. Nashville, Tenn.: Kingswood Books, 1993.

———. *The Methodist Conference in America: A History.* Nashville, Tenn.: Kingswood Books, 1996.

Richey, Russell E., and Kenneth E. Rowe, eds. *Rethinking Methodist History: A Bicentennial Historical Consultation.* Nashville, Tenn.: United Methodist Publishing House, 1985.

Robins, Roger. "Vernacular American Landscape, Methodists, Camp Meetings, and Social Respectability." *Religion and American Culture* 4 (1994): 165–91.

Roediger, David R. *The Wages of Whiteness: Race and the Making of the American Working Class.* New York: Verso, 1994.

Rowe, Kenneth. *Black Methodism: An Introductory Guide to the Literature.* United Methodist Bibliography Series No. 3. Madison, N.J.: General Commission on Archives and History, the United Methodist Church, 1984.

Rydell, Robert. *All the World's a Fair: Visions of Empire at American International Expositions, 1876–1916.* Chicago: University of Chicago Press, 1984.

Saxton, Alexander. *The Rise and Fall of the White Republic: Class Politics and Mass Culture in Nineteenth-Century America.* New York: Verso Books, 1990.

Schmidt, Jean Miller. *Grace Sufficient: A History of Women in American Methodism.* Nashville, Tenn.: Abingdon Press, 1999.

Schneider, A. Gregory. *The Way of the Cross Leads Home: The Domestication of American Methodism.* Bloomington: Indiana University Press, 1993.

Scott, Daryl Michael. *Contempt and Pity: Social Policy and the Image of the Damaged Black Psyche, 1880–1996.* Chapel Hill: University of North Carolina Press, 1997.

Scott, James C. *Domination and the Arts of Resistance.* New Haven, Conn.: Yale University Press, 1990.

Silber, Nina. *The Romance of Reunion: Northerners and the South, 1865–1900.* Chapel Hill: University of North Carolina Press, 1993.

Silk, Leonard, and Mark Silk, eds. *The American Establishment.* New York: Basic Books, 1980.

Sledge, Robert Watson. *Hands on the Ark: The Struggle for Change in the Methodist Episcopal Church, South, 1914–1939.* Lake Junaluska, N.C.: Commission on Archives and History, The United Methodist Church, 1975.

Smith, John David, ed. *Racial Determinism and the Fear of Miscegenation, Post 1900*, Anti-Black Thought: 1863–1925, vol. 8. New York: Garland Publishing, 1993.

Smith, Mark M. *How Race Is Made: Slavery, Segregation, and the Senses.* Chapel Hill: University of North Carolina Press, 2006.

Smith, Rogers M. *Civic Ideals: Conflicting Visions of Citizenship in U.S. History.* New Haven, Conn.: Yale University Press, 1997.

Steinberg, Stephen. *Turning Back: The Retreat from Racial Justice in American Thought and Policy.* Boston: Beacon Press, 1995.

Stepan, Nancy Leys. *The Idea of Race in Science: Great Britain, 1800–1960.* New York: Archon, 1982.

Stewart, Jeffrey, ed. *Race Contacts and Interracial Relations: Lectures on the Theory and Practice of Race.* Cambridge: Harvard University Press, 1992.

Stocking, George. *Race, Culture, and Evolution: Essays in the History of Anthropology.* New York: Free Press, 1968.

Stoll, Jay S. *Methodist Adventures in Negro Education.* New York: Methodist Book Concern, 1972.

Stowe, David W. "The Rise of Whiteness Studies." *Lingua Franca* (September/October 1996): 68–77.

Straughn, James H. *Inside Methodist Union.* New York: The Methodist Publishing House, 1958.

Sweet, William Warren. *Methodism in American History,* 2d edition.. Nashville, Tenn.: Abingdon Press, 1961.

Thomas, I. L. *Methodism and the Negro.* Cincinnati, Ohio: Jennings and Graham, 1910.

Thomas, James S. *Methodism's Racial Dilemma: The Story of the Central Jurisdiction.* Nashville, Tenn.: Abingdon Press, 1992.

Tolnay, Stewart E., and E. M. Beck. *A Festival of Violence: An Analysis of Southern Lynchings, 1882–1930.* Urbana: University of Illinois Press, 1995.

Trueblood, Roy W. "Union Negotiations between Black Methodists in America." *Methodist History* 8, no. 4 (July 1970): 18–29.

Tuveson, Ernest. *Redeemer Nation: The Idea of America's Millennial Role.* Chicago: University of Chicago Press, 1968.

Tweed, Thomas A. "John Wesley Slept Here: American Shrines and American Methodists." *Numen* 47, no. 1 (2000): 41–68.

Van Deburg, William L. *Slavery and Race in American Popular Culture.* Madison: University of Wisconsin Press, 1984.

van Dijk, Teun A. *Elite Discourse on Racism.* London: Sage Publications, 1993.

Vaughan, Alden T., and Edward W. Clark, eds. *Puritans among the Indians: Accounts of Captivity and Redemption, 1676-1724.* Cambridge: Belknap Press, 1981.

Veltman, Laura J. "(Re)Producing White Supremacy: Race, the Protestant Church, and the American Family in the Works of Thomas Dixon, Jr." In *Vale of Tears: New Essays on Religion and Reconstruction,* ed. Edward J. Blum and W. Scott Poole. Macon, Ga.: Mercer University Press, 2005.

West, Cornel. *Race Matters*. Boston: Beacon Press, 1993.

White, Walter. *Rope and Faggot: A Biography of Judge Lynch*. New York: Knopf, 1929; reprint, Notre Dame, Ind.: University of Notre Dame, 2001.

Williamson, Joel. *New People: Miscegenation and Mulattoes in the United States*. New York: Free Press, 1980.

Wilson, Charles Reagan. *Baptized in Blood: The Religion of the Lost Cause, 1865–1920*. Athens: University of Georgia Press, 1980.

Wilson, John. "A New Denominational Historiography?" *Religion and American Culture* 5, no. 2 (1995): 249–63.

Zangrando, Robert L. *The NAACP Crusade against Lynching, 1909–1950*. Philadelphia: Temple University Press, 1980.

Zerubavel, Eviatar. *Time Maps: Collective Memory and the Social Shape of the Past*. Chicago: University of Chicago Press, 2003.

Index

About the Author

Morris Davis is Assistant Professor of the History of Christianity and Wesleyan/Methodist Studies at Drew University.